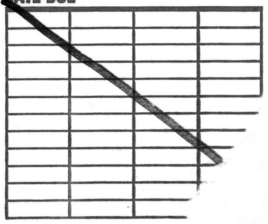

MARXISM AND IMPERIALISM

To
John Saville

in gratitude for much stimulating encouragement, and as a small tribute to his long years of service to socialism.

MARXISM AND IMPERIALISM

studies by
V. G. Kiernan

St. Martin's Press   New York

Contents

Foreword

Imperialism is a major theme of world history, and one that offers more glimpses than almost any other of the nature of man and of human society; that is, of the hierarchies of unequal classes that have made up all human societies but the most primitive. It has gone through Protean shapes and variations, in some of which it persists today, openly as in Portuguese Africa or clandestinely as in the countless spheres of influence of the United States. Questions relating to it and its history are therefore far from being merely academic. Strictly academic history-writing, indeed, has shown a disposition of late to edge the subject out of court; to put imperialism in inverted commas in its examination-papers, as if it were some quaint fallacy or old wives' tale. At this rate we might before long, with the aid of the philosophers, put most of history in inverted commas, and allow ourselves to forget most of its unpleasantnesses.

My own interest in the subject began many years ago, when the British, French and other empires were still intact and seemingly unshakable. It was in my student days in the 1930s that I first made the acquaintance of nationalist Indians, Chinese, Africans, among my fellow-students at Cambridge, and that I first struggled with the works of Lenin and Bukharin on imperialism: works then even younger than myself, far off in the past as they may seem to lie today. In the first study in this collection, written by way of introduction to it, I have tried to survey some leading strands in the development of the theory associated with Lenin; really a cumulative body of ideas to which a whole generation of thinkers contributed, not all of them socialists, and some of them British. Whatever its shortcomings, it is virtually the only serious theory of imperialism ever put forward. My aim has been to try to distinguish what may be of permanent value in it from what was ephemeral, or has been discounted by later history.

When we look back from today, Leninist theory may seem to take too little account of change, and to confound distinct epochs, one of armed competition for colonies, and a later, less warlike overflowing of political boundaries by migrant capital. Its strength lay in economic analysis; in its more specifically Marxist forms it is most vulnerable to criticism through its comparative neglect of other motive forces, political or psychological. In this preoccupation Marxism continued Marx's own turning away (in his finished, published work at any rate) from a many-sided approach to history and society towards a narrower concentration on their economic structure. Non-Marxist writings on empire, on the other hand, have often displayed a still more restricted and abstract concern with political factors of one sort or other, to the neglect of economic. Marxism is faced with the task of broadening its perceptions by taking stock more fully of the diverse forces at work. Some small attempt in this direction is made in the other six essays collected here, all written during the past ten years, and all from what I may venture to call an independent Marxist standpoint.[1]

The earliest of these, *Farewells to Empire*, contrasts the views of a number of writers, each in his own way an authority, and nearly all of them influenced more or less strongly, either by attraction or by repulsion, by the Leninist or Hobson-Lenin theory. In the writings here considered they were looking back on imperialism, and the British empire in particular, about the time when this empire was being, in a fairly orderly way, wound up. Britain had a unique and extraordinary record as a colonial power, which ought not to be hastily forgotten, or left to melt into myth, if only because Britain is still far from having disentangled itself from neo-colonialism, that *alter ego* of imperialism; and because Britain now has racial problems to solve which are legacies from its days of dominion over palm and pine.

---

[1] I have tried to sum up briefly my impressions of the character and consequences of empire in the preface to the 1972 (Pelican) edn. of my book *The Lords of Human Kind* (pp. xxiv ff.).

How little the meaning of imperialism can be confined to direct colonial rule is most forcibly evident from the annals of the United States; and the next study seeks to explore some causes of the divergence between modern European empire-building and the obstinate rejection of direct colonialism by America's corporate digestion. This rejection has been accompanied by a quickening advance towards an ascendancy, more oblique and disguised, over a greater part of the globe than any other land has ever exercised, and more often than not at least as malignant as any other in its effects. The counter-revolution of September 1973 in Chile is only the latest in a long series of similar events up and down Latin America and the world, highly gratifying to the interests that have most weight in determining American policy. However much or little these may have done to bring about each successive defeat of a people's struggle to throw off the chains of poverty and reaction, can only be guessed; but the observer may well say to himself, like Banquo contemplating Macbeth and his crown, 'I fear thou playdst most foully for it.'

The Peasant Revolution is an approach from the point of view of the undeveloped world and its mostly peasant peoples, and of the guerrilla movements through which many of them in our time have attempted to emancipate themselves. It was written in the hope of adding a little to the interest aroused by the resistance movements in Portuguese Africa in particular. Basil Davidson's reports from Guinea, and then the few but pregnant writings of its leader Amilcar Cabral, made me an admirer of that great African. Cabral was murdered early this year, but he left his achievement behind him in the form not only of his ideas but of a free nation, already recognized by many governments. By now, also, revolt in the two much bigger Portuguese territories, Angola and Mozambique, has made very considerable progress.[2] It has seemed to many socialists in recent years that the working classes of the advanced countries have let the time go by when they might have overthrown class rule, as Lenin in 1917 feared that the Russian workers might miss a unique chance; that their mission has passed to a successor, the colonial peasant mass. If so, the mandate can be at best only

[2] See especially on this Basil Davidson, *In the Eye of the Storm. Angola's People* (London, 1972).

partially fulfilled: the 'third world' may liberate itself, but it cannot liberate all humanity, as early Marxism too hopefully counted on the proletariat single-handed to do.

The three other studies relate to India, a country of primary importance in the story of the British and European empires, and of special interest to me because I lived there for some years, in the last epoch of British rule, and was able to see something of the Raj and of the national movement against it. About the relevance of Marxism to India I learned much from my old friend P. C. Joshi, then general secretary of the Communist Party, for whom many years later the essay on *Marx, Engels and the Indian Mutiny* was written. This and the preceding one, written in the centenary year of Marx's *Capital*, are concerned with the interest that he and Engels themselves took in India. That region may be said to have done more than anything else to stimulate their—very tentative—thinking about imperialism. But it contributed also in a good many, sometimes roundabout, ways to the development of their general thinking, especially on world history.

In 1907 when a new governor of Egypt was wanted, that left-wing trade-union stalwart John Burns said to an aristocratic acquaintance: 'Appoint me, I will rule Egypt like a Pharaoh! You will not be disappointed.' His hearer was quite ready to believe him.[3] In 1908 the fiery socialist Keir Hardie visited India. Lady Minto, the Viceroy's wife, was indignant: 'It is monstrous these men coming out and trying to create further agitation. . . .' To the relief and amusement of officialdom, Hardie's incendiarism did not go beyond suggesting in the *Labour Leader*, when he got home, that a Viceroy who had 'won golden opinions' might win India's still fuller confidence by appointing 'an educated Indian gentleman' as one of his private secretaries.[4] The evolution, or failure to evolve, of Labour Party attitudes to British rule in India was surveyed a few years ago in a masterly and very detailed manner by Georges Fischer. It was his book that suggested my final article. On such imperial issues the outlook of the non-Marxist Left in Britain and elsewhere, after the split in the Socialist

---

[3] Lord Hardinge of Penshurst, *Old Diplomacy* (London, 1947), p. 142.
[4] M. Gilbert, *Servant of India . . . Sir James Dunlop Smith, Private Secretary to the Viceroy* (London, 1966, p. 130). The book covers 1905–10.

International, was more sharply divided from the Communist than on almost anything else. To its opponents 'reformism' seemed to mean, for the colonies at least, leaving things as they were. Those old issues survive in new shapes, for the Labour Party has often seemed nearly as insensitive as Britain at large to the risks of involvement in neo-colonialism, or of serving as camp-follower to American ambition.

Of the six essays previously published, the first four (those numbered 2 to 5) appeared in *The Socialist Register*, which this year reaches its tenth annual number; an occasion when its editors, Professor R. Miliband and Professor J. Saville, may be thanked for the labour they have devoted to establishing this forum of socialist discussion. No. 6 was a contribution to a volume published in India to mark the hundred and fiftieth anniversary of Marx's birth.[5] No. 7 appeared in *New Left Review*, 42 (1967). Acknowledgments are offered to all the editors and publishers concerned. I have revised the text throughout; one or two pages formerly omitted have been inserted, and some passages left out, chiefly to avoid repetition.

Edinburgh,
7 November 1973

[5] *Homage to Karl Marx. A Symposium*, ed. P. C. Joshi (Delhi, 1969).

I

The Marxist theory of Imperialism and its historical formation

I   THE AGE OF IMPERIALISM

Every type of society in history has had its characteristic
pattern of aggressiveness, and civilization and empire-building
were twin brethren. From the sixteenth century Europe was
going through a series of expansionist phases; not until the 'age
of Imperialism' of the late nineteenth and early twentieth
centuries did this name come to be attached to one of them, and
the meaning it then took on was not, and has never become,
very clear-cut. To countries like Britain with many overseas
possessions it meant most naturally the ambition of adding
field to field, colony to colony. To other Europeans it was
likely to signify something more general: power-politics,
Weltpolitik, any use or threat of force to achieve national
objects, including such objects as the defeat of trade rivals.

With this 'new imperialism' came a luxuriant advertising
or mythologizing which moved a German statesman to compli-
ment Britain, France, Russia—the three biggest colony-owners
—on their skill at 'cloaking practical motives and instincts in
high sounding words which make them seem beautiful'.[1] What
was really happening was tumultuous and hard to decipher,
but some relevant features of the situation stood out. One was
the 'second industrial revolution'[2]: higher technology, new
industries drawing on it, piling up of capital into larger and
larger units under the direction of fewer and more powerful

[1] Prince von Bülow, *Imperial Germany* (English edn., London, 1916), p. 320.
[2] H. Gollwitzer, *Europe in the Age of Imperialism 1880–1914* (London, 1969),
p. 73; cf. H. Magdoff, *The Age of Imperialism* (New York, 1969), p. 28.

individuals. Another was foreign investment, or export of capital, as the German economist Rodbertus noted before his death in 1875.[3] Britain and France went in for it well before that date, Germany started later; but in the years before 1914 there was an astonishing acceleration of the outflow of funds, carrying the British total to something like £4000 million, the German to about £1200 million.[4] It was not hard to see that money placed abroad like this would often be desirous of support from its government. In some episodes like the seizure of Tunis or the Transvaal it was transparently plain that financial interests 'hauled the political and military power of their governments behind them'.[5]

On their side statesmen readily found reasons for joining in imperialistic courses. Bismarck for instance can be convincingly represented as a 'Bonapartist' ruler launching his Germany into world politics in order to cement its new-found unity and disguise its still archaic political structure.[6] With motives harmonizing so well, finance and government were coming together in a marriage as close as that of Church and State in former days. Their leaders shared 'a common attitude of mind and spirit'.[7] Very often capital operating abroad was doing so in unconcealed unison with designs of State. Either partner might take the lead, the other sometimes hanging back. German businessmen helped to push Bismarck into the colonial hunt: in William II's reign 'the banks often drew back from the impetuosity of official purposes'.[8] It was the same in Britain, where Grey as Foreign Secretary might take steps to ginger up British commercial activity in Turkey.[9] Military men with their own swords to grind often furnished a catalyst; armies like industries were swelling in size and influence.

---

[3] See H. B. Davis, *Nationalism and Socialism. Marxist and Labor Theories of Nationalism to 1917* (New York, 1967), pp. 99–100.

[4] See figures in E. Mandel, *Marxist Economic Theory* (trans. B. Pearce, London, 1968), Vol. 2, p. 450.

[5] H. Feis, *Europe the World's Banker 1870–1914* (Yale, 1930), p. 467.

[6] H.-U. Wehler, 'Bismarck's Imperialism 1862–1890' (*Past and Present*, No. 48, August 1970), p. 153, etc.

[7] Gollwitzer, *op. cit.*, p. 80. Cf. A. S. J. Baster, *The International Banks* (London, 1935), p. 236, on 'the close personal connection between banking and political personages in the England of the 19th century'.

[8] Feis, *op. cit.*, p. 167.

[9] Feis, *op. cit.*, p. 331.

2   SOME BRITISH REACTIONS

Watching big business assume the port of Mars, many wondered uneasily whether all this was going to end in war. If England always had the biggest empire, it was the least militarized among the big nations, and for a long time its faith was pinned to free trade and peace. To this faith the imperialist creed came as a painful challenge, a relapse into the mentality of bygone days. In the years before 1914 many of the realities of the new age were explored by a number of British radicals, whose attempts to elucidate them remain valuable both on their own account and by way of comparison with the Marxist ideas emerging in the same period and interacting with them.

J. A. Hobson's *Imperialism* was in advance, in 1902, of any comprehensive socialist treatment. It portrayed capitalism as led astray by the self-interest of dealers in arms, war contractors, financiers and stock-jobbers. He laid great, very likely too great, stress on export of capital. Investments in weak, backward countries required political control as an insurance, and they knew how to inveigle politicians into backing them. Hobson attributed the exodus of capital to lack of investment opportunity at home, due to low wages and inadequate purchasing power. His remedy was to improve living standards. This was to be the favourite prescription of liberals; its impossibility, under capitalism, became one of the leading tenets of Marxism. It was repudiated as firmly, if less outspokenly, by businessmen and most economists, who agreed with Marxists that the masses could never be anything but poor; also that world trade was too limited for all countries to prosper, so that there too some must be poor in order that others might be rich. These two convictions had a kindred character, and each tended to reinforce the other. Together with the rapid strides of technology and output, they were bound to make the problem of markets an urgent one.

Hobson's book made little impression on British socialists or Fabians, who had no objection to the empire in principle.[10] On the continent it helped to give currency to the word 'imperialism', which often served as an abusive description of British

[10] R. Koebner and H. D. Schmidt, *Imperialism. The Story and Significance of a Political Word, 1840–1960* (Cambridge, 1965), p. 262.

doings.[11] By the time Norman Angell published the first
version of his magnum opus *The Great Illusion*, in 1909, Britain
was deep in foreign political entanglements, with an uneasy
alliance with Japan and a veiled alliance with France and
Russia. It was with imperialism in the sense of great-power
rivalries and the search for wealth through armed might, not
with colonial issues, that he was preoccupied. What appalled
him was the habit, very marked in Britain among the advocates
of protectionism in place of free trade, of picturing commerce
as a species of warfare, 'an unending duel for raw materials',
with armies and navies as the weapons and a warlike vocabulary
of markets invaded, supplies captured, competition killed.[12]
Apologists for capitalism might defend it against socialist
strictures as everything rational and sensible, but they depicted
all capitalists except their own as embodiments of ferocity and
guile.

Angell filled a chapter with an anthology of bellicose
declarations of faith in armaments as the keystone of the wealth
of nations, by men in uniform and leaders of opinion, mostly
British and German. Later on he was to find fault with
Marxists for swallowing all this stuff and taking as gospel the
fantasy of a world doomed to cut-throat competition. He himself dismissed it as out of date. 'Wealth in the modern world is
not a limited stock of goods, any part of which if taken by one
is lost to others. . . .'[13] Nowadays the commercial interests of
all nations were interdependent, and none could attack
another without injuring itself. No war, even if victorious,
could be economically profitable.

These arguments were widely discussed, on the whole with
incredulity, as akin to the ingenious paradoxes of W. S.
Gilbert. Today many of them seem very hard to controvert;
but as Croce was to say of them, such novelties often fail to
carry conviction until harsh experience has cleared the way.[14]
Two serious deficiencies in Angell's case helped to make it

[11] R. Koebner and H. D. Schmidt, *op. cit.*, p. 256.
[12] B. Semmel, *Imperialism and Social Reform. English Social-Imperial Thought
1895–1914* (London, 1960), p. 153.
[13] Norman Angell, *The Great Illusion 1933* (London, 1933; expanded
edition), p. 137.
[14] B. Croce, *History of Europe in the Nineteenth Century* (English edn., London,
1932), Chap. X.

unconvincing to left-wing opponents. He was at pains to demolish, as 'completely false', the thought of 'nations as rival units competing against one another'.[15] Here he was influenced by his British background, still largely one of small-scale competitive enterprise, and took too little heed of the agglomerations of capital, closely linked with the apparatus of State, that were increasingly typical of the age. Secondly he displayed, and never lost, a remarkable myopia about the seamier sides of colonialism, refusing even to consider any hypothesis of colonies being exploited: they were only being *administered*, for their own and the common good—best when administered by Britain, which derived no private advantage from performing the service. This complacency was sure to strike many, in as well as out of Europe, as British smugness and hypocrisy. There were enough gaps in his logic to weaken the force of his assertion: 'it can be shown, quite indubitably, that capitalism is not the cause of war'.[16] *Capitalists*, he would have admitted, *may* be the cause. His pronouncement is still repeated in varying guise today, as is the Marxist counterstatement. If either could really be demonstrated so plainly, by now after three quarters of a century of polemics the truth, it may be supposed, would be known.

Writing in 1914 on the verge of the war which he tried to believe was not coming, H. N. Brailsford in *The War of Steel and Gold* paid tribute to both Hobson and Angell; he dissented from the latter on the colonial issue, agreeing rather with Angell's Marxist critic Kautsky.[17] He was acutely aware of the international anarchy that socialists were complaining of. 'Europe is in perpetual flux, and peace is preserved only by a constant readjustment of the strains and tensions which hold it together.'[18] He had no doubt that economic appetites were at the bottom of the malady; and like Hobson he held that imperialism benefited only a minority, though he extended this from sectional interests to the plutocracy as a whole. 'Regarded as a national undertaking Imperialism does not pay. Regarded as a means of assuring unearned income to the governing class, it emphatically does pay.'[19] Like Hobson too

---

[15] Angell, *op. cit.*, pp. 171–2.   [16] *Ibid.*, p. 252.
[17] H. N. Brailsford, *The War of Steel and Gold* (London, 1914), p. 164.
[18] *Ibid.*, p. 22   [19] *Ibid.*, p. 78.

he singled out excessive investment of capital overseas as the root of the mischief, and proposed the same cure. 'Raise wages, raise with them the standard of comfort, and this restless capital need no longer wander abroad.'[20]

3   EARLY MARXIST THINKING

Marx and Engels were deeply interested in some aspects of imperialism, mainly in Ireland and in India. It cannot be said that they arrived at anything like a systematic view of imperialism, or that such a view can be derived in any straightforward way from Marx's dissection of capitalism. In their later years they felt with regret that capitalism was gaining a new lease of life by spreading outward over the world. But Marx died in 1883 when the scramble for colonies was only reaching its climax, and Engels in 1895 before its consequences were fully unfolded; and many of their ideas were left buried in heaps of old articles or letters. They may be said to have left a loophole for an indulgent attitude to colonialism, because in their eyes, although colonial rule was bad the old feudal stagnation it broke into was worse still. A rude, painful jerking awake of the other continents by European technology might indeed be called their version of the 'civilising mission' that Europe credited itself with.

The big carve-up of the late nineteenth century dealt primarily with the most backward continent, Africa, while in Asia a nationalist protest was only dawning. As regards the menace of war, for a good many years the search for colonies could be thought a useful safety-valve for European tensions. It was a striking contrast with the many colonial wars of earlier epochs that partition of the earth was being completed now without giving rise to any major war, except the remote Russo-Japanese war in 1904. Meanwhile to ardent socialists, as to early Christians, the end of an old bad world was so close at hand that it might appear a waste of time to pore over minutiae of what imperialism was doing far away. How much harm it might be doing psychologically, by infecting common people with the ideology of their rulers, left-wing socialism with

[20] H. N. Brailsford, *op. cit.*, p. 81.

its incorruptible working class and irreconcilable class struggle was slow to perceive.

Britain and France, with the largest empires, had few Marxist thinkers, and their socialists were mixed and divided. It was the big, well-organized German party that presided over the international movement and over socialist speculation, and this was to give the theory of imperialism as it took shape a heavy list to the side of the schematizing, universalizing tendency of German philosophy. In a country with negligible colonies but the most dynamic industrial machine in Europe, and with an authoritarian regime, Germans found it easy to contemplate imperialism as an impersonal force, an over-riding power in itself. They were accustomed to having their history made for them, instead of making it themselves. Englishmen by comparison had more of an instinctive sense of how economic imperatives may be modified by political inter-ferences. They had a long familiarity with the detail of colonial events, even if their multiplicity of colonies of every sort and size sometimes made it hard for them to see the wood for the trees. They lacked the guiding thread of theory that Marxism could supply, but they had more freedom, if at times an erratic freedom, to hit on insights of their own. A blend of English pragmatism and German doctrine was to be desired; as it was the two things remained far apart. Russian Marxism, while indebted to Hobson, was to borrow too heavily from the Germans. It imbibed a habit of abstracting the economic too much from the political aspects of imperialism; while its general reliance on the experience of more advanced countries further west made it prone to jumble together features specific to Britain or France or Germany.

In England there was a 'Fabian imperialism' which saw no harm in Europe bestowing its civilization on tropical lands and receiving their products in return: a fair exchange of glass beads for gold could not be called robbery. To Fabians like Wells 'there was something terribly impressive about imperi-alism, about its power, its science, its ideal of a world subdued and organized. . . .'[21] But an Englishman, Belfort Bax, made an energetic protest against the willingness of some of his fellow-

[21] A. L. Morton, *The English Utopia* (London, 1969 edn.), p. 240.

socialists to regard the new capitalism and the new colonialism as progressive. '*Capitalist-national imperialism*', he declared with great prescience, 'is capitalism's reply to international Social-Democracy. . . . World history is now at the crossroads.'[22] And it was not in unphilosophical England alone that the heresies he attacked were finding a footing. In Germany Bernstein had lately started his campaign for 'revision' of Marxism by recommending a parliamentary instead of revolutionary approach to socialism. Whether his main thesis was convincing or not, most of his book was a reasoned plea for taking note of contemporary changes and moving with the times. It was when he came to colonialism that he showed the cloven hoof, by wanting socialists to accept it as part of the age they were now living in. By entering the race for colonies Germany was only taking 'its honourable share in the civilizing work of the world', and socialists could not but wish to see their country 'represented in the council of nations'. Bernstein saw nothing wrong with the recent German seizure of the Chinese harbour of Kiaochow, and no reason to suppose that European rule need do any harm to native peoples.[23] On this the Herrero war in south-west Africa six years later failed to open his eyes.

In 1900 the Boer war was raging, and a combined invasion-force drowned the Boxer rebellion in blood and sacked Peking. It was about this time that German socialists entered on serious consideration of imperialism, with the struggle against revisionism to whet their concern. Some of the main lines of subsequent Marxist thinking were already roughly anticipated. A socialist organ was stating what was to be Lenin's basic principle when it declared: 'The man or party who talks of opposing imperialism and expansion without attacking capitalism is so manifestly insincere or ignorant as to be unworthy of consideration.' Phrases were heard about imperialism as 'the policy of a dying capitalism', 'a phenomenon inherent in the highest stage of capitalism'.[24] In 1904 a French writer said, much as Bax had done, that 'imperialism and socialism to a very large

[22] Cited in V. I. Lenin, *Notebooks on Imperialism* (*Collected Works*, English edn., Vol. 39; Moscow, 1968,) p. 590.

[23] E. Bernstein, *Evolutionary Socialism. A Criticism and Affirmation* (1899; English edn., New York, 1961), pp. 170, 174, 178.

[24] From an editorial in *International Socialist Review*, October 1900, cited in *Monthly Review* (New York), April 1964, p. 650.

extent form the fundamental contradiction of our age', and
that for capitalism the former was 'its last card', 'last refuge'
against the collapse threatening it.[25]

Left-wing German socialists were taking the lead. Lebedour
censured Bernstein's defence of colonialism, and identified
Weltpolitik with capitalist acquisitiveness.[26] In 1907 Karl
Liebknecht touched on imperialism in a book denouncing the
reign of militarism and armaments. He had no faith in any
safety-valve for Europe in the search for colonies. He thought,
as did Brailsford seven years later, that while some lessening of
threats to peace was discernible within the continent, over
trouble-spots like Alsace-Lorraine, there were 'new and highly
dangerous sources of tension' in rivalries overseas.[27] He glanced
at the notion which Hobson helped to set afloat, and which had
a good deal of attraction in these years for European and
American liberals, that the Powers might come together and
agree to pool their overseas holdings. Realistically Liebknecht
treated 'the formation of a trust governing all possible colonial
possessions by the colony-owning states' as only a very distant
possibility, and disarmament as no better.[28]

4   KAUTSKY ON IMPERIALISM (1909)

A good many Marxist ideas on the subject were already
floating in the air, but the task of working them out and fitting
them together was taken up slowly—and never completed
before 1914, thanks to the widening rift within socialism even
before it was struck down by the Great War. Its foremost
thinker, Karl Kautsky, could claim to have been first in the
field as a student of the 'new imperialism', and to have drawn
attention to the significance of capital export as early as 1898.[29]
In a work of 1902 he predicted that a major war would mean
revolution, but hoped that war could be avoided and a better

[25] P. Louis, cited in *Notebooks on Imperialism*, pp. 250–51.
[26] See L. Basso, 'An Analysis of Classical Theories of Imperialism', in a
symposium on the Age of Imperialism: *The Spokesman* (Nottingham, Nos.
24–5, Winter 1973–4), p. 115.
[27] Karl Liebknecht, *Militarism and Anti-Militarism* (1907; trans. G. Lock,
Cambridge, 1973), p. 18.
[28] *Ibid.*, p. 19; cf. pp. 114–15.
[29] See *Notebooks on Imperialism*, p. 267.

way to socialism found.[30] He left some room for hope by under-
lining discords within capitalism, between high finance, which
could pull the strings of political influence, and industry, for
which its reign meant only armament-taxes and risks of war.
'Where the financier is rash, extravagant and violent the
industrial manager is frugal, timid and peace-loving', well-
disposed to parliamentarism and prepared to make some
concessions to his workmen.[31] Kautsky was conscious however
that the gap between the two was narrowing.

He was still very much a pillar of the left in 1909 when he
wrote his short book *The Road to Power*: it grew out of polemics
against reformist hopes of a peaceful transition to socialism. He
gave imperialism a leading place, and had much in common
with Hobson and Brailsford so far as diagnosis of the disease
was concerned, though not over its cure. Why, he asked, had
Europe's chronic political upheavals, lasting until 1871, been
replaced in recent years by tranquillity, even torpor? His chief
answer was that after 1887 a long economic depression gave
way to an epoch of industrial expansion and prosperity. This he
attributed to a huge extension of railways, and with them of
trade, bringing colonial policies and the world market to the
front.[32] We may ask how closely this economic growth and
imperialism really went together. Germans and others were
drawn into the scramble for central Africa by dreams of a rich
market to be found there, as in eastern Asia.[33] But this was a
will-o'-the-wisp, and Kautsky conceded that not much
railway-building was going on in Africa. Indeed his railway
statistics for 1886–1906 show that vastly the biggest extension
was in the U.S., with Russia far behind in second place and
India third: all the rest, including all the newer colonial
territories, totalled a relatively insignificant figure.

Still, Kautsky was undoubtedly right in saying that the bulk
of the middle-class public everywhere believed in a connection
between imperialism and the return of prosperity, and also
that from early in the recovery the ruling classes were learning

[30] Karl Kautsky, *The Social Revolution* (1902; trans. A. M. and M. W.
Simons, Chicago, 1916), p. 97.
[31] *Ibid.*, pp. 56–8.
[32] See French edition, *Le Chemin du Pouvoir* (Paris, 1969?), pp. 101–2,
106–8.
[33] Wehler, *loc. cit.*, p. 137.

to set up imperialism as an ideology, a counterblast to the socialism whose progress in the previous lean years alarmed them so deeply.[34] Once started, the jingo hubbub of tub-thumping or drum-beating could not easily be halted; and rulers could feel no assurance that trade improvement would go on, so that this psychological distraction was not lightly to be discarded. There were vested interests besides to make sure that it was not abandoned. Collectively the propertied classes must have come to be carried away by their own rhetoric. No dominant group can make successful use of any creed, religious or other, to bemuse its subjects, without catching some of the contagion itself.

Imperialism took for granted, and so did some socialists, Kautsky went on, that all the other races were and would always be mere children; whereas in fact their backwardness was not due to any innate inferiority, and they could and would acquire the white man's skills. They would do so all the quicker, he believed, because industrial countries were now exporting to the backlands not merely their commodities, but their means of production and transport; their own flourishing industry was bound up with this, although it meant turning the other races into competitors as well as enemies.[35] As far too often in Marxist writings, not in that period alone, what particular regions are contemplated here is left very hazy. Kautsky refers to Japan leading the field and all Asia following it into revolt against Western dominion.[36] It is true that free Japan was building a capitalist economy of its own, and also that its progress was lending wings to nationalist aspirations in other lands. But none of these, whether nominally free or under foreign rule, were being industrialized, with the very imperfect exception of India; least of all the Muslim lands whose rebellious mood Kautsky alludes to, but whose outlook remained religious and atavistic.

In various corners of Europe itself, like Spain and Portugal, where also modern industry was planted by foreign capital, it was growing very slowly. Further afield it was and is a basic trait of imperialism that the capital it has invested in retarded areas develops them only in a very lop-sided and inadequate

[34] Kautsky, *Le Chemin du Pouvoir*, p. 110.
[35] *Ibid.*, pp. 155-7.   [36] *Ibid.*, p. 158.

fashion. They have for the most part lingered in a broken-backed condition, a limbo between old and new, with a money economy but not an industrial one, and forming a passive appendage to the advanced countries. Imperialism before 1914 has even been credited with a primary purpose of holding back industrialization overseas, in order to preserve the industrial monopoly of the West.[37] On this view Britain might be said to have used its empire to keep some part of the industrial monopoly it enjoyed not many years before. It must be added that Britain was setting the pace in financing the industrialization of Europe's grand competitor the U.S.; but the multitude of British investors were not all of one mind, and their money was not shepherded as carefully as that of some other countries, either by big financial corporations or by political guidance.

Kautsky judged India closest to revolt, and was convinced that its loss would bankrupt Britain. He was agreeing too completely with British empire-men on India's indispensability; and he must have been over-impressed by the agitation then in progress, over the partition of Bengal. Indian nationalism was still in a very early stage, and Kautsky's vision of most of Asia and Africa sliding into a state of chronic resistance that would end by shaking off foreign rule[38] was more accurate as a forecast than in actuality. It may have owed something to his being an Austrian by birth, familiar with the discontents of nationalities that were threatening to disrupt the Hapsburg empire. Uncomfortably aware, as he could not help but be, that some revolutionary virtue was going out of the working class and the International, he was in effect looking for a fresh reservoir of revolution outside Europe, as socialists have been doing again of late years.

Tumult in Asia would help to dislocate the precarious equilibrium of Europe;[39] the burden of armaments would mount towards the point of exhaustion; imperialism would be deadlocked, yet it could not be given up because there was no other alternative to socialism.[40] To make things worse there was corruption and irresponsibility in high places, part of which he

[37] Mandel, *op. cit.*, Vol. 2, p. 479; and see pp. 459 ff. on the raggedness of colonial economic development.
[38] Kautsky, *Le Chemin du Pouvoir*, p. 159.
[39] *Ibid.*, p. 162.   [40] *Ibid.*, pp. 149–50, 154.

put down to capitalists being too busy, unlike earlier ruling classes, to run the State themselves.[41] This may appear to underrate the intimate links between them and the men in office, yet many of these really were stragglers from earlier times, blinking in the daylight of the twentieth century. Here again Kautsky as an Austrian, brought up under the dawdling Hapsburg aristocracy, might well be impressed by this anomaly. There had just been an Austro-Russian crisis over the Balkans.

Such a line of thought left on one side the crucial question of whether capitalism as such had an inbred and ineradicable urge towards conflict. He was expecting war very largely as a consequence of imperialism, but he often seemed to be thinking of it more as a political than an economic necessity. War would not be inspired by rational aims of getting a better share of world markets, it would come about haphazardly, as Europe sank deeper into hysteria, through some act of folly, some sudden provocation, by scatterbrained ministers.[42] July 1914 does look very much like this, whatever deeper calculations may have lurked under its surface. After the War when Kautsky was commissioned to inspect the German records of 1914 he found weighty reason to blame Europe's governors, the Kaiser most of all;[43] by that time he was predisposed to put the responsibility more on them than on capitalism.

In 1909 he was still positive that war would mean revolution, and that it would have come long since if the rulers had not been held back by fear of the workers.[44] This was no new thought with him. In 1902 he was even prepared to reproach the old regimes for shelving problems and leaving Europe cluttered with anachronisms, because they nervously shrank from any resolute policies that might embroil them in a war. Only countries free of revolutionary mass movements, he wrote then—Britain, the U.S., Japan—felt confident enough to go in for buccaneering, under the control of 'an unscrupulous, brutal clique of men of the "high finance"'.[45] In this phrase

[41] *Ibid.*, pp. 165–7. On this question of ruling class and governing class cf. his *The Social Revolution*, pp. 25 ff.

[42] *Le Chemin du Pouvoir*, pp. 168–9.

[43] See Kautsky, *The Guilt of William Hohenzollern* (English edn., London, 1920).

[44] *Le Chemin du Pouvoir*, p. 154.

[45] *The Social Revolution.*, pp. 95–6.

too was the implication that the spirit of conquest was not engendered by capitalism as a whole, but by vicious elements in it. All the same he held that imperialism, after giving the capitalist order a long respite, would end by helping to drive it to suicide. Of the Hapsburg empire, which started the war in 1914, it was literally true that war meant revolution, and therefore suicide. But this would come about through national-ist, not socialist revolt, and only after defeat of the Hapsburg armies. The Russo-Japanese war might have warned Marxists that revolt is caused not by war, but by military failure. 'Defeat in war is almost certain to cause revolution of one sort or another', as Angell was to say after 1918,[46] and it was a lesson that sober capitalists would ponder in their hearts.

5   IMPERIALISM AND THE SOCIALIST RIFT

Kautsky was firmly orthodox in holding that the only cure for the world's feverish condition was abolition of capitalism. Amid many uncertainties the one thing certain, he concluded his book in 1909 by saying, was that Europe was entering a period of upheaval which could only end with the working class in power. With the spectre of war more and more the leading participant at socialist conferences, it was an urgent task to thrash out the alternatives that Kautsky's presentation left open. Socialists might, like the English radicals, treat imperial-ism as a siren luring mankind on to reefs where neither it nor capitalism was obliged to follow. Or they might make up their mind that no accidental morbidities were driving it on, but its own intrinsic nature. Socialists of the more moderate file were instinctively drawn to the more hopeful answer, that capitalism under pressure of public remonstrance, and through recog-nition of its own longer-range interests, was capable of growing more pacific. Kautsky himself was very soon to be found on this side of the fence.

Fresh fuel for the debate, which also could be made use of on either side, was furnished in 1910 by another Austrian, Hilferding, in his book *Finance-capital, the latest stage of capitalist development*. His term 'finance-capital' was coined to denote a

[46] N. Angell, *Must Britain Travel the Moscow Road?* (London, 1926), p. 34. He was replying to Trotsky's book on Britain.

convergence of the two wings of capitalism that for Kautsky in 1902 were so widely separate. He associated it with the spread of cartels, and regarded finance as acquiring the superior position: 'industry becomes more and more dependent on the banks', whose money is invested in it. Dominance of finance, and intensified tariff contests, promoted export of capital, and thereby were responsible for 'spreading the capitalist system throughout the world'. Capital export in turn stimulated industrial production, because it meant export of goods on credit, which then created fresh markets abroad; the result was fuller employment and better wages, and appeared to demonstrate at last how 'the tendency to create poverty, immanent in capitalism', could be overcome. The price of this prosperity was a violently competitive and rapacious spirit in foreign trade, a thirst for unlimited domination, accompanied by racialist and authoritarian leanings. Hilferding was clear-sighted too about the price paid by colonial peoples expro-priated from their land and subjected to forced labour.[47]

Historically the primacy of the big banks was to prove only a passing phase,[48] like sundry other phenomena that successive thinkers picked out as the master-key to their epoch. Quite apart from this, there are several links in Hilferding's reasoning where the ambiguities of meaning of the word 'imperialism' are visible. So far as the colonial side was concerned, Germany had very little part in it, though it might desire a bigger one. Financial ascendancy over industry he saw had less application to Britain. Tariffs had less still. Capital was not being exported from Britain and France in the form of goods on credit nearly as much as from Germany, and therefore could not have the same stimulating effect on production, since to a great extent they were only re-investing abroad their income from earlier loans. In short, like other theorizing of that time Hilferding's exposition brought out very well certain important things, but failed to take account of national divergences or to provide a framework for judging European 'imperialism' as a whole.

In the more speculative domain of future prospects, Hilfer-

[47] See the extracts from Hilferding's book in the anthology edited by D. K. Fieldhouse, *The Theory of Capitalist Imperialism* (London, 1967), pp. 74 ff.

[48] P. M. Sweezy, *The Theory of Capitalist Development* (London, 1949), p. 268.

ding saw possibilities of capitalism attaining an equilibrium, both at home and internationally, and he himself was moving towards the reformist camp.[49] So were other socialists in increasing numbers, and in the anti-war movement left-wing resolutions were matched with right-wing tactics. At the Chemnitz conference of the German party in September 1912 the leading ideas of the anti-imperialist left, by now fairly familiar, were all endorsed, and capital export, competition for fields of investment, designs of economic hegemony, denounced. But on the right wing willingness to compromise with the expansionists, and defend Germany's colonial record and rights, was going very far.[50] Much was made too of the prospect, or mirage, of an arrangement for some kind of condominium over the backlands. To welcome this as a safeguard against war was a long step towards reformism. If capitalism's title to rule the backlands were legitimized, its divine right to rule at home would be harder to challenge.

After successive international crises were surmounted during 1911–13 optimism burgeoned, and Marxists vied in proving 'the impossibility of a world war'.[51] German socialists were hopeful of big business exercising restraint over the government.[52] In tsarist Russia there was less room for comfortable illusions. As a militant of the left in the International, Lenin was bound to follow closely the controversies over imperialism. It was in 1912 that he began filling the bulky series of notebooks on the subject that he worked diligently at for the next four years. They contain extracts from 148 books and 232 articles in four languages, German heavily preponderating.[53] Notes on Hobson run to thirty-two printed pages, on Brailsford to fifteen. Among Lenin's few marginalia on the latter is an endorsement of Brailsford's critique of Angell for underrating the clash of colonial cupidities;[54] and this is virtually Angell's

[49] See E. M. Winslow, *The Pattern of Imperialism. A Study in the Theories of Power* (New York, 1948), p. 164; cf. G. Haupt, *Socialism and the Great War. The Collapse of the Second International* (revised English edn., Oxford, 1972), p. 149.
[50] See P. Frölich, *Rosa Luxemburg. Her Life and Work* (trans. E. Fitzgerald, London, 1940), Chap. 9: 'The Struggle against Imperialism'.
[51] Haupt, *op. cit.*, p. 107; cf. p. 123.
[52] *Ibid.*, p. 43
[53] *Notebooks on Imperialism*, p. 20.
[54] *Ibid.*, p. 646.

only appearance in the whole collection. Lenin of course knew about him, but must have felt there was nothing in him to take seriously—which can only be regretted. He was not making any such detailed study of a colonial area as Marx made of India, but he read about India, Persia, Egypt, Russian Turkestan. In most of these places nationalist unrest was astir, and for him as for Kautsky in 1909 could help to buttress confidence in the coming revolution of Europe. He was far from realizing, and could not have allowed as conceivable, that nationalism was a more pregnant revolutionary force than socialism, both in Europe and outside.

6 ROSA LUXEMBURG'S STUDY (1913)

Not Lenin, but Rosa Luxemburg, a participant in both the Russian and the German spheres of socialism, and the most remarkable woman perhaps of this century, was the next Marxist to attempt a searching enquiry into imperialism. Her book *The Accumulation of Capital, a contribution to the economic elucidation of imperialism*,[55] was published early in 1913 as an instalment of the current debate. Its intention was to confute reformist illusions, and at the same time to settle an abstruse but fundamental crux of Marxist economics: the problem of how the surplus could be consumed and converted into profit, in Marx's schematic universe, 'a society consisting exclusively of workers and capitalists'.[56] She put forward as the 'solution envisaged by Marx himself' that capitalism could not in reality function as a closed system, but only through inter-action with a realm outside itself. It was compelled to gain control of primitive lands, 'non-capitalist social organizations', and to subvert these in order to supply itself with fresh markets.[57] (An example might be Britain conquering India and crippling native handicrafts so as to be able to sell there manufactures which could not be sold at home.) Two clear implications were that imperialistic expansion was not some-thing a capitalist economy could indulge in or throw aside at

[55] See the English translation by A. Schwarzschild, London, 1963 edition.
[56] *Ibid.*, p. 337.
[57] *Ibid.*, p. 366.

will; and that before very long the process would reach its limits, and capitalism cease to be viable.

Rosa Luxemburg's theory has the great merit of emphasizing that capitalism has never existed in isolation; and that 'the extension of capitalism into new territories was the mainspring of . . . the "vast secular boom" of the last two hundred years.'[58] Or, as English children were taught to lisp in honour of their empire, turning economics into song—'Wider yet and wider shall thy bounds be set': an undisguised warning to all and sundry that British annexations were not yet at an end. Capitalism as seen by Rosa Luxemburg had no choice but to stretch out and ransack the globe.[59] Germany was selling half its indigo in undeveloped countries.[60] Inevitably though contradictorily, 'the old capitalist countries provide ever larger markets for, and become increasingly dependent upon, one another, yet on the other hand compete ever more ruthlessly for trade relations with non-capitalist countries.'[61]

In outline if not in detail, the theory is lucid and elegant. Its agreement with the tangible stuff of history is not always so clear. Among countries reduced to colonial status India and Algeria are discussed in detail, a welcome new departure, and often illuminatingly, but placed overmuch side by side, so that the basic contrast of Algeria unlike India being a colony of white settlement is obscured. With British-Indian circumstances Rosa Luxemburg does not always show sufficient acquaintance. She traces the same subversion of an old natural economy in the penetration of the U.S. and Canadian countryside by mill products as in possessions like India. It ought to have struck her that the outcome in the two cases was totally different, because social and political conditions were different. Elsewhere too, variability of human factors, including the cultural and psychological, was bringing about varying results from similar economic starting-points.

Like Marx and Kautsky, she thought of the irruption of capital into the stagnant backlands as causing capitalist production to sprout there. Imperialism had for outcome 'the industrialization and capitalist emancipation of the hinter-

[58] Joan Robinson, Introduction to *The Accumulation of Capital*, p. 28.
[59] *The Accumulation of Capital*, pp. 357–8.
[60] *Ibid.*, p. 362.   [61] *Ibid.*, p. 367.   [62] *Ibid.*, pp. 395 ff.

land'.[63] It was obliged to seek a 'rapid change-over to capitalism of the pre-capitalist civilisations',[64] yet the operation was self-cancelling, since it sterilized the former virgin lands as markets. Experience seems rather to indicate that imperialism or neo-colonialism may be quite content to leave the backlands indefinitely in an intermediate condition. The Third International put forward a convincingly uncomplicated definition in 1922—applicable to both 'colonialism' and 'imperialism'—by saying that 'the essence of imperialism consists in exploiting the different stages of development of the productive forces in the different areas of world economy to gain monopoly super-profits.'[65]

Where capitalism was being superimposed on—rather than replacing—pre-capitalist society, the resulting exploitation might often be worse, Rosa Luxemburg knew, than anything to be found in the industrial countries.[66] To think of an 'increasing misery' of the colonial world, or of semi-colonial regions like Latin America, might not be unrealistic; and it might be taken to explain at least as well as her more recondite logic the poor markets they offered, and the continual need for fresh ones. Where a transition to modernism did take place, its mechanics are hinted at, more than described, in her survey. The book, it should be kept in mind, was written in four months;[67] there was no time now for Marx's leisurely meditations. But she was well aware that modernization could not occur automatically or smoothly. Export of capital to undeveloped countries promoted development, but also held it back. 'Though foreign loans are indispensable for the emancipation of the rising capitalist states, they are yet the surest ties by which the old capitalist states maintain their influence, exercise financial control and exert pressure'[68]—or, as we should say, bolster a neo-colonial tutelage. Better than Kautsky she understood how much must change inside a newly develop-

---

[63] *Ibid.*, p. 419.

[64] *Ibid.*, p. 446.

[65] Theses of the 4th Congress on the Eastern Question, November 1922; text in J. Degras, *The Communist International 1919–1943. Documents* (London, 1956), Vol. 1, p. 384.

[66] *The Accumulation of Capital*, p. 365.

[67] Frölich, *op. cit.*, p. 186.

[68] *The Accumulation of Capital*, p. 421.

ing region before modern industries could spring up. It was not
a mere matter of ability to learn technical skills; 'obsolete
political organisations' must be replaced by 'a modern state
machinery'. This could not happen peacefully. 'Revolution is
an essential for the process of capitalist emancipation.'[69] She
instanced the recent upheavals, all inadequate, in Russia
(1905), Turkey (1908), and China (1911), and might have
looked back to the civil broils in Japan during its first modern-
izing phase.

All these examples were of countries which never formally
lost their independence, and indeed were all imperialist on
their own account. It was to countries like them that her
remark about foreign loans was relevant. The revolutions she
was considering, as the inclusion of Russia stresses, were internal
events, even if all of them were ignited in one way or other by
foreign contact. She went on to say that 'A young state will
usually sever the leading strings of older capitalist states by
wars'.[70] Direct illustrations of this do not come readily to mind,
but she was right at any rate in saying that military reorganiza-
tion was a further condition of economic autonomy. Japan had
proved the point, Turkey and China were trying to. None of
this had much bearing on the colonies, and their desire for
freedom drew her attention less than Kautsky's earlier or
Lenin's now. So far as legal or institutional conditions requisite
for capitalism are concerned, it might fairly be said that India
under British rule had for a long time been better equipped
than any of the free nations she mentioned. Yet industry was
blossoming in India very slowly. How things went in any such
case depended very much on non-economic factors, first and
foremost the complex of things making up 'national character'.

Overlooking it may be some complications of this order,
Rosa Luxemburg sketched a world where centres of capitalism
were multiplying, and its horizons shrinking. Its frenzied
behaviour in international affairs marked an intuition that it
was approaching the end of its tether, where collapse must come
'inevitably, as an objective historical necessity'. Imperialism
was 'the final stage of its historical career'.[71] It was at once (as
with Kautsky, though not for the same reasons) an effort to

[69] *The Accumulation of Capital*, p. 419.
[70] *Ibid.*, p. 419.   [71] *Ibid.*, p. 417.

prolong its existence and 'a sure means of bringing it to a swift conclusion'; though capitalism might never actually reach its terminus, since the catastrophes it was breeding might destroy it first.[72]

It might be war that would write its *finis*. Years earlier Rosa Luxemburg like many socialists thought of militarism as an excrescence, 'a capitalist disease', which would produce war 'in spite of the complete inconclusiveness of the objectives and motives of the conflict'.[73] Now she devoted a long section of her book to armaments, considered in a new light as underpinning capitalism by providing it with a special, artificial market. Here was an early recognition of something that has since gained steadily in importance. She was thus integrating the growth of armaments with the capitalist system, and making it, with the burdens it imposed and the tensions it inflamed, one of the contradictions that must eventually destroy the system. Imperialism she warned her readers, under stress of these contradictions, was turning more and more to 'lawlessness and violence'.[74]

However, it was mass impoverishment that she thought, or hoped, would precipitate socialist revolution. She was convinced that capitalism was spreading mass misery in Europe as well as outside. It may be noted that she (like most Marxists) did not enquire how the surplus-value of the colonial world was being realized, or who, if not the ordinary man in Europe, was consuming the wealth extracted from it, largely in the form of consumer commodities. 'The more ruthlessly', she wrote, 'capital sets about the destruction of non-capitalist strata at home and in the outside world, the more it lowers the standard of living for the workers as a whole.'[75] By including peasants, and hand-workers still being pressed down by machine competition, she gave this assertion more persuasiveness. With many other socialists in those years she was impressed by rising taxes, rents, prices, all swelling the cost of living. Even so, there was a touch of the doctrinaire in her insistence on the impover-

[72] *Ibid.*, p. 446.
[73] An article of 1899, cited by Sweezy, *op. cit.*, p. 310.
[74] *The Accumulation of Capital*, p. 446.
[75] *Ibid.*, pp. 446–7; cf. Rosa Luxemburg's pamphlet of 1906, *The Mass Strike, the Political Party and the Trade Unions* (trans. P. Lavin, 1925; London edn., n.d.), p. 82.

B

ishment of the European masses, the more so as she made no exception, as Lenin was to do, for any favoured minority among them. She was reading into the present some of the effects of her anticipated future of capitalist decline, in her eagerness to block every way out, except for what temporary relief one power-group might win by snatching colonies from another.

The practical moral stood out: the 'necessity for the international working class to revolt against the rule of capital',[76] before it collapsed and buried mankind under its ruins. On the level of theory the upshot was equally unmistakable: imperialism belonged inseparably to capitalism, and there could be no getting rid of one without the other, as English liberals and reformist socialists dreamed of doing. The book came in for hot discussion, and met with censure both from moderates who did not want to be made to face a capitalist dragon breathing fire and smoke, and from some on the left. Among these was Lenin, who found fault with her economic analyses as she did, on several pages, with some of his. What was to become his most salient disagreement was with her restriction of annexationist appetites to undeveloped areas alone.

7   THE COMING OF THE GREAT WAR

Prodigious research into the summer crisis of 1914 has done little to clarify the 'vital interests' that made Europe's masters, from the Hapsburg in his palace to the huckster in his counting-house, think the gamble of war worth trying. After all these years the Great War looks less like an act of men than a moment in a vast chaotic change, as elemental as the sinking of a mountain range or the drying up of a sea. No big war manifestly economic in its motives had been fought since the advent of industrial capitalism, and businessmen were in no better position than military men to tell what the balance-sheet would be at the end. War aims could only be sketchy; governments had to start working out lists of objectives, with finance and industry throwing in their advice or instructions. In Germany there was much talk of expansion and 'autarchy', the

[76] *The Accumulation of Capital*, p. 467.

creation of 'a large self-sufficient whole' as Sombart put it.[77] 'Mittel-Europa' would be such a whole. Its prophet Naumann painted its inspiration as political, federative, idealistic, not economic or imperialist, 'although'—he admitted to a critic— 'in the present age all historical facts automatically assume an industrial and capitalist character'.[78] Bethmann-Hollweg the chancellor was under opposite pressure from annexationists and socialists, and in sum the colloquy about what Germany was fighting for was muddled, often indiscreet. This did not escape the astute Dr Goebbels, and led him during the Second World War to prohibit public canvassing of war aims except in the most glowingly non-committal language.[79] In 1914–18 the Allies were keeping most of theirs shut up in secret treaties.

When hostilities began the Bureau of the International was busy organizing a conference to be held at Vienna which would go intensively into the problems of imperialism.[80] Caught unawares by the crisis, in the dark about what was going on, socialist leaders called for peace until the last moment, when most of them, more or less gloomily, espoused the cause of patriotism, like the lady who swearing she would ne'er consent consented. Even at the outset a small minority refused. The dividing line was very much as it had been in recent years over imperialism and its connections with capitalism. Those who condoned the war as a defensive one for their own countries were free to blame foreign capitalists, but could not blame capitalism at large, and preferred not to say too much about it. For some of their opponents the issues were perplexed by the ostensible causes at least of the war having nothing to do with any colonies.

Friction over colonies and spheres of influence had indeed seemed to be abating, and Britain and Germany not unwilling to end it by compromise. Kautsky had just been writing about

[77] Nicolai Bukharin, *Imperialism and World Economy* (English edn., London, n.d.), p. 38. On war-time discussions in Germany on war aims, see H. W. Gatzke, *Germany's Drive to the West* (Baltimore, 1950), and F. Fischer, *Germany's Aims in the First World War* (English edn., London, 1967).

[78] Prince Lichnowsky, *Heading for the Abyss* (English edn., London, 1928), p. 132.

[79] See W. A. Boelcke, *The Secret Conferences of Dr Goebbels 1939–43* (English edn., London, n.d.), pp. 38, 41, etc.

[80] Haupt, *op. cit.*, pp. 136-8.

this in an article which he humourlessly published with few alterations in September 1914, when Lenin read it with a sardonic eye.[81] It forecast a happy concord among colonial powers, which Kautsky was christening 'ultra-imperialism'. One good reason he could give for them to close their ranks was colonial resistance. But he went on to traverse the whole left-wing Marxist conception of imperialism which had been taking shape, and which departed from his 1909 guidelines by identifying it with cartels, tariffs, all the paraphernalia of up-to-date capitalism. This approach was mere tautology, he complained: imperialism required more specific definition, such as English writers gave it. By narrowing the subject to colonialism he was evading the broader economic feuds that paved the way for the war. There was substance nevertheless in his charge that imperialism was being treated too largely and loosely, and too much as one and the same thing with capitalism. He was giving his answer in advance to Lenin, who on his side could feel only contemptuous indignation at Kautsky's nostalgia for 'a cleanish, sleek, moderate and genteel capitalism'.[82]

Lenin too must have been taken by surprise by the war. In an often-quoted letter shortly before it he was lamenting with gloomy humour that the Tsar and the rest were not likely to play into socialist hands by falling out with one another. Yet in October 1914, in a statement drafted for his party committee, he accused the rulers of going to war partly in order to distract the minds of the workers from their discontents.[83] This suspicion was not a socialist invention; the German fire-eater General Bernhardi had warned his countrymen that Russia, 'deeply tainted with revolutionary and moral infection', might seek relief before long by going to war, either in the Far East again or in Europe.[84] In the October document Lenin found plenty of room for political motivations, so as to put all Europe's ruling groups in the dock together. He was bracketing 'the

[81] *Notebooks on Imperialism*, pp. 264-6.
[82] *Ibid.*, p. 116.
[83] Lenin, *C. W.* (*Collected Works;* English edn., Moscow, 1964), Vol. 21, p. 27.
[84] Gen. F. von Bernhardi, *Germany and the Next War* (1911; trans. A. H. Powles, London, 1914 edn.), p. 93. On how far fear of mass unrest was a motive for the war, see Haupt, *op. cit.*, pp. 243 ff.; he does not reach a definite answer.

struggle for markets, in the epoch of the latest, the imperialist, stage in the development of capitalism in the foremost countries, the dynastic interests of the most backward East European monarchies. . . .' In other pronouncements too he showed awareness that the world crisis was a highly complex thing. 'There are *no* "pure" phenomena, and there can be none, either in nature or in society. . . . There is no "pure" capitalism in the world, nor can there be. . . .'[85] There can then it would seem be no 'pure' or solitary explanation of any big war.

Russia and Austria-Hungary were following Serbia before long into the background; this war, unlike its successor, was decided on the western front, where the antagonists all fitted far better into Marxist formulae. Lenin's own bent of mind carried him to the economic bedrock that these formulae were mainly concerned with. He took far less interest than Marx or Engels in international politics. To him diplomats were no more than heralds in fine costumes blowing flourishes on their trumpets before the battle. Conundrums about ministries and their mental workings intrigued him not much more. This as well as an agitator's tactics made for some over-simplifying, and failure to eliminate lurking inconsistencies—a defect possibly not unconnected with the difficulties he was to run into late in 1917 when writing *The State and Revolution*. In the October 1914 statement, for instance, the German bourgeoisie was placed 'at the head' of one of the coalitions, not merely welcoming the war but choosing the moment for it; yet in the same breath it was described as 'servilely cringing' to Kaiser and Junkers.[86]

We might say either that he and his few allies on the left blamed capitalism, not this government or that, for the war, and therefore wanted war to be transformed into social revolution—or that they wanted revolution and therefore blamed capitalism. Over niceties of this kind they were in no mood to split hairs. The stock of ideas already built up about imperialism came in pat to their purpose, even if they may have

[85] Lenin, *The Collapse of the Second International* (May-June 1915), in *C. W.*, Vol. 21, p. 236.
[86] *C. W.*, Vol. 21, pp. 27–8. Seven years later, the Allies having won the war, Lenin in his preface to the 1921 edition of his *Imperialism* rather capriciously fixed on Britain as the chief villain, with only a casual mention of Germany among the other criminals.

over-estimated the effectiveness for popular propaganda of what had hitherto been intellectual disputation. A conference of Russian socialists abroad in March 1915 denounced all belligerents impartially as aggressors, spoke of imperialism as the latest phase of capitalist evolution, and went on to capital-export and to war as a struggle for the repartition of the colonial world.[87] Abstract and incomplete as this was, it must be said to compare well for realism with most non-socialist explanations. The official British historian of the peace conference started by defining the war as 'a conflict between the principles of freedom and of autocracy, between the principle of moral influence and of material force, of government by consent and of government by compulsion.'[88] Hilaire Belloc managed still more heroically to present it as a duel between the Catholic faith and its opponents. In either case it would be hard to guess unaided which side was which.

Disputes about the nature of imperialism were wrapped up with the burning question of what to do about the war. Kautsky and Bernstein were at one now in recommending a peace without annexations, to be agreed on by all governments. Hilferding developed the more optimistic side of his study of capitalism, urging that world trade ought to draw nations together, not set them at odds; he pointed out (like Angell) that British colonies could be sources of profit to Germany too.[89] Lenin demanded revolutionary defeatism. Just as for capitalism war was the only way out, social revolution was the only way out for humanity. To throw away this opportunity, and be content with a mere peaceful return to peace, would only mean another conflagration before long, and so on and on until capitalism was demolished. Early in 1915 he disagreed with the slogan of 'united Europe', on the ground that it would only be a union of capitalist countries to exploit colonies jointly, or to prop up obsolete monarchies; and that in this 'epoch of the highest development of capitalism' Europe would in reality be coming together to protect its loot against an envious and more quickly growing Japan and U.S.[90]

[87] *C. W.*, Vol. 21, pp. 159 ff.
[88] H. V. Temperley, cited ironically by Angell in *The Great Illusion*, p. 157 n.
[89] An article of 1916; see abstract in *Notebooks on Imperialism*.
[90] *C. W.*, Vol. 21, p. 339.

Even on the left, others including Rosa Luxemburg, Bukharin, and Trotsky found Lenin's attitude too rigid. As war dragged on he himself must have had some misgivings, and there are signs that by 1916 he was beginning to modify an all-or-nothing stand for revolution at once that was in danger of becoming negative and sterile.[91] If he miscalculated the practical chances, one main cause was his incomprehension of nationalism as a mass sentiment. It was deepened by his isolation during the war years in Switzerland, most of the time shut up in libraries, which fostered a certain dogged one-sidedness. He persisted with what must seem a touch of the spirit of a flat-earth fanaticism in declaring the 'fundamental truth' of the Communist Manifesto that 'the workingmen have no country';[92] shutting his eyes to the complex and tenacious web of links that history had woven between citizen and State. They were entwined with national feelings far older than monopoly capitalism, and easily perverted into the jingo mood they were never very distinct from. To Lenin the break-up of the international socialist movement that was his country of adoption was a traumatic blow, more appalling than the war itself; it infused into his nature an embitterment not characteristic of it in earlier days. Despite his preoccupation with economics he could speak of capitalism's hopes of super-profit from the war as less important than its 'political advantages in that it has split and corrupted the proletariat'.[93] Struggling to unravel what black magic was enabling Europe's rulers to drug the workers into obedience, he was turning to imperialism for an answer to this riddle too, and putting his voluminous jottings on it to account in a series of shorter or longer writings, culminating in 1916 in *Imperialism*.

8 BUKHARIN ON IMPERIALISM AND WAR (1915)

Lenin left it to his ally Bukharin, a rising intellectual among the Bolsheviks, who was in Switzerland in 1914–15, to essay first the task of synthesizing afresh the floating ideas of Marxism

---

[91] See an illuminating article by B. Pearce, 'Lenin and Trotsky on Pacifism and Defeatism', in *Labour Review* (London), Vol. 6 No. 1, 1961.
[92] *C. W.*, Vol. 21, p. 32.
[93] *The Collapse of the Second International, C. W.*, Vol. 21, p. 233.

about imperialism, and of proving that the war now raging was
the one that its teaching had foreshadowed. Bukharin did so in
1915 by expanding an article he had written into a treatise,
Imperialism and World Economy. It was intended for publication
in Russia, where it failed to pass the censor, and was not
printed until after the Bolshevik seizure of power. Lenin wrote
a preface to it, and evidently approved its leading arguments.
Bukharin was primarily an economist, and not always as
much at home on other ground. It was as an economist that
Lenin esteemed him; politically, in the contentions about the
correct line of anti-war agitation, he judged him 'devilishly
unstable.'[94] So far as a theory of imperialism was concerned
the two men could see more or less eye to eye, and their
ability to agree about basic economic factors may have helped
to confine each of them to a somewhat narrowly economic
approach.

Bukharin's title announced his firm association of imperialism
with capitalism. Unlike Rosa Luxemburg he was not bringing
forward any novel reason for capitalism having to resort to
aggression.[95] War was natural to it in this epoch of concentration and monopoly. Contemporary imperialism was quite
distinct, he laid down, from all earlier forms of expansion and
conquest; though at one point he admitted a likeness by
referring to it as a 'new mercantilism'[96]—an analogy that had
struck other writers, Thorold Rogers in England among the
first.[97]

Asking why colonialism had 'become a veritable mania of
all modern capitalist states', Bukharin drew both on Hobson's
capital export and Hilferding's finance-capital. In doing so he
neglected some incongruities, because he put all types of
foreign investment into one and the same category, from
German industrial goods exported on credit to Anglo-French
re-investment of interest. Britain had a net inflow of capital in

[94] *The Letters of Lenin* (trans. E. Hill and D. Mudie, London, 1937), p. 388.
The letters give other hints of disagreement; e.g. pp. 395–6, on the national
question, and p. 411.
[95] Basso, *loc. cit.*, p. 123, remarks that he gives three explanations, without
linking them together.
[96] Bukharin, *op. cit.*, p. 125.
[97] See M. Dobb, *Political Economy and Capitalism* (London, 1937), p. 223
(in Chap. VII, 'Imperialism').

almost every year between 1875 and 1907.[98] Re-invested funds, floating free above the productive process, had a kinship with the usurer capital of old days, or of Asia. Loans to profligate Oriental despots, followed by an occupation of Egypt or some other mortgaged estate—the sort of transaction Hobson was most concerned to censure—were more congenial to it than to 'finance-capital' in Hilferding's sense of bank money invested in industry. Not all British investments took this direction, of course. To clinch the connection between capital export and imperialism, Bukharin cited figures showing half Britain's overseas investment to be within the empire.[99] But he like Rosa Luxemburg was drawing no distinction between areas like India and areas like Canada; it was one that foreign observers often missed, Russians maybe more easily because in their own empire native peoples and Russian settlers were mixed up together. British investment was healthily drawn away from the carcasses of tropical kingdoms by the lure of vast English-speaking regions scattered over the globe, all hungry for development capital.

In white settlement areas of the British empire political control from London was disappearing, while in the U.S., or anywhere under the Monroe Doctrine, it could not be aspired to. The sudden pre-1914 flood of British investment went largely to the U.S., and the amount invested there and in Latin America became almost as large as in the whole empire including Canada.[100] Altogether a far higher proportion of the British than of the French total was playing a constructive rather than a parasitic role. It might even be said that just as many of the more enterprising Britons emigrated to newer, less cramped countries, British capitalism was putting forth vigorous new shoots abroad, while at home it was rapidly being left behind by the Germans.

No doubt by helping to build American and Japanese capitalism, already displaying bellicose tendencies, it was helping to generate fresh imperialist tensions of the future. But for the time being a great deal of surplus European capital, not

[98] For detail see C. K. Hobson, *The Export of Capital* (London, 1914), p. 204.
[99] Bukharin, *op. cit.*, pp. 42–3.
[100] See figures in Feis, *op. cit.*, Chap. 1.

British alone, was being drawn off, and this was relieving its congestions and reducing its readiness to resort to 'imperialistic' activities in the Hobsonian—or common-sense—meaning of the word. Nearly a quarter of German investment in 1914 was in the U.S. and Canada, or else in France and Britain.[101] Of the remainder a large part was in neighbouring territories of Austria, which Pan-Germans could look upon much as Britons looked on their white dominions. Another English liberal, writing in 1914, admitted that capital export had often been used to 'drain countries of their resources', but on balance he was convinced that it functioned constructively and added to the world's wealth.[102] Bukharin's conviction was that any good it did—if deserving to be recognized at all—was merely marginal. He may be excused for not foreseeing a day when capitalist States would invest huge amounts of capital in a socialist Russia that he helped to build.

What imperialism was doing in the colonies he was not studying in any detail; he referred summarily to 'its barbarous, destructive, wasteful activities'.[103] He felt no inconsistency between this and the mistaken estimate he shared with the Kautsky of 1909 of the rate at which backward lands under Western rule were being inducted into capitalism. Nowadays 'the industrialization of the agrarian and semi-agrarian countries proceeds at an unbelievably quick tempo', he wrote;[104] which led him to another fallacy, that all social relations everywhere were being transposed into one uniform pattern, a confrontation of capitalist and workman.[105] He did not mention Kautsky's book, or Rosa Luxemburg's which ought to have enlightened him about obstacles in the way of industry in retarded societies.

Inside national limits Bukharin admitted that the coming of trusts and cartels represented a kind of 'organization process', but internationally there was still chaos. 'This anarchic structure of world capitalism is expressed in two facts: world industrial crises on the one hand, war on the other.'[106] We

---

[101] See figures in Feis, *op. cit.*, p. 74.

[102] C. K. Hobson, *op. cit.*, pp. xix–xx; cf. Feis, *op. cit.*, Introduction to Part III.

[103] Bukharin, *op. cit.*, p. 167.   [104] Bukharin, *op. cit.*, p. 39.

[105] Bukharin, *op. cit.*, p. 27.   [106] Bukharin, *op. cit.*, p. 53.

might find an analogy in political history in the discipline imposed on disorderly feudalism by the absolute monarchies of the sixteenth century, and the diversion of its restless energies outward into dynastic wars. Economic life was taking on a more and more international character, but this instead of bringing the nations closer—as Kautsky and Hilferding now thought it should—only sharpened competition among national groups of capitalists. Tariff policies, formerly defensive, were now weapons of offence, and 'tariff wars' were preliminary skirmishes leading to wars of gunpowder.[107] Bukharin noted that (then as today) exported capital could overleap customs barriers,[108] but this too he regarded as a kind of invasion: 'it subjugates new territories with the greatest ease', intensifying rivalries to an extreme where they can be settled only 'by fire and sword'.[109] Here reasoning seems to lose itself in rhetoric, or to waver between consideration of foreign capital invested in an industrial country, and of capital from two industrial countries disputing control over a colony. As in a number of other places, a concrete example of what Bukharin is aiming at would be welcome.

He allowed too that numerous international combines or agreements had been taking place, but he reckoned them, correctly enough, as very unstable, and derided the hopes built on them as remedies for the world anarchy. He made the general charge against reformists of blinking the contradictions of capitalism and exaggerating its adaptability;[110] a valid criticism, but Marxism must be said to have erred as far in the opposite direction. He agreed with the Hilferding of 1910 that in pure theory the tendency towards amalgamation of capital might continue until a single universal cartel bestrode the planet, but that in practical terms this was not feasible.[111] 'A series of wars is unavoidable', therefore. World capitalism would move towards a single domination, but this would be brought about through the stronger aspirants crushing the weaker by force.[112] European union would not be a step towards peace, he added, following the lead given by Lenin, but rather 'a colossal struggle between Europe on the one

[107] Bukharin, *op. cit.*, pp. 74, 83.   [108] Bukharin, *op. cit.*, p. 97.
[109] Bukharin, *op. cit.*, p. 103.   [110] Bukharin, *op. cit.*, p. 143.
[111] Bukharin, *op. cit.*, pp. 135–6.   [112] Bukharin, *op. cit.*, pp. 136–7, 139.

hand, America and Asia on the other'.[113] Today it can hardly
be denied that such a struggle, commercial if not military, is
very much in the offing.

Capitalism by its nature must at all costs expand, or go to the
wall. 'Imperialist annexation is only a case of the general
capitalist tendency towards centralisation of capital. . . .'[114]
Now that earth's disposable areas were pre-empted, nothing
could be got except at someone else's expense. Bukharin
quoted Marx's adage about all economic history turning on
the antithesis of town and countryside, and observed truly that
this was being reproduced on a vaster scale between industrial
and undeveloped regions.[115] Spread of industrialism must
mean a relative falling off of agricultural resources, and therefore an impetus towards acquisition of agrarian regions to
provide industrial economies with an 'economic supple-
ment'.[116] (In fact in recent decades the opening up of new land
in autonomous countries like Canada and Argentina had given
rise to an embarrassing flood of cheap grain.) But to suppose
that agrarian appendages alone were needful to capitalism, as
Kautsky was saying (and as Rosa Luxemburg's theory implied), would be half way to accepting the contention that this
war was unnecessary, and that imperialism was a menace only
to the backlands. Bukharin accused it of seeking with omnivor-
ous greed to engulf and absorb indiscriminately. Its appetite
was not confined to overseas territories (among which he
unreasonably rejected any distinction between 'tropical' and
'settlement' colonies):[117] it commenced with these because they
were the most accessible, but the time had come for 'a fundamental revision', or tearing up of frontier lines. Germany's
seizure of Belgium was on a par with Britain's of Egypt, except
that the former was an instance of 'horizontal' expansion, the
latter of 'vertical'.[118] Bukharin expected the war, if not ended

---

[113] Bukharin, *op. cit.*, p. 120.   [114] Bukharin, *op. cit.*, p. 120.
[115] Bukharin, *op. cit.*, pp. 20–21.
[116] Bukharin, *op. cit.*, p. 105 and Chap. VIII.
[117] Bukharin, *op. cit.*, pp. 107–8.
[118] Bukharin, *op. cit.*, p. 121. Among later Marxists, Sweezy (*op. cit.*,
p. 320) writes that 'the annexationist urge of imperialist nations is by no
means confined to backward non-industrialized regions'; M. Dobb, on the
other hand, in *Capitalism Yesterday and Today* (London, 1958), p. 30, speaks
of 'that economic and political penetration . . . of undeveloped countries
which goes by the name of modern imperialism.'

by revolutions, to wipe the slate clean of smaller states;[119] instead it was to have the opposite effect of bringing a number of them back into existence, a development continued after the Second World War in other continents; few of them it is true have been genuinely independent. He was astray again in expecting the British empire to fuse into one economic entity, a parallel to Mittel-Europa.[120]

For him each nation at any rate was evolving into one great capitalist corporation, 'an entrepreneurs' company of tremendous power'.[121] With the war, the bonds between State and finance and industry were everywhere drawn closer still; bureaucratic capital might be said to be joining banking and industrial capital as a third partner. But the inclination to over-schematic thinking, and to 'reductionism', or neglect of all but directly material causation, which Gramsci was to stigmatize in his later work on Marxist philosophy,[122] is visible in his treatment of the State; though it stands to his credit that he was not leaving it out of his equation, as Marxists have too often done.[123] 'State power has become the domain of a financial oligarchy . . . an exact expression of the interests of finance capital.'[124] An *inexact* expression, rather; fortunately for mankind its overlords have never succeeded in devising methods of government entirely and exclusively satisfactory to themselves. Directing a State is a different matter from directing a bank or brewery, on whatever scale; and besides the many alien incrustations, whether represented by Kaiser or by Demos, that clog the 'pure reason' of capitalism, there is the fact that it does not always know, any more than its simpler-minded forerunners, what is best for it. It may have to be saved from itself. A state run wholly by and for big business would not be long in capsizing.

Overlooking all this, Bukharin thought that democracy and

---

[119] Bukharin, *op. cit.*, p. 144.
[120] Bukharin, *op. cit.*, p. 80.
[121] Bukharin, *op. cit.*, p. 155.
[122] See Q. Hoare and G. N. Smith, *Selections from the Prison Notebooks of Antonio Gramsci* (London, 1971), pp. 419 ff.
[123] Basso, one of the few recent commentators on Bukharin's book, commends him for giving fuller weight than either Rosa Luxemburg or Lenin to the rôle of the State in economic affairs (*loc. cit.*, p. 122). He considers the book richer in ideas than Lenin's *Imperialism* (p. 125.)
[124] Bukharin, *op. cit.*, p. 108.

parliamentary life would soon be things of the past: their function of providing for adjustments between diverse propertied interests was coming to an end, as all property converged in one mass, and what imperialism required was some type of dictatorship.[125] He was again echoing Hilferding, and hitting the mark in so far as dictatorship was to prove the norm in capitalist societies in crisis; yet formal democracy has survived, and best in the most advanced countries, where parliaments have not served as camouflage alone but have adapted their old function to smoothing out dissensions among capital and labour and the middle classes.

Bukharin did Angell an injustice when he taxed him (at second hand) with forgetting that nations are made up of groups, and that policies harmful to the whole may benefit sectional interests.[126] He was losing moreover some of the force of his own case, for on his showing each national complex was now so closely welded that there were no longer any significant sectional interests, unless those of the man in the street might be reckoned such. But the man in the street too was being drawn into the amalgam represented by what we might call 'national capitalism', and was soon to disguise itself as 'National Socialism'. It is to Bukharin's credit once more that he was alive to this, even if he failed to throw much light on it. Skilled and well-paid workers like Ford's, he wrote, were apt to identify their own and their bosses' interests, as craftsmen did in the patriarchal days of manufacture. He threw out an allusion to America and Australia, not of much relevance to European history, but went on to argue that by the end of the nineteenth century capitalist encroachment had 'to a large degree destroyed the bond of unity between capitalists and workers': it had not however yet broken the bond 'between the working class and the great organization of the bourgeoisie, the capitalist state.'[127] Here is another proposition much in want of illustration, to clarify how and when workers who in the Communist Manifesto had no fatherland came to acquire one. Their link with the State was a new one still being forged, as

[125] Bukharin, op. cit., p. 128.
[126] Bukharin, op. cit., p. 61. Bukharin, like Lenin, virtually ignored Angell's case.
[127] Bukharin, op. cit., p. p162-4.

well as an old one not yet worn out. With the war it was being reinforced by cooperation between trade union leaders and governments.

Bukharin was close to an important part of the truth, of which Lenin took less notice, when he dwelt on the 'grandiose ideological formulation' that accompanied imperialism, and how it was instilled into the masses.[128] Speaking of the flood of propaganda about the war as a conflict of races, he commented with much insight that such fantasies were meat and drink to ruling classes 'directly interested in utilising the remnants of old psychological stratifications' for their own advantage.[129] Every age is swaddled in left-overs from the past, and it is out of these draperies, the mental stuff of former days, that the illusions necessary for the business of government are chiefly woven.

So far as colonies or semi-colonies were prized as markets, the 'mania' for grabbing them might be regarded as a desperate effort to put off the evil day when capitalism would have to make a better market for itself at home by allowing wages to rise, as the English liberals proposed. Bukharin was positive that this would never come to pass; a belief central to the left-wing Marxist philosophy, and in the light of later history one of its most vulnerable joints. He declared that capitalism would no more think of such a programme than of trying to drag itself out of a swamp by its own hair.[130] Any trifling improvement there might be in the workers' lot he put down to their being granted a small portion of imperial profit. He had consequently to attack any suggestions of colonies being not worth having. 'The colonial policy yields a colossal income to the great powers, *i.e.* to their ruling classes', out of which something could be bestowed on the workers, or some sections of them, chiefly the more skilled.[131] He was harking back to Kautsky's summary of recent history in 1909, but forcing it into a narrower mould, when he asserted that 'All the relative "prosperity" of the European-American industry was conditioned by nothing but the fact that a safety-valve was opened in the form of colonial policy.'[132] As Marxists too

[128] Bukharin, *op. cit.*, p. 109.
[130] Bukharin, *op. cit.*, p. 79.
[132] Bukharin, *op. cit.*, p. 165.

[129] Bukharin, *op. cit.*, pp. 110–11.
[131] Bukharin, *op. cit.*, p. 165.

habitually did, he was lumping together as 'colonial' profit each and every gain from the proliferation of world trade anywhere and everywhere. Years later he repeated, just as sweepingly, that capitalism survived and flourished through its ability to disarm working-class hostility, 'paying higher wages to labour by plundering and mercilessly exploiting the colonies', and thereby fostering a sense of community between workers and capitalist State.[133]

It might sound doubtful wisdom for Marxism to tell the workers, exactly as conservatism was telling them, that if they wanted anything better than a bare subsistence they could only get it, short of revolution, by backing the imperialist struggle for existence. On the morrow of the war there were 'National Bolsheviks' in Germany. Bukharin hugged the hope that harsh war-time experience was delivering the working class from its delusions, by revealing the cost of imperialism as far higher than its reward—for the workers, that is, not for their employers, for otherwise he would be agreeing with Angell that no nation at war could be gainfully employed. Hitherto imperialism confined its barbarities mostly to 'savages' in the backlands; 'now it thrusts itself upon the toilers of Europe. . . . The war severs the last chain that binds the workers to the masters, their slavish submission to the imperialist state.'[134] No doubt it ought to have been doing this. Bukharin rubbed the lesson in by saying, as Rosa Luxemburg did, that the future of capitalism must in any case be a gloomy one, with 'A deep-going tendency towards decreasing real wages . . . not a relative, but also an *absolute* worsening of the situation of the working class.'[135] Impoverishment in other words had only artificially and temporarily been interrupted by imperial profiteering.

Whether much or little gain awaited the winners in this war, he could not admit any option for capitalism of altering its fated course. There could be no further evolution for it on any new lines. Imperialism was its final, full-blown phase, beyond which could lie only the worsening delirium of a sick world, or socialism. He ended with the vision of the Communist Manifesto, the expropriation of the expropriators.

[133] N. Bukharin, *Historical Materialism* (English edn., London, 1925), p. 256.
[134] Bukharin, *Imperialism and World Economy*, p. 167.   [135] *Ibid.*, p. 159.

9   LENIN'S 'IMPERIALISM' (1916)

Soon after completing his book Bukharin found himself serving
a prison sentence in Sweden, after which he shook the dust of
Europe off his feet and withdrew, as Trotsky and others had
done, to America, until the fall of the Tsar summoned him
back to Russia. All this time Lenin was wrestling with the same
problems. Some of his thoughts took shape in a pamphlet, *The
War and the Second International*, written in the summer of 1915
while Bukharin was still at work. Early next year, with
Bukharin off the scene and his book gone aground in Russia,
Lenin felt called on to provide a substitute for it, and the outcome was his longer pamphlet or short book *Imperialism*,
repeating or improving his previous arguments. While busy
with it he moved in February 1916 from Berne to Zürich in
search of better libraries;[136] by early August he was trying to
arrange for the sheets to be smuggled to Russia, hidden inside
book-bindings.[137] They did not get into print until the following
April, when the Tsar had fallen and it was Lenin who was
being smuggled into Russia.

    In both these compositions he was seeking to test what was
true in the heap of ideas current, as he said in his foreword
to *Imperialism*, since the beginning of the century: he singled out
Hobson and Hilferding as having given the best lead, but as
suffering from political errors. He himself as a Marxist
thinker was not a great originator, but rather a great system-
atizer: one of those minds, also indispensable, that deepen and
consolidate a body of thought and give it firmer anchorage. It
was a talent that went with his genius for practical organization.
Since the catastrophe of 1914 he was being forced back on
fundamentals, retreating to Marxist philosophy as an impreg-
nable line of defence, as he had done after the failure of the
first Russian revolution when he composed his attack on
Empirio-criticism. His notebooks show how wide-ranging his
intellectual curiosity was, in certain directions, when he felt
free to indulge it. He made notes on Lassalle on Heraclitus the
Obscure,[138] to whom can be traced the dialectical concept of

---

[136] *The Letters of Lenin*, pp. 384–5.   [137] *Ibid.*, pp. 398–9.
[138] See Lenin, *Philosophical Notebooks* (*Collected Works*, English edn., Vol.
38; Moscow, 1961), pp. 341 ff.

contradiction which must have had a special meaning for
Lenin in this dark hour. All his chief undertakings in the field
of theory belonged indeed to intervals of defeat or solitude.
Each was a justification of what Lenin took to be the true
Marxist position, rather than an attempt at innovation. The
last two, *Imperialism* and *The State and Revolution*, were addressed
to immediate problems of action, and this was bound to influence their character, in some ways crampingly.

In his preface to Bukharin's book Lenin recorded again his
awareness that a serious analysis of the war required 'a full
understanding of imperialism, both from its economic and
political aspects'.[139] He reiterated that one must look at things
all round; social life being so complex, 'it is always possible to
select any number of examples or separate data to prove any
proposition one desires.'[140] He admonished himself and his
readers of the merely 'conditional and relative value of all
definitions'.[141] He noticed briefly how factors belonging to a
'non-economic superstructure' could intensify imperialist
quarrels; he even quoted from a French author the remark
that modern life generates psychological irritations that may
find an outlet in war.[142] He had to keep off various subjects
because he wanted *Imperialism* to circulate legally in Russia,
and tsarist censors, although he must have thought them
remarkably broad-minded or slack, would have to draw the
line somewhere. How many of these other topics he would
have liked to explore, or how successfully he would have done
so, can only be conjectured. History meant much less to him
than to Marx, and in spite of his self-warnings he shared in
some degree Bukharin's tendency to isolate economic factors.
An ascetic self-restraint, besides, made him want to put before
readers the plainest and most convincing case, and make sure
of capitalism being brought once for all to the gallows by
saddling it, as the Allies at Versailles were to saddle their
defeated foes, with the entire load of war-guilt.

All this brought him to invest capitalism with too universal
and omnipotent a direction of events, to make it too un-

---

[139] Bukharin, *Imperialism and World Economy*, p. 9.
[140] Preface to 1920 edn. of *Imperialism*; *C. W.*, Vol. 22, p. 190.
[141] *Imperialism*, *C. W.*, Vol. 22, p. 266.
[142] *Ibid.*, pp. 262–3.

questionably the All-Highest of the age, dominating men and things like the Immanent Spirit in Hardy's *Dynasts*. On his stage many other factors in imperialism—restlessness of displaced aristocracies, ambitions of soldiers, momentum of earlier conquest—were relegated so far into the background as to be almost out of sight. Capitalist purposes themselves did not all spring so directly as he was ready to assume from the pure intrinsic nature of capitalism, and they were modified in their turn by many other impulses at work. Economic history can never be a self-contained process moving along a predestinate track of its own. Capitalist society was still in the making, and had needs not reckonable in cashbooks and ledgers. It suffered from instability at the apex, where diverse social groups were coalescing into a plutocracy, as well as at the bottom. Of this coming together too imperialism was a necessary part.

Imperialism had for sub-title 'The Highest Stage of Capitalism', implying also its *final* stage. Lenin followed Hilferding in giving prominence to the trend of capital towards concentration and monopoly, which he could claim for Marx the credit of having foreseen.[143] He was carrying to its furthest limit, complete integration of capital of all types, a progress that Marxists had been observing for years. Kautsky left a wide though diminishing gap between two principal types, banking and industrial capital; Hilferding narrowed it by putting the first in command; Lenin abolished it. He made frequent use of the phrase 'finance-capital', but he was altering its import, compressing its content, so much that he would have done better to find a new one. [144] His monist conception of capitalism did away with any question of different sections of it having different outlooks and modes of behaviour; there was only one capitalism, which could have only one criminal career, and one fitting punishment. Its connection with war, fortuitous in Rosa Luxemburg's early thinking, semi-accidental in Kautsky's in 1909, was now a marriage that no man could put asunder.

It was common sense, if not strict logic, to postulate a relationship between monopoly capitalism and imperialism as 'beyond doubt', on the ground that they were manifesting

[143] *Ibid.*, pp. 198–200.
[144] Sweezy, *op. cit.*, p. 269.

themselves at the same time.[145] Yet objections are not hard to find, and Lenin himself did not succeed in excluding discrepancies from his argument. His picture of a trustified, monopolistic economy derived chiefly from Germany and the U.S., and was much less faithful to realities in Britain, where he admitted that concentration began later than in the protectionist countries, but only he thought a little later: he considered it as having achieved 'complete supremacy' everywhere by about 1900,[146] the date which he took as inaugurating the world-reign of monopoly capitalism.[147] It might be argued on the contrary that Britain's unique array of colonial possessions, mostly acquired long before that date, furnished it with an alternative to concentration of capital, and hindered its arrival at the 'highest stage'. If so, here is one of those variations or mutations, instances of the adaptability of an economic system to its environment, which Lenin could not disregard altogether but wanted to allow no more than a nominal place. In another way too British capitalism did not fit very well into his scheme. City bankers were content with the pickings of their long-established international business, and had little desire to turn aside into new paths of industrial financing.[148]

Lenin introduced a second dichotomy when he spoke of heavy industry's ability to 'exact tribute' from all other branches of the economy.[149] Yet further on he declared that French colonial expansion since 1880 stemmed from a weakening of industrial capital, and commented: 'The characteristic feature of imperialism is *not* industrial *but* finance capital.'[150] In the context he could only be thinking of banking, or moneylending, capital, certainly hypertrophied in France at the expense of industrial. This means that he like Bukharin was unconsciously juggling with the two senses of Hilferding's term. France was the usurer of Europe, he wrote.[151] But usury is not the highest stage of capitalism, whatever else may be. We must suppose a regression of French capitalism, under the spell of colonial tribute, and France's empire like Britain's may be classed as a divagation, an alternative to the logical progress

---

[145] *Imperialism, C. W.*, Vol. 22, p. 255.
[147] *Ibid.*, pp. 200–201.
[149] *Imperialism, C. W.*, Vol. 22, p. 217.
[151] *Ibid.*, p. 233.

[146] *Ibid.*, pp. 298–9.
[148] Semmel, *op cit.*, p. 145.
[150] *Ibid.*, p. 268.

of capitalism towards its finishing-point that Lenin was
impatient to find everywhere.

'The old capitalism has had its day. The new capitalism
represents a transition to something.'[152] Towards what, he
described bourgeois economists as uneasily asking? Towards its
supplanting by socialism, was of course his own reply. In fact
the transition was to be a very halting, groping one, by way
of two world wars, towards welfare- or prosperity-capitalism;
a mediocre prospect happily hidden from Lenin. For him the
capitalism of his day was 'highly developed, mature, and over-
ripe',[153] ready in short to give up the ghost, though he was in
far less haste than his later disciples to dismiss it as techno-
logically exhausted.[154] What he was most positive of was that
the new capitalism was a far worse master than the old; its
oppression was 'a hundred times heavier, more burdensome
and intolerable'.[155] Did he ask himself whether anything could
be a hundred times worse than the capitalism branded by
Karl Marx? He dwelt as Bukharin had done on the lagging of
agriculture behind industry[156], and fully endorsed the opinion
common in the International for several years before the war
that things were getting worse for the workers. It was not at
that date absurd for Lenin to reaffirm that so long as capitalism
lasted the poverty of the masses, or the great bulk of them, was
irremediable. Socialism had always drawn much of its vitality
from this simple conviction, and when men like Bernstein
began to leave it behind they were, unwittingly, beginning to
leave their socialism behind too. Now more than ever Lenin
was bent on guarding it firmly. A man of action must have
some unarguable axioms to sustain him. That of working-class
solidarity was proving not unshakable; but if workers were less
virtuous than Lenin had believed them, capitalists could not
be allowed to be less wicked.

He seems as a rule to be arguing from the poverty of the
masses, and consequent anaemia of the home market and
investment incentives, to the flow of capital abroad, very much
as Hobson did. A later Marxist has sought to absolve him of

[152] *Ibid.*, p. 225; cf. p. 219.
[153] Preface to Bukharin's *Imperialism*, p. 9.
[154] See e.g. *Imperialism, C. W.*, Vol. 22, p. 204.
[155] *Ibid.*, p. 205.   [156] *Ibid.*, p. 217.

anything so crude as under-consumptionism, and to show him as relying instead on finance-capital as the driving force behind expansionism.[157] This sounds a little abstract, the more so as the term finance-capital is in some respects equivocal. At any rate Lenin was always eager to discredit the panacea put forward by Hobson and Brailsford of a raising of living standards to induce capital to stay at home. Against the relevant extract from Hobson in his notebooks he scribbled: 'ha-ha!! the essence of philistine criticism of imperialism'; he was derisive too of Hobson's related wish for democratic social planning.[158] On Kautsky's patronage of the proposed higher wages he wrote now that it was nothing more than 'a very fitting topic for a churchman to preach on to the financiers'.[159] Lenin was no church-goer, or he would have known better than to suspect clergymen of being so tactless. Another later Marxist will not allow the proposal to be feasible even in theory, because any attempt to regulate investment merely 'sets off a series of new dislocations'.[160] This objection scarcely puts out of court a gradual long-term change, such as we have actually witnessed. Lenin in any case appears to throw out the liberal remedy as politically, more than economically, impracticable.

10   CAPITAL-EXPORT IN LENIN'S THEORY

He devoted five pages of *Imperialism* to capital export, somewhat schematic, as well as brief, to bear the weight of the book's entire thesis. That Britain and France in this period were mostly re-exporting old investment income did not strike him as calling for notice,[161] though it might be said to cast doubt on the congestion he took for granted in the home market, where newly-formed capital apparently continued to find scope. Or

[157] G. Lichtheim, *Imperialism* (London, 1971), p. 117. For a Marxist critique of Hobson's under-consumptionism, see Dobb, *Political Economy and Capitalism*, pp. 268 ff.

[158] *Notebooks on Imperialism*, pp. 414, 432.

[159] *The Collapse of the Second International*, C. W., Vol. 21, p. 230.

[160] Magdoff, *op. cit.*, p. 24. For an opposite view, that Lenin was wrong to dismiss the possibility of wages being raised, see J. Strachey, *The End of Empire* (London, 1961), pp. 109–12.

[161] Lenin's Notebooks show that he knew of C. K. Hobson's book, but he does not seem to have read it.

we may conjecture a double flow of funds, with older, mellower investors turning into contented clippers of colonial coupons, as the rich merchant of English tradition turned into an ease-loving landowner, while newer, sharper-toothed men gathered money and sent it abroad. Holdings of foreign and colonial stocks by the advanced countries were in any case accumulating, as Lenin said. He adhered to his monist system by making as little distinction as Bukharin between investment in areas sociologically the most heterogeneous. He referred to shares in U.S. railways held by English millionaires as an instance of 'concentration of finance capital'.[162] Wherever capital flowed, the aggressive instincts of monopoly capitalism were at work, and the revenue it brought in was the solid basis for imperialist oppression by 'a handful of the wealthiest states'.[163] Present-day capitalism was not merely the cause of, it was identical with, imperialism. 'Call it what you will, it makes no difference.'[164] It was this kind of definition that Kautsky understandably objected to, as going round in a circle.

Capital was attracted most compellingly, in Lenin's opinion, to backward regions like Turkey, with untapped resources and unprotected labour, where 'the financier reaps a triple profit' as compared with what he could look for in developed countries like the U.S.[165] Yet nearly a quarter of British overseas investment was in the U.S., while high profits in the backlands often went with high risks. True, investors were always eager to reduce these risks, while keeping up the profits, by enlisting official aid. This might come from the local government, if there was one capable of upholding what financiers call Order. Where none such existed, the investor would importune his own government to step in.

Several peculiarities helped to make France both an adventurous foreign lender and a restless forager for colonies, though very little of French investment went into French colonies. On the other hand colonies might be coveted by countries with little or no capital to export. Lenin specified as three new baits

[162] *Imperialism, C. W.*, Vol. 22, p. 257.
[163] *Ibid.*, p. 243.
[164] *Ibid.*, p. 270. Cf. p. 202: 'Capitalism has been transformed into imperialism.'
[165] *The Collapse of the Second International, C. W.*, Vol. 21, p. 230.

added to the '"old" motives of colonial policy', fields of investment and markets and raw materials.[166] None of these was new in kind, though all were taking on fresh significance. If congestion of capital and falling profit-rates at home may be called the *subjective* economic cause of colonialism, then need of raw materials from outside and markets in which to earn money to pay for them can be dubbed *objective* causes: they must affect every industrial economy, capitalist or not. Lenin and later Marxism were not always careful enough to see where one began and the other ended. Poor, vigorous countries wanting to stake a claim to their share of what was going might well see in colonies a short cut to prosperity. Japan was the typical nation here, with its annexation of Taiwan in 1895 and Korea in 1910. In any such case forces other than strictly economic would exert a heavier leverage, as the Japanese army did. Tsarist Russia was another such anomaly. In an article written about this time Lenin pigeon-holed its expansionism as *'military-feudal* "imperialism"'[167], a label which betrays some uncertainty, like the special category of Aryan that Nazi savants had to invent for Dr Goebbels to fit into. The Russo-Japanese war in 1904 was a quarrel over colonial spoils, but decisive among these was the Yalu River timber on which the Tsar's private investment was staked, and which made him deaf to his ministers' remonstrances.[168]

Portugal, to consider one further exception, stood at the opposite pole from Japan, both as an ancient intruder into other continents and as now socially and economically derelict, though they were alike in suffering from no plethora of capital. In the course of the scramble for Africa its sphere was greatly enlarged, army officers and other sectional interests dragging the country into what was really a reduction to absurdity of imperialism. Portuguese life perpetuated much of an old feudal climate, its habits of wasteful display and prodigal

[166] *Imperialism, C. W.*, Vol. 22, p. 299.

[167] *C. W.*, Vol. 21, p. 420. Rosa Luxemburg thought Russia was acting more from needs of State than of economy (see Lenin's *Notebooks on Imperialism*, p. 309). In his *History of the Russian Revolution* (London edn., 1967), Vol. 1, p. 190, Trotsky took the opposite view; but on p. 33 he wavered, and in his *Stalin* (London edn., 1969), Vol. 1, p. 243, he returned to the view that Russia went to war to stifle working-class unrest.

[168] Brailsford, *op. cit.*, p. 51. See further A. Malozemoff, *Russian Far Eastern Policy, 1881-1904* (California, 1958).

spending, its blend of liberality and rapacity, readily translated into a 'civilising mission'. Something of this pre-industrial mentality may have lingered among ordinary folk in the industrial countries too, and coloured their hazy feelings about empire. But with every allowance for all this 'quixotry', a recent historian goes much too far when he says that Portuguese empire-building made 'nonsense of the Hobson-Lenin theory of economic imperialism before that theory could even be propounded.'[169] How great Powers act cannot be judged by any dwarfish apings of them. Besides, considerable amounts of foreign capital were being invested in Portuguese Africa, as well as in Portugal itself, largely by its old bear-leader England. A direct take-over of the colonies by England and Germany was more than once in prospect; an example of how economic penetration might lead towards political ascendancy. A Foreign Office memorandum in 1919 remarked that 'The policy pursued by the Germans in Turkey, Russia and elsewhere before the war has shown how it is possible for a foreign people to exploit the resources of a country of which they have not the political control'; but it went on to express suspicion of Japan's motives for acquiring property in India.[170]

That most capital exported was not invested in colonies could not be gainsaid, but Lenin saw no proof here that colonies were a superfluity. There were all kinds of auxiliary purposes for them to serve, for instance as places where surplus goods could be dumped.[171] The world he looked out on appeared to him, as to most businessmen—in spite of Angell—, one of limited resources and openings, where each competing nation must perforce grab as much as it could and fence it off with tariffs or boundary lines. He wrote of the scramble all over the globe by big corporations anxious to make sure of their supplies. He was by no means alone in surmising that some raw materials, oil among them, might be nearing exhaustion.[172] Even the most unattractive territory was worth snapping up, because it might turn out later on to contain

[169] R. J. Hammond, *Portugal and Africa 1815–1910. A Study in Uneconomic Imperialism* (Stanford, 1966), p. x; cf. pp. 72, 335.

[170] D. Dignan, *New Perspectives on British Far Eastern Policy 1913–1919* (University of Queensland, 1969), pp. 295–6.

[171] *Notebooks on Imperialism*, pp. 195–6.

[172] *Imperialism*, C. W., Vol. 22, pp. 248–9.

valuables.[173] Gambling is part of all business activity, it has been remarked.[174] Over and above this, Lenin could have argued against Angell that buying raw materials from someone else was less profitable than cornering one's own sources, as capitalists were learning to do inside their national limits by the practice of 'vertical integration'.

Altogether, Lenin can be said to have had firm ground under his feet when he linked colonialism with the appetites of big business, even without the aid of a capital-export theory which in a good many ways hampered rather than assisted him. To Kautsky's cavil that Germany's trade was growing faster than Britain's with some British colonies, Lenin retorted that 'German imperialism is younger, stronger, and better organized'.[175] 'Imperialism' seems to signify no more here than business efficiency; and a Hamburg trader forging ahead of his Liverpool competitor might agree with Kautsky that Britain's empire was not doing it much good. But he might be likelier to conclude, with Lenin, that it would be better transferred to his own custody, since he would know how to make more use of it. Almost any fact of the times could lend itself to opposite interpretations, and businessmen were as prone to fashionable crazes or dreams of Eldorado as anyone else.

We may regret Lenin's omission from his treatise of any detailed discussion of colonial areas that had come into his reading. In the heat of wartime neither he nor his readers could have much thought to spare for such matters, and later on he never had occasion to come back to them. Like Bukharin he took for granted that imperialism must have a blighting effect on native peoples, just as the 'new capitalism' was having on the majority at home. The imperial relationship was essentially predatory, its purpose the extraction of tribute or loot; railways were the 'summation' of capitalism by virtue of serving as its instrument for plundering the continents.[176] But

---

[173] *Imperialism, C. W.*, Vol 22, p. 261.

[174] From one point of view imperialism may be thought of as an outlet for a gambler's instinct that is one component of the complex psychology of capitalism. Scott, who shared this instinct, described it graphically in Chap. 1 of *Rob Roy* in his picture of the hero's father, the great merchant whose 'health and spirits and activity seemed ever to increase with the animating hazards on which he staked his wealth . . . .'

[175] *Imperialism, C. W.*, Vol. 22, p. 290.

[176] Preface to 1920 edn. of *Imperialism, C. W.*, Vol. 22, p. 190.

this was only one side of the story. Just as Marx thought of capitalist industrialization as a painful but necessary stage of progress, Lenin thought the same of capital injected into backward regions. Export of capital might retard industrial growth at home, but would initiate or accelerate it in the areas of investment.

Marx seems to have expected the capitalist mode of production to spread like a germ-culture wherever introduced, and his successors, independently of him, were of the same mind. Visualizing an irresistible outflow of capital from the industrial countries, they were in a way leaving themselves no choice. Once an adequate infrastructure of railway stations and police stations was in being in any colonial area, there could be little further employment for capital except in creating industry. After saying that the extension of railways had been quickest in the colonies and other undeveloped lands of Asia and the Americas, Lenin continued, as if no more evidence were requisite: 'Capitalism is growing with the greatest rapidity in the colonies and in overseas countries.'[177] The only one he mentioned, under this omnibus heading, was the highly atypical Japan, and apart from Japan it was only to countries like the U.S. or Canada that his dictum properly applied. Once again he was ignoring the potent influence of each region's local character and history, and crediting capitalism with too sovereign a sway.

To the extent that new industrial raw materials like rubber and oil were being tapped, they might be supposed to stimulate industry at home in the advanced countries. Lenin's emphasis was on the opposite tendency of imperial tribute to promote the rise of a 'rentier stratum' divorced from production, and with it a drift of whole countries towards a parasitic style of 'living on the exploitation of the labour of several overseas countries and colonies'. He quoted a description of Holland as 'the model "rentier state"', already in the condition towards which England and France were moving.[178] But Holland never was a hearth of modern industry, and the empire that must have been partly the cause of this was an inheritance from the seventeenth century. France was industrializing slowly, grudg-

[177] *Imperialism*, C. W., Vol. 22, p. 274.
[178] *Ibid.*, pp. 277-8.

ingly. Whether a country once fully in the grip of modern industrialism could relapse into a more primitive condition must appear far more doubtful than Lenin thought it. Many social impediments would hold up the free readjustment of capitalism, even assuming that this was its natural direction. So would the need for heavy industries to keep up armed strength, on Lenin's other assumption of a perpetual war to the knife among all capitalist countries, to say nothing of the maintenance of Order in colonies.

Furthermore, decline into parasitism would seem to negate the dynamic, aggressive marriage of 'finance-capital', and to represent a later, if not a higher, phase of capitalist evolution. Active, industrializing capital would be banished to newly-emerging lands, which could scarcely then be regarded as hapless victims of exploitation. Lenin was trying to have it both ways when he took up Hobson's speculation about a happily united Europe of the future living on the toil of a subject China. Hobson was careful to add, and Lenin to repeat, that the future is always too incalculably complex for safe prediction[179]—a caution that Marxists as well as others have too often forgotten. History is strewn with unrealized might-have-been's, often worth making cautious use of as magnifying-glasses. Lenin would not in any case anticipate that colonial regions could be kept in chains for long: once industrialized by foreign masters they would soon become ungovernable from outside. This amounted to something very like the 'decolonization' theory debated (and repudiated) by the Third International in the 1920s. It could find warrant both in Kautsky's *Road to Power* and in Hilferding, from whom Lenin borrowed the aphorism: 'Capitalism itself gradually provides the subjugated with the means and resources for their emancipation.'[180] But to wait for capitalism to generate liberation movements would mean waiting a very long time. India was virtually the only big colony to be led to freedom by a national bourgeoisie; none was led by an industrial working class. Pre-capitalist forces—peasants, intellectuals—rejuvenated

[179] *Ibid.*, pp. 279–80. Strachey (*op. cit.*, pp. 101–2) points out that Lenin had far more awareness than Hobson of colonial nationalism as a limiting factor, especially in China.

[180] *Imperialism, C. W.*, Vol. 22, p. 297.

by modern ideas would provide most of the recruits to the cause of colonial revolt. Lenin was relying overmuch on the automatic play of economic forces, with too little allowance for the play of ideas, which—whether progressive or reactionary—can be hatched only in a very specific environment but can then spread to many others.

I I LENIN ON CAPITALISM AND THE WAR

To pine with Kautsky for a peaceful stay-at-home capitalism was to ask, Lenin repeated, for a return from monopoly to the stage of small-scale competition, which even if feasible would mean going backward.[181] He rejected as equally false, but more plausible and therefore more harmful, the notion of a peaceful accommodation among capitalist nations. 'The most subtle theory of social-chauvinism, one that has been most skilfully touched up to look scientific and international, is the theory of "ultra-imperialism" advanced by Kautsky.' This was undeniably an ill-chosen term, as Lenin said, but what enraged him was Kautsky's deduction that 'ultra-imperialism' might be in a position to create 'an era of new hopes and expectations within the framework of capitalism.'[182] Any dreams of a tranquil tomorrow could only distract socialists from wrestling with the hideous realities of today. There could be no lessening of contradictions within the new capitalism; uncontrollable pressures drove it towards violence and conquest.[183] Ultra-imperialism in short was 'ultra-nonsense'.[184] A well-regulated world laid out among a few law-abiding empires was 'the cant of English parsons'[185]—a class of individuals for whom Lenin must have had for some reason a particular disrelish.

He ridiculed a French economist for fancying that the network of international investment would prevent war.[186] Concentration of capital only made international relations more unbalanced and explosive. By stifling at home competitiveness inherent in capitalism, monopoly fostered in it a morbid aggressiveness which had to find vent externally, by way of

[181] *Ibid.*, p. 289.
[182] *The Collapse of the Second International, C. W.*, Vol. 21, pp. 223-4.
[183] *Ibid.*, p. 226.   [184] *Imperialism, C. W.*, Vol. 22, p. 271.
[185] *Ibid.*, p. 284.   [186] *Ibid.*, p. 288.

imperialism.[187] With the world already carved up, great-power greeds could only be satisfied by a forcible redivision of the spoils. Hence the Great War. For some years after 1871 capitalism was in a relatively pacific mood, though tyrannous in its rule over the masses, especially in the colonies.[188] Capitalists then had no need to fight one another, because there was room for all. If we apply Lenin's criteria rigorously, the partition of the world was not really 'imperialism', because finance-capital or monopoly capitalism was not fully in the saddle before about 1900, when most of it was complete. Imperialism properly so-called began when the earlier colonialism ended, and its business was to re-partition the world.

As to whether this could be repeated indefinitely, as Lenin assumed, one doubt is suggested by his own belief that colonial resistance movements would soon be entering the arena in greater force. It lends more weight than he was willing to grant them to some other words he quoted from Kautsky: 'India may cease to be a British possession, but as an integral empire it will never fall under the sway of another foreign power.'[189] Kautsky—that 'beastly, rotten, smug hypocrite'[190]—was now for Lenin the arch-forger of spurious Marxism, and here Lenin was repelling the prediction that nations would give up the struggle for colonies, as not worth the candle. Also, as at many other points, he did not feel impelled to explore far-off vistas, because all his hopes and resolves were fixed on the destruction of Western capitalism here and now. All the same, he was leaving something out when he pictured the Great Powers fighting war after war to divide and re-divide the world, with colonies passively changing hands among them like provinces of Europe in the days of Napoleon or the Congress of Vienna.

Meanwhile Europe found itself condemned to spend four years partitioning and re-partitioning a few square miles of its own familiar Flanders mud. Lenin was still going on the dubious presumption that in any major conflict one side would start with a sufficient superiority to achieve its aim at a not prohibitive cost. As to what these aims were, Lenin even more

[187] *Imperialism, C. W.*, Vol. 22, pp. 265–6.
[188] Preface to Bukharin's *Imperialism*, p. 10.
[189] *The Collapse of the Second International, C. W.*, Vol. 21, p. 229.
[190] *The Letters of Lenin*, p. 342.

firmly than Bukharin was convinced that they were not limited, as Kautsky would have it, to annexation of agrarian or undeveloped regions. To him it was as patent as to Angell nonsensical that French capitalism should strive to regain Alsace-Lorraine, or German capitalism to swallow Belgium. How the inhabitants of an industrial country like Belgium would be handled if annexed, he did not speculate. Alsace-Lorraine offered the nearest precedent; its people were politically in some degree of subjection, but as wage-earners they could scarcely be said to fare worse than ordinary Germans. In the British empire Lenin might have taken note that white settlers (even Boers) and native inhabitants were on a very unequal footing, and wondered whether conquered Europeans could in practice be treated, and exploited, like Asians or Africans. True, Poles in Russia, Slovaks in Hungary, and other minorities eastward were on something like a colonial level, and Nazism was to demonstrate how much further this could be carried, how completely the equality of the white race abrogated. But all this related to an agrarian, not an industrial setting.

Lenin's reply would probably be that a strongly unified German capitalism benefited by having Alsace-Lorraine, and would benefit by having Belgium, incorporated in its structure; this would be another step in the process by which capital was piling up into bigger agglomerations. Presumably this would mean that Belgian capitalists rather than workmen would be the losers; also that only colonial tribute, not the gains of imperialism in the larger sense, had the effect of reducing capitalism to a parasitic condition (and otherwise Kautsky would be right to say that capitalism was healthier without imperialism). Some equivocations creep in, nevertheless, when Lenin touches on particulars. A country may wish to annex territory, either industrial or undeveloped, less for its own advantage than to injure a rival; thus Germany wants Belgium as a 'base' against England, England wants Baghdad as a base against Germany.[191] It is easier to equate these two calculations in strategic than in economic terms, and the argument seems to stray bewilderingly to and fro across the borderline. All sorts of considerations jostled in the minds of those who took

[191] *Imperialism, C. W.,* Vol. 22, p. 269.

decisions, but the historian has to try to disentangle them. Lenin was using the butt-end of his economic pistol when he quoted the verdict of a German business expert that the grandiose Berlin-Baghdad railway project was a huge blunder, due to the vainglorious Kaiser's trip to Palestine.[192] If so it was a consequence of Germany having a stupidly archaic government, not of the basic requirements of its capitalists. These might indeed come to believe that they needed a Berlin-Baghdad railway, if rosy enough images of it were dangled before them. Between the authentic and the fancied requirements of any dominant group the line must often be nebulous.

At bottom Lenin held that whatever other things helped to fix the shape of the struggle for world power, its essential content was the drive of monopoly capitalism. Here lay the decisive force in all economic and international relations.[193] (Capitalism once out of the way, he reckoned on socialism being able to transform any country much faster than it has proved able to do; on this side too inertias from the past were heavier than he bargained for.) He sometimes, though not always, forgot that financial and military strength may be very uneven; and he often spoke as if international relations were far more plastic, more readily moulded by the master-hand of finance, than history shows them. Just as no amount of investment in the U.S. could give Britain political control there, neither could French investment in Russia, except that it might bind wayward Russia more closely to the French alliance. Britain and France had the biggest investments in Turkey, but in 1914 this helped to push Turkey, in search of escape from the stranglehold, onto Germany's side.[194] As a crucial test we may take the opposing coalitions that were fighting the Great War. Lenin thought of international cartels giving way to quarrels, as the participants' financial strength fluctuated and the stronger demanded a bigger share, and he referred casually to State alliances running 'parallel with this and in connection with it.'[195] But only an endless series of 'diplomatic revolutions' could have kept the two in step. His-

[192] *Imperialism, C. W.*, Vol. 22, p. 237.
[193] *Ibid.*, p. 259; cf. p. 253.
[194] See W. W. Gottlieb, *Studies in Secret Diplomacy during the First World War* (London, 1957), Part I.
[195] *Imperialism, C. W.*, Vol. 22, p. 253.

torically it was the politico-military combinations, like the Triple Alliance of 1883, that came first, and once in being they became far too fixed and rigid, thanks in part to the elaboration of armies and of strategies like the Schlieffen Plan, to be altered and reshuffled from year to year as the shifting inclinations of financial centres might dictate.

If Germany was fighting for 'Mittel-Europa', it was, para-doxically, fighting to subjugate mainly its own allies, Austria-Hungary and Turkey. German enterprise had been encouraged by the alliance to flow into the Hapsburg empire, but it would have been nearly as ready to flow into the tsarist empire, and the choice was made not by the bankers but by Bismarck and the generals. It would besides often be quite awkward for the most powerful interests in one country to agree on which other country was the 'enemy'. Among Lenin's own illustrations we find that in electricity Germany and the U.S. were hand in glove, and together supreme, while in oil Germans had been defeated by Americans and their associates.[196] This, as well as necessities of war planning, must compel each set of capitalists to hand over a good deal of the responsibility for decisions to their political heads and military advisers. From the standpoint of public relations this had at least to seem to be happening. Ordinary Germans might fight for Kaiser or Führer, but they would not be fired by a clarion call of 'Your Krupp and country need you!'

Altogether, so far as economic interests were concerned a large-scale war could only be a clumsy, confused mêlée, not a neatly scientific operation to register changes of strength like the mimic battles of the Stock Exchange. What it might accomplish was to register now and then in a rough and ready way a general alteration of military and economic power, and award the lion's share of markets and investment-fields to those with the most leonine appetite for them. From this angle it might not matter too much what enemies were being over-thrown, so long as the right lion came out on top and there was plenty of game to gorge him. In some such way as this both Lenin and capitalism, in its corporate self, may be supposed to have thought about the Great War—both heavily under-estimating its costs.

[196] *Ibid.*, pp. 247 ff.

C

12   LENIN ON IMPERIALISM AND THE WORKING CLASS

In 1916 Lenin was no nearer to comprehending the passions of
nationalism, and was still obsessed by the need to explain what
had gone wrong with the working class. He might be suspected
of inventing a riddle for himself, where for most spectators none
existed. But the scheme of salvation that he inherited from
Marx depended on the revolutionary mission of the working
class. He was capable of invoking the spirit of class loyalty in
passionately idealistic or ethical terms; but as a good materialist
he must attach it to economics, and he was not always circum-
spect enough when it came to reconciling the two. He was
trying to fit into a unified materialistic pattern a bundle of
impulses, some of which derived from class relations or the
mode of production only at several removes. For him the spirit
he admired in the working class sprang from its being doomed,
under capitalism, to be always poor and miserable; which was
a little too much like saying that any workers not poor and
miserable must have come by something discreditably, or sold
their souls to the devil. Their falling off could be rationally
explained, Lenin had been saying since the war began, by
capitalist bribery, which could only come out of the extra
profits of imperialism. And a second material pressure, the
hardships of the war, would remedy things by disillusioning the
workers and bringing them back to the right path.

It was a mountainous slice of modern history that Lenin was
trying to squeeze into the four corners of a theory of imperialism
restricted to the past two or three decades. Some uncertainty
is revealed by the fact that when, in *Imperialism*, he set himself
to work out his solution in more detail than Bukharin had
ventured on, he did so chiefly with reference to the workers
of Britain, the country which had the biggest colonial empire
but was by no means the most amenable to his definition of
imperialism. He could not fail to see that the 'corruption' of the
English workers went back to the mid-nineteenth century, when
Britain had already plenty of colonies and foreign trade and
investments, but no monopoly capitalism, or true imperialism.
It might seem to follow that parasitism, proletarian as well as
bourgeois, had its essential roots in colonial policies; yet
Germany had next to no colonies, and German workers, if less

parasitic, were no less patriotic. We are brought back to the
dilemma that if there was a net inflow of capital, as into
Britain, foreign investment was not relieving capital congestion:
if a net outflow, as from Germany, it was not producing an
unearned income out of which the workers could be bribed.
Hilferding's claim for capital export of the credit for stimulating German industry and creating more jobs was very
reasonable, but could scarcely be twisted into bribery and
corruption. As regards Britain, Lenin might have reflected that
much of its comparative comfort could be due to its having got
through industrialization gradually, over a long period.
Angell remarked that in France, with little of Germany's
febrile industrial expansion, the common man lived more com-
fortably than the common German.[197] A Britain that was
neither investing heavily at home nor adding much on balance,
in most years, to its investment abroad, could afford some
limited concessions to its workers, besides supporting its
pampered rulers in more than oriental luxury.

In 1892 Engels ascribed the feebleness of socialism in
Britain to the benefits of an industrial monopoly enjoyed by the
country until not long before, benefits shared to a certain
extent by the workers.[198] Whether the natural monopoly that
accrued to England from its being the first industrial country
can be equated with the monopoly any industrial country
might now aspire to by crushing its rivals, and both called
'imperialist', seems questionable. Ten years later Kautsky, who
had lived in Britain, gave an exceedingly gloomy account of a
British working class completely sunk in torpor and ignoble
content, lost to anything higher than football or betting on
horses.[199] Lenin could not have brought himself to write off a
whole national working class like this, and Kautsky's disgust
with it foreshadowed a later disenchantment with the revolutionary proletariat at large, and with it virtual abandonment
of socialism.

Patriotism as well as industrialism was older in Britain than

[197] Angell, *The Great Illusion*, pp. 223–4.
[198] Engels, Preface to the 1892 English edition of *The Condition of the
Working-Class in England in 1844* (reprint, London, 1936), p. xvii.
[199] Kautsky, *The Social Revolution*, pp. 100–102. He had written sadly
about the demoralisation of the British workers in 1899; see Koebner and
Schmidt, *op. cit.*, p. 246.

anywhere else, and when labour unrest was stirring in the later nineteenth century jingo propaganda was an antidote ready to hand. A satire of 1881, 'Demoralising Effects of Modern Liberalism', accused Tories of fomenting imperialism and militarism in order to confuse class feeling and have an excuse for a bigger army to protect them. A large standing army 'is, after all, the only protection which the few possess against the many'.[200] How far the working class did succumb to the spell of empire is exceedingly hard to make out. On the whole it would seem that it let itself be persuaded that the empire was somehow a good thing for it, without troubling its head much about the matter or sharing the positive enthusiasm of the small middle classes. Amid the hysteria of the Boer War no anti-war speakers in working men's clubs were howled down, as they were outside.[201] But workers with no ballast of socialism might ordinarily, in foreign concerns outside their ken, tail behind the social groups just above them.

Imputing the disease to too many fleshpots, Lenin was making his task harder by painting the new capitalism as vastly more oppressive than the old; this might seem to prove the workers vastly more foolish than their fathers in submitting to it. When the left wing asserted in the pre-war years that working-class conditions were everywhere worsening they put a great part of the blame on the cost of imperialism, and with this was bound up their confidence that when imperialism brought war, war would bring revolt. In 1909 Kautsky considered that most of the burden of armaments in Germany was being foisted onto the workers.[202] In 1914 C. K. Hobson was puzzled to decide whether export of capital from Britain improved things on balance for labour, or the reverse; he came to the conclusion that over the course of a century it had been beneficial, but during the last dozen years its short-term effects might have been adverse.[203] Both a desire to make the most of

[200] Anon. (London, 1881), p. 10.
[201] R. Price, *An Imperial War and the British Working Class. Working-Class Attitudes and Reactions to the Boer War 1899–1902* (London, 1972), p. 96.
[202] *Le Chemin du Pouvoir*, p. 150.
[203] C. K. Hobson, *op. cit.*, pp. xiii ff., 66–7. Cf. S. B. Saul, *The Myth of the Great Depression 1873–1896* (London, 1969), p. 53: 'The effect upon investment of changes in consumption at home is unfortunately a completely open question. Indeed we know far too little about the forces affecting the supply and remuneration of labour.' Dobb, *Political Economy and Capitalism,*

the harm done by imperialism to the workers, and his trust in the soundness at heart of the majority of them, compelled Lenin to restrict the moral corrosion to a minority, which for the time being was in the lead with renegade socialists or 'opportunists' for spokesmen.

When Engels talked of workers and fleshpots in 1892 his opinion was that 'the privileged minority pocketed most, but even the great mass had, at least, a temporary share now and then'.[204] This was more than Lenin could bring himself to admit. Nor was he willing to think of the 'crumbs of imperialism' being partaken of (and magnified in their imagination, very likely) by all workers at least in special industries, such as armaments, steel mills supplying rails, cotton-mills exporting to India. Instead he preferred to spread them over the top layer of the working class at large. What precisely constituted this top layer is not made entirely clear. At one moment he seems to cast the net very wide, by including the bulk of membership of cooperative societies and trade unions and chapels, all he remarks citizens with votes[205]—but all Englishmen had votes. Elsewhere he includes shopkeepers, white-collar workers, and the like. But he dwells chiefly on the scarcity of the sharers, or black sheep. 'Morsels of the loot . . . fall to the share of certain sections of the petty bourgeoisie and to the working-class aristocracy and bureaucracy . . . an insignificant minority of the proletariat and of the toiling masses.'[206]

Kautsky in 1902—even when writing off the whole British working class as politically moribund—inferred from official statistics that only one fifth of it enjoyed the amelioration about which there was so much complacent talk.[207] If we make a very rough guess at the total number of beneficiaries as a million

pp. 232–3, discusses good and bad effects of foreign investment and imperialism for the working class. Sweezy (*op. cit.*, p. 315) thinks of it benefiting in the nineteenth century generally from the expansion both of England's trade and of its foreign investments. E. Varga, *Twentieth Century Capitalism* (London, n.d.), p. 32, supports Lenin by arguing that real wages were falling in Britain before 1914 because of rising prices.

[204] Engels, Preface to the 1892 English edition of *The Condition of the Working-Class in England in 1844*, p. xvii.

[205] *Imperialism, C. W.*, Vol. 22, p. 282.

[206] *The Collapse of the Second International, C. W.*, Vol. 21, p. 223. Basso (*loc. cit.*, pp. 128–9) finds this explanation unconvincing: 'the roots of opportunism are more general and deeper';—a comment with which one must agree. [207] Kautsky, *The Social Revolution*, p. 40.

families, or something like one ninth of Britain's population, how much was there for distribution among them? Giffen's well-known estimate in 1899 of the country's annual receipts from foreign and colonial investment put them at £90 to £100 million. Lenin took the same figure in 1916,[208] when it was far too low. A later calculation brought it up to £200 million for 1914, a rate of growth vastly quicker than that of the national income.[209] If we take this sum, and—again very roughly—suppose one quarter of it to have been converted into 'crumbs', then each of one million families would get an extra £50 a year; and this at a time when a solicitor's clerk might start work in the Temple at seven shillings a week. A boy on a Suffolk farm might start at half a crown a week; yet farm labourers were highly patriotic,[210] evidently not from any material inducement, but through careful conditioning by their temporal and spiritual betters. For those who got it, an extra pound a week deserved to be called a substantial loaf, instead of a few crumbs.

Colonial profits, it has been said, do much to strengthen a ruling class at home,[211] and it may be that we ought to look for the political effects of the enormous investment-income (all of it in Lenin's eyes ill-gotten gain, wherever it came from) first and foremost on those who put most of it in their own pockets. They gained not only in opulence but in self-confidence, bringing with it a degree of flexibility, willingness to make concessions here and there. Lenin was not unreasonable however in thinking that Britain's imperial prosperity enabled, or assisted, the luckier wage-earners to better their condition. This category did include the opinion-forming or guiding sections of the working mass, and its relative well-being did give it a more favourable attitude towards its superiors and their State, and their gospel of empire; a feeling that it was after all a passable world they were living in. No Chinese wall, Lenin commented, divided workers from bosses.[212] As regards

---

[208] *Imperialism, C. W.*, Vol. 22, p. 277.
[209] Feis, *op. cit.*, pp. 23, 27. Brailsford (*op. cit.*, pp. 77–8) thought Sir George Paish's estimate of £140 million in 1907–8 reasonable.
[210] See R. Blythe, *Akenfield* (Penguin edn., 1972), pp. 39, 41–2.
[211] B. Lasker, *Human Bondage in Southeast Asia* (Institute of Pacific Relations, 1950), p. 265.
[212] *Imperialism, C. W.*, Vol. 22, p. 285.

the working class proper, wage differentials were rising before 1890, and perhaps later, though the social prestige of the 'aristocracy of labour' was diminishing with the rise of other groups such as white-collar workers or local government employees.[213] All these more comfortable sections together would be able to set a 'patriotic' tone for the working population at large, if they knew, or if they only fancied, that their blessings were coming out of imperial profit of one sort or other. They would conclude with Lenin that to be on the losing side in this war would 'deprive the petty bourgeoisie of their dominant-nation privileges and additional incomes'[214]—though they would certainly not put it to themselves in any such language. As a further link in the chain of influence we may reckon the small middle-class investors whom Lenin had in mind when he quoted a statement made in the Reichstag in 1900: 'the one pound share is the basis of British imperialism'.[215]

All this might go far towards explaining a heady Britannia-mood, proof against disagreeable evidence of the high price paid even before 1914 in the way of taxation, rising costs, and in most countries compulsory service. If Lenin's allusions to the 'privileges' enjoyed by the great Powers in world commerce sometimes sound hazy, the public mind was (as Angell found) hazier still. He himself wrote that the Boer War left both middle and lower classes in Britain in need of consolation for higher taxes and lost relatives.[216] Colonies might be profitable—to more than capitalists—when they only required a small effort against weak native peoples, but not at the cost of an arms race or a serious conflict. When these were involved, Lenin can be understood to mean, imperialist policies good for bosses and better-off workers were bad for everyone else.

Crumbs were not being bestowed in the straightforward fashion of the corn dole in imperial Rome. Their most direct recipients were the legion of domestic servants, or the more dignified ranks among them; these were far removed from the 'aristocracy of labour', though their social influence may not

[213] See E. J. Hobsbawm, 'The Labour Aristocracy in Nineteenth-century Britain', in his *Labouring Men. Studies in the History of Labour* (London, 1964), pp. 272 ff.
[214] *The Collapse of the Second International, C. W.*, Vol. 21, p. 229.
[215] *Imperialism, C. W.*, Vol. 22, p. 228.
[216] *Ibid.*, p. 294.

have been negligible. Lenin did not enter into the devious
channels through which a proportion of remittances from
plantations in Assam or railways in Argentina found its way
into pay-packets in Birmingham or Glasgow. He had to rule
out firmly any appreciable rise of earnings from the proceeds
of legitimate trade or industry—if he can be said to have
recognized any such thing. He is never explicit about why
capitalism should be able or willing to pay its workers a bonus
from its foreign-investment income, but not from any other
source. He had much to say about high profits derived from
monopoly, for instance by German cement syndicates.[217]
Employers preferred, one may surmise, to let their workers
think that trade unions and agitation would do them no good:
perquisites would only be forthcoming if the country could,
with their loyal support, enlarge its place in the sun: 'Little
England', or 'Little Germany', could afford them only the
meagerest living. Here again capitalism and Marxism were
looking through the same spectacles.

13   MARXIST THEORY AND POST-1918 HISTORY

Lenin was buoyed up by a too hopeful faith that nowhere else
could 'opportunism'—the working class whoring after the
strange gods of plutocracy—be so widespread and tenacious
as in Britain. He ended his book on the same sanguine note as
Bukharin. It would be instructive to know the response of the
Russian readers it was designed for to this work, austerely
academic in plan yet highly charged with emotion. It was
Lenin's last-ditch stand in defence of the principles of irrecon-
cilability and revolution that he had been preaching since 1914.
After this there was nothing left for him but to return to
Russia and vindicate his thesis in another way, by making a
revolution.

The theory of imperialism enshrined in his book, even if
here and there in this 1916 version it may wear a look of
improvisation, was a slow growth of two decades, in many
minds. In the history of ideas it is a good specimen of how large,
complex hypotheses come into being. It illustrates too the
working of the Marxist rule that theory and practice should go

[217] *Imperialism, C. W.*, Vol. 22, pp. 207–8.

hand in hand. Demands of political strategy may well invigorate theory, but will often compel it to take second place to them; and amid the welter of controversy within a political movement rating ideas so highly, any theory risks being squeezed too much into the polemics of opposite factions. Meanwhile the rapid unfolding of events taught many lessons, but each in turn tended to overshadow the learners. Hobson wrote too much under the vivid impression of the Boer War, Lenin's presentation was forged on the anvil of the Great War.

The theory developed into a penetrating commentary on capitalism in our century, its reckless pursuit of profit, its perilous ascendancy over governments and armies and men's minds. On the other hand it was neither an all-round survey nor a fully integrated one, and it is far from easy to extricate its living ideas from their confinement in the desperate circumstances of 1916. War was for Lenin the hallmark of the capitalism of his day. Yet in every phase of its long march since the late middle ages capitalism has pushed or helped to push peoples into strife, and it is not self-evident that Lenin's generation was entitled to appropriate such a term as 'imperialism' to its behaviour in one epoch. Now that we look back on it from a distance, the imperialism of that day may seem the outcome less of capitalism's own inner structure, as it was then, than of a peculiar, unique amalgam in Europe and Japan of feudal-monarchical elements still strong and industrial capitalism young and ambitious but still unsure of itself, because only in two countries had its coming to power been inaugurated by the overthrow of an older regime. Curiously enough, also, in those more purely 'bourgeois' countries, Britain and France, capitalism was less advanced in size and in structural evolution than in politically retarded Germany. Seen in this way Lenin's 'highest stage' was not the last, but only last but one, or more, and our latter-day imperialism, with the U.S. as its exemplar, falls into a different category.

America was already looming up. Marxist theory took too little note of novel features there or in Japan; it was too Eurocentric, its horizons failing to match those of an expanding world. One symptom of this was its preoccupation with export of capital from Europe, along with inadequate enquiry into the impact on particular regions outside. Foreign investment was, no doubt, playing a large part in world affairs, but in very heterogeneous ways, and a great deal of its activity lay outside what the analysts of imperialism were trying to elucidate. This goes with the most pervasive weakness of the whole body of theory, its uncertainty of focus, always shifting and wavering between the narrower field of colonialism and the far broader one of 'imperialism'. This latter has to be understood as embracing the sum total of all aggressive impulses directed to the winning of abnormal profit beyond national frontiers by exertion of superior strength, economic or political or, in the last resort, military. Such a conception suffers by its subject-matter being neither readily demarcated nor readily correlated with the plainer subject of colony-hunting. Much misunderstanding might be avoided if two separate words were available to distinguish the two themes.

Two main streams of experience and reflection converged to form the Marxist theory, colonizing activity outside Europe and industrial growth inside. They never dovetailed very smoothly. Something more coherent might have emerged if Marxism had incorporated more of the socio-political lessons of colonialism, to be found in writers like Hobson, instead of taking from them little but the capital-export thesis. As it was, the theory left itself too open to the kind of criticism, already sketched by Kautsky, that Schumpeter was maturing during the Great War and published in 1919.[218] For him capitalism could get on perfectly well without imperialism, whose roots were to be found rather, where Angell was looking for them, in social psychology. There was no lack of objections for him to raise about individual colonies like Morocco and how they came to be taken, in contrast with the Rhodes-and-Chamberlain land-grabbing in southern Africa, which Hobson and the Marxists treated too much as a standard pattern. Against such criticism it has been urged that cavillings about this colony or

---

[218] See J. A. Schumpeter, *Capitalism, Socialism, and Democracy* (3rd English edn., 1950), pp. 49–55. Schumpeter thought of the Marxist theory of imperialism as the work mostly of 'Neo-Marxists' after 1900 with their centre at Vienna. His critique of it is trenchant, but far too brief; and he is himself at least equally open to objection when he writes that the causes of imperialism have had nothing to do with class struggle or class structure (p. 54), or that 'very little influence on foreign policy has been exerted by big business' (p. 55).

that only cover odd corners of the subject, whereas the Marxist conception 'views history as a unitary whole, without separating either economic or political, much less ideological, motives.'[219] But any conception or definition, if sufficiently broad, can be made like a Tudor treason statute to cover almost anything. As applied by Marxist writers then and later, the theory was couched almost exclusively in economic terms;[220] and it has seldom carried conviction except to those predisposed on other grounds to accept it. To the student of empires and their rise and fall it must appear that Lenin does not really offer him a theory of imperialism at all; or only one about as helpful for study of a specific colonial case as Newton's law of gravity for shooting an arrow through an apple.

What Lenin modestly called a 'popular outline' was stamped by the triumph of the Bolshevik revolution, along with the rest of his writings, as the legitimate continuation of Marxism. In its own province *Imperialism* stood out all the more in solitary splendour because Kautsky and Hilferding lay under the black cloud of apostasy; Rosa Luxemburg's memory was tarnished by her disapproval of Leninist tactics in the revolution; Bukharin was eliminated before long from the Soviet pantheon, and his book, the precursor of Lenin's, ignored or crudely falsified.[221] Elevated thus to the level of a canonical text containing all needful or admissible truth on the subject, for a good many years Lenin's essay did more to restrict than to foster research, and lingered on in a state of artificial preservation like Lenin's body in its mausoleum. Meanwhile imperialism formed a chronic topic of controversy between the old Second and the new Third Internationals, but chiefly in a style which elicited little fresh thinking, communist denunciation of right-wing socialists for not condemning colonial regimes or for giving no more than verbal support to freedom movements.

To this failure of theory to go on developing and keeping up

[219] Basso, *loc. cit.*, p. 112.
[220] An example of this economic approach will be found in J. Eaton, *Marx against Keynes* (London, 1951). For a criticism of the wholesale use of 'imperialism' by Marxists, see Strachey, *op. cit.*, pp. 191, 278 N.
[221] The editorial notes to Lenin's *Imperialism* in the *Little Lenin Library* series (London, 1934), evidently taken from a recent Russian edition, invest the work with a shining halo, while Bukharin's (though he is still 'Comrade Bukharin') is very cavalierly and misleadingly treated.

with the times, as it had before 1914, many communist mis-
calculations and practical errors can be traced. By 1922 the
Third International was pronouncing a new world war, to be
fought out in the Pacific, unavoidable unless forestalled by
world revolution.[222] Trotsky was counting on America to go
to war with Britain, in order to preserve its 'economic domination'—just as British and German capitalists thought of
going to war with each other before 1914, Angell commented.[223]
This was looking to history to repeat itself with a woodenness
in line with the marked infusion of economic determinism in
Leninist teaching; it presupposed that capitalism was governed
not at all by free will but wholly by blind necessity. War
preparations undeniably continued, and armaments and
suppression of colonial revolt had to be paid for. Marxism
hesitated between contemplating colonies (as in duty bound)
as purveyors of tainted crumbs to the masses, or as a dead
weight on their backs; it sometimes took one line, sometimes
the other, occasionally both in the same breath. By and large
it may be said to have laid stress on the crumbs when theorizing,
on the drawbacks when haranguing. Sectarianism was stiffened
by the intransigence of a Leninist doctrine which began life
as a political manifesto. Lenin treated it as petty-bourgois
reformism and illusion to condemn only particular imperialistic
actions like the seizure of the Philippines, without condemning
capitalism root and branch; the Third International went on
too long repeating that there could be no genuine anti-war
movement which was not also anti-capitalist. Deficiencies in
the theory of imperialism also stood in the way of an all-round
appraisal of fascism, which might be called a higher, if not the
highest, stage of imperialism. To this failure Hilferding's death
in a Gestapo prison added a grim footnote.

While Marxism floundered, so did the capitalist camp,
victors and vanquished of the Great War alike. Had Germany
won, there would have been a re-ordering of Europe and the
world on a far grander scale, the repartition that Lenin wrote
of; how German enterprise would have fared in digesting its
spoils would be a question worth going into. As things were, it
was open to Angell to claim striking confirmation of his case:

[222] See Degras, *op. cit.*, Vol. 1, p. 391.
[223] Angell, *Must Britain Travel the Moscow Road?* p. 176 n.

the winning side was making very little out of its success, and whatever satisfaction it felt at crippling German competition was quickly damped by discovery that it needed a recovering Germany to trade with; also that German capitalism had to be rescued and brought back into the family, to prevent Germany from going the same way as Russia.

It may be permissible to look back on the Great War as a monument to a frantic adherence to instincts and habits of the past, a convulsive refusal to face an unescapable remoulding of society, in one way or another, to enable it to contain the demonic energies released by science. A system, or class, like an individual, learns, if it learns at all, by trial and error. Even if capitalism was reponsible for 1914, it might not be in haste to try the same gamble again. But any real turning over of a new leaf meant acquiescence in the two highly unpalatable recipes that liberals had long been advocating: welfare instead of scarcity at home, reciprocal enrichment instead of beggar-my-neighbour abroad. In 1926 Angell joyfully announced 'something like a revolution in the employer mind', starting in America, a recognition for the first time of 'high wages generally as an indispensable element in the maintenance of the market'.[224] In 1927 an English Marxist could see no sign of any such change of mind.[225] If there was any, it was feeble and fitful; and the interwar years as an epoch have the air of a twilight zone in the evolution of capitalism, a time of doubt when old maxims were discredited but new ones given only a jaundiced welcome. A fumbling League of Nations presided over it, advertising the admission by the capitalist States of some need for reform, along with their apparent inability to achieve even the harmony of 'ultra-imperialism'.

In its external conduct fascism was more open to Marxist scrutiny than in its social composition. In face of its challenge capitalism of the more moderate or responsible type showed a heartfelt conversion to the creed of pre-1914 Marxism, that war meant revolution. Whereas in 1914 both sides went to war *le coeur gai*, now one entered the lists with extreme reluctance. It was defeated Germany, baulked as yet of a chance to see what it could make of an empire, that clung to the old philos-

---

[224] *Ibid.*, p. 46.
[225] Dobb, *Political Economy and Capitalism*, p. 268.

ophy and behaved as Marxism predicted. With all the three aggressor states motives of a 'political' order were at work besides the purely economic. All the same, events from the occupation of Manchuria in 1931 to the end of the Second World War can be presented not unconvincingly as the second grand conflict for the repartition of the world.[226]

After 1945 there was acceptance by capitalism, less grudging at least than before, of the twin principles that classes at home and nations abroad ought to pursue mutual affluence. It began to look as if the class conflicts and wars of the twentieth century were the preface after all not to social revolution but to a new-model capitalist society. In somewhat the same manner long ago the wars and civil broils of the late middle ages brought popular revolution in sight, but ended instead in an overhaul and consolidation of the old order by the new monarchies. For its part however Marxist theory, awakening from its state of suspended animation, was also turning over a new leaf. Of late years it has been re-examining its ideas about imperialism, if not as yet thoroughly enough. It is not ill-equipped to deal with the neo-colonialism which since 1945 has replaced direct colonial rule over vast areas. In terms of the concentration of capital, the influence of huge monopolistic corporations over governments, the contemporary scene fits into Leninist categories even better than that of the earlier part of the century did, because capital in all the advanced countries is now more nearly of one kind than when Lenin tried to force conflicting species of it into one mould. Export of capital is on a still bigger scale; Marxism has not yet learned to distinguish adequately between its effects on undeveloped regions and on the industrial countries to which most of it flows, and is still too apt to think of it all as 'imperialistic'—a label very intelligible to workers in Chile, but baffling to workers in Scotland. It may be remarked in passing that capital export, as export of goods on credit, has found an analogue in the domestic market in hire-purchase, which started tentatively in the interwar years and now marches in seven-league boots.

[226] Sweezy, *op. cit.*, pp. 323–4. He defends in general 'the consistency and appropriateness of Lenin's conception of imperialism' (p. 308). Cf. Dobb, *Political Economy and Capitalism*, p. 261: 'the economic policy of Fascist States represents the essence of Imperialism'.

Most of the flow of capital is from the U.S., and all perplexities about it and about the nature of today's 'new
capitalism' find their summing up in the grand problem of
America and where it is going. There a driving energy and a
concentration of economic power reminiscent of Lenin's
Germany is combined with a political structure still more free
than those of his France or Britain from relics of a pre-capitalist
past. Yet the old question still remains, whether America's
behaviour in the world is dictated by basic requirements of
American capitalism as a whole, or by sectional interests able
to manipulate irrational factors, from private corruption to
public hysteria.

None of Europe's problems was solved in any fundamental
way by the new monarchies of the sixteenth century. We cannot yet see how radically our newest capitalism has been
overcoming those of today. Imperialism is very far from having
come to the end of its protean transformations. In relations
among capitalist States it may have reached some kind of
stable 'ultra-imperialism'; even this is not beyond doubt, if
only because the prospect of a grave shortage of the raw
materials vital to our very artificial civilization, a bugbear in
Lenin's day, now grows threateningly real. Cut-throat competition for dwindling resources may before long be anything but
a figure of speech.

Modern imperialism has been an accretion of elements, not
all of equal weight, that can be traced back through every
epoch of history. Perhaps its ultimate causes, with those of war,
are to be found less in tangible material wants than in the
uneasy tensions of societies distorted by class division, with
their reflection in distorted ideas in men's minds. Capitalism is
at bottom a relationship among human beings, and no human
relationship, or its consequences, can have the logic of
geometry. Lenin tried to draw out the consequences of capitalism too symmetrically. Still, his argument was built on the
bedrock of what was happening in his day, which was our
yesterday. Its belittlers have found no better interpretation,
and some have wanted to save trouble and embarrassment by
banishing the term 'imperialism' from use, as meaningless.
Marxist usage has given some colour for this, by making one
word—as it has done with the term 'feudalism' also—cover

such a multitude of sins. But to pretend that there is no such thing as imperialism in modern history is mere obfuscation; while any attempt at explaining it without recourse to Lenin must be more incomplete than his own.[227] He himself pointed to a wide range of cognate questions that he could not follow up, and that his disciples ignored. And the more attentively we study his commentaries the more other queries start up under our feet. When all these have been gone into, and answers synthesized with what is valid in Lenin's, we shall have a more comprehensive picture; not a final one, for the subject exemplifies only too well the immense complexity of history, the labyrinth of accident or coincidence through which historical necessity must make its way.

[227] D. C. M. Platt, in 'Economic Factors in British Policy during the "New Imperialism" ' (*Past and Present*, No. 39, 1968, pp. 120 ff.), sensibly concludes that the Hobson-Lenin emphasis on capital-export was overdone, but that imperialism is much more satisfactorily explained in economic terms than in the merely political terms to which it has been fashionable of late to reduce it. A similar conclusion is suggested by T. Lloyd's article 'Africa and Hobson's Imperialism' (*Past and Present*, No. 55, 1972, pp. 130 ff.).

2
Farewells to Empire
Some recent studies of Imperialism

Imperialism has already begun to be thought of as a thing of the past, with not much relevance to the present day. It appears in this light in some, though not all, of the books that have come out in this country in the last few years, in which the modern empires, chiefly the British, are weighed up and their epitaphs variously written. *The Imperial Idea and its Enemies*, by A. P. Thornton (1959), stands out as more than an epitaph, almost a requiem. If it is in the end a disappointing book, it disappoints because it is in various ways exceptionally good, not least in vivacity of style. Its best feature is a lucid and sustained criticism of the political errors, malpractices, or extravagances of imperialism; so much so that it only gradually dawns on the reader that this is the work not of one of the enemies of imperialism but of a convinced imperialist—in the unashamed sense that the word enjoyed sixty or seventy years ago, when empire-builders in their primitive Edens had not yet felt the need to sew together fig-leaves and make themselves breeches.

It would not be doing him justice to say that his head is screwed on properly but his heart is in the wrong place. What is wrong is outside him: it is the Idea he comes both to bury and to praise. What this Idea really is, or was, or whence it arose, he never explains; and as with nostalgic regret he traces its long decline there is a constant blurring between two quite distinct British empires, those of the white settlements and of the black or brown colonies. Or rather it might be said that Thornton's is an empire never built at all, and therefore—for purposes of academic romanticism—built for ever.

Because the Idea is so unsubstantial, the book lacks unity,

and large sections of it wander into general European politics and the international power-struggle, or party attitudes to the League of Nations. But the guiding light, when it peeps out now and then from under its bushel, proves to be a belief in an English mission: a duty imposed by some Providence on Englishmen to use their power in the world as a power for good, without asking anyone else whether they wanted to have good done to them or not. It was 'an immense responsibility for human welfare and the opportunity for human betterment that it represented' (p. 305); it belonged to Britain as 'chief exponent of the cultures and values of Western civilization' (p. 313). But by 'Britain' we must understand a select few, not a whole nation. If Thornton believes that colonial peoples have been in need of firm handling for their own good, it may be because he seems disposed to believe much the same about the mass of people at home in England. Looking backward he sees generations of the best upper- or upper-middle-class elements devoting themselves with a noble disinterestedness to the task of guiding and rescuing from their own base instincts the un-clothed native abroad and the unwashed native at home. True imperialists and true socialists (respectable Fabian socialists from the same seminaries) he feels to have had much in common; the concern of both has been caring for the masses of mankind, helpless to care for themselves.

Indian nationalists used to calculate that at the rate the British Raj was going it would give the whole country literacy within another 800 years. British socialists may sometimes have wondered whether the Labour Party was likely to give this country socialism quite so quickly. To Thornton any such impatience would be distasteful. The advent of nationalism in the colonies and of democracy at home both strike him as nuisances, witless forces getting in the way of wise and benevolent purposes; 'noisy jingoism' as a morbid symptom that came in with democracy, to the distress of all 'true workers' in the vineyard of empire (p. 268). But this is treating democracy as an abstraction, something learned at school from Plato. Of capitalist democracy, as a phenomenon of modern times, and the powerful interests bent on controlling and perverting it by every device of propaganda, Thornton seems to know nothing. He fancies that the ruling class was dislodged from power when the Liberals won the general election of 1906 and embarked on their trifling social reforms (p. 132). Academic unrealism could not go much further than his dictum on the 'thirties: 'No one led the democracy because no one knew where the democracy wanted to go' (p. 307).

Thornton is less urbane than usual when he talks of the Left in the 'thirties (who wanted socialism in less than 800 years), and their 'confused battle in Spain,' and their 'tastes and emotions . . . expertly catered for and formed' by the Left Book Club (p. 294). Books like his own, with their dream-world distortion of how history has been made and progress won, might with at least as much truth be said to cater to the taste of a new middle class of technocrats, not unwilling to see themselves as heirs of a fine old middle class once the backbone of England, and to be flattered with the notion that *they* are now in power, keeping troublesome millionaire and troublesome shop steward well in hand. There is an old joke about laboratory rats successfully training their professor to ring a bell whenever they want food.

Thornton's fundamental weakness is his neglect of the whole economic meaning of empire; it remains for him an 'idea,' or at most an ideal of sound administration. Thus he recognizes no such thing as an American imperialism, because the U.S. 'had no tradition of any imperial idea' (p. 327). No blood-relationship between imperialism and capitalism comes into his mind at all. Lenin is only once mentioned; Hobson oftener, but no serious attention is paid to his economic analysis; or to that of H. N. Brailsford, whose *War of Steel and Gold* (1914) is given a paragraph. There is only one casual reference to the opium trade and the century-long campaign against it in Britain (pp. 97–8); yet the opium trade was a keystone of the structure of British power in Asia. There is the same failure to understand that an empire marches on its stomach in most of what he says about India—where Ernest Jones, half a century before Lenin, would have been well worth a place among the 'enemies'[1]— and Egypt, whose cotton, flourishing since Mehemet Ali, helped to prolong the British occupation if not to start it. In a detailed survey of British and French activities in the Middle

[1] See J. Saville, *Ernest Jones, Chartist* (1952), pp. 65–6, 211–13; P. C. Joshi (ed.), *Rebellion, 1857* (Delhi, 1957), pp. 302 ff.

East after 1918 virtually nothing is said about filthy lucre. Oil is mentioned; but about the fact that British oil interests were planning to achieve a world monopoly and hold the U.S. to ransom—with the result that war between the two countries was a possibility seriously thought about—there is silence.

The utmost Thornton can admit is that there was in the history of the empire one bad phase, of 'mischievous exploiting "imperialism"' (p. 299). When and why this began or ended is not made clear, but the Boer War was its central episode, and the revulsion of feeling afterwards left good and bad imperialism (white magic and black magic, as it were) equally discredited and out of fashion; for opponents of the Boer War were as 'emotional' and 'irrational' as its supporters (p. 101). The 'proconsular idea' (p. 135) may indeed have gone out of fashion with the public, but the taste for high colonial dividends was very far from having evaporated. Thornton writes excellently of the betrayal of the Africans in 1906 when South Africa was handed over to Boer management (pp. 135 ff.). But he does so only in terms of political justice, and the antithesis of good government against self-government; not in terms of the partnership that was being struck up, and that has subsisted ever since, between London capitalists and white settlers acting as their overseers and policemen. Capitalist democracy was aware that its dirtiest work was best done by delegation, and by not letting its left hand know what its right hand was doing.

One does not gather from this book much impression of the author having ever watched the workings of British imperialism with his own eyes. His notion of enlightened officials in India protecting the weak against the strong is to a great extent mythical. In order to keep itself afloat the Raj was obliged from first to last to join hands with reactionary interests inside India. It provided law and order (not always even this at village level), and so protected the poor man against open violence of the old feudal sort; but law and order included those economic laws whereby the rich hold the poor at their mercy without any need of cudgel or club. Some Englishmen in India might deplore the fact, but their machinery protected the strong against the weak, the boss against the worker, the zemindar against the ryot, the man of caste against the untouchable. To say that by giving India independence Britain 'handed over the masses to the classes' is unqualified nonsense. 'An Indian bureaucracy that was the enemy of the princely houses did not promise well for the future of democracy . . .' (p. 329). The reader who knows his Indian princes will smile at this, or charitably blame a sleepy printer. Intellectually Thornton recognizes that independence had become inevitable; his emotional reluctance to do so comes out in his comments on it, and it is at these moments when Thornton is brought to put his own cards on the table that one sees what a very poor hand of cards he holds.

Down to 1940 the imperial idea was drooping: no new 'crusader' came forward to revive it (p. 203). (Poor Lord Beaverbrook! never even mentioned.) Then it was splendidly revived by national crisis. Was it? After 1945 the Middle East was the only big stage left for a resuscitated Pax Britannica. Thornton thinks it had to be protected against Russian meddling (pp. 338–9): in point of fact the U.S.S.R. left it alone for an astonishingly long time, and only began 'meddling' in self-defence when hostile capitalist manoeuvring there, on the Russian doorstep, had gone on for years.[2] Coming to the Persian oil dispute, he complains that Britain seemed to lack 'the nerve and the power to defend her own legitimate oil interests' (p. 349); a remark which shows how little in practice his 'true imperialism' differed from the 'exploiting "imperialism"' he supposes to have vanished years before. Anyone curious about these 'legitimate interests' should turn to L. P. Elwell-Sutton's *Persian Oil, a Study in Power Politics* (1955)—a very remarkable study of imperialism in horny-handed practice, as distinct from cloistered theory.

It all ends with the Suez adventure of 1956 (pp. 350–51). One would wish to feel more certain that Thornton considers the adventure not only idiotic, because England was going to war with 'wooden guns,' but flagrantly immoral as well. This dismal *finis* leaves him still hankering for some new version of the imperial Idea to replace the old, some new mission or function to win back England's status in the world. He toys

---

[2] W. Z. Laqueur, *Communism and Nationalism in the Middle East* (London, 1956), p. 260, remarks on the 'great measure of caution' shown by Russia in making no moves here until 1955.

with the thought of England playing the part of a 'moral leader.' 'Not all imperialism is power-imperialism—religions and ideologies are but part of an imperial process' (p. 355). Haziness has grown hazier. Imagination conjures up a latter-day Don Quixote sighing like Alexander for new windmills to conquer, a Union Jack on his shield and a sluttish Dulcinea of Threadneedle Street in his dreams; or a Sancho Panza jogging about on his donkey in search of an island somewhere to govern; or a new Tory premier fidgeting about in a fancy-dress establishment, trying to decide what costume might go well with his figure. Moral leadership is not likely to; but as Thornton has remarked earlier (p. 325), 'another kind of imperial idea' is a private stock of nuclear bombs.

To R. Robinson and J. Gallagher, authors of *Africa and the Victorians* (1961),[3] imperialism is 'one of the most evocative myths of our time.'[4] What is 'mythical' is not that empires have recently existed—this has not yet been doubted even in academic circles—but any explanation of them in terms of economic greed. Hobson and Lenin are singled out for disparagement, though no attempt is made to meet them fairly on their own ground. A long note (p. 15) rebuts them by appealing to business scepticism about trade potentialities in Africa at the time of the partition. But the capital-export theory is not concerned with trade in the old-fashioned sense. There was no knowing in advance what raw materials any unexplored area might turn out to contain; the Sahara itself has turned out to contain undreamed-of riches. In any case a study confined to Africa, and which labours to prove that Africa was a backwater, a mere sideline, can provide no firm basis for conclusions about imperialism in general.

Territorial acquisitions in tropical Africa, we are told, were 'little more than by-products' of something quite different, a

[3] Various of this work's shortcomings are pointed out in an excellent review by G. Shepperson in the *Revue belge de philologie et d'histoire*, Vol. XL, 1962, No. 4; others in a review of it and other books on Africa by J. D. Hargreaves in *Victorian Studies*, September 1962. More recently it has been criticized in the *Journal of African History*, Vol. III, 1963, No. 3, by J. Stengers (pp. 469 ff.) and by C. W. Newbury (pp. 493 ff.), who likewise pay tribute to its striking qualities but find very serious faults in its arguments.

[4] Foreword.

search for strategic security in quite different regions (p. 463). They were touched off by the British occupation of Egypt in 1882, whose consequences governed the whole subsequent partition. It was all a game of diplomatic chess with the French. Egypt itself was not occupied for any motives of sordid gain; nor, twenty years later, were the Boer republics. The reasons lay in local crises. African régimes were weakening or collapsing, and thus jeopardizing Britain's two routes to India: the one via the Suez Canal, the other via the Cape.

There is an elegant symmetry about this theorem, but some of the logic it involves is as artificial as the frontiers that were being ruled in straight lines on the map of Africa by statesmen far away. The Khedive's rule in Egypt collapsed under the weight of its debts to bloodsucking Anglo-French bondholders. To say that the British occupation went on and on 'because the internal crisis remained unsolved' (p. 463) seems an odd way of saying that with a foreign army in possession the Egyptians could not organize a new political system. In the case of southern Africa the local crisis has to be understood as the growing inferiority of the British colonies to the gold-rich Transvaal, which endangered Britain's 'influence' or 'paramountcy.' Here is a sort of Morton's fork, on one of whose prongs or the other any independent part of Africa could be impaled. Egypt had to be taken over because it was too weak. The Transvaal had to be taken into custody because it was too strong. The former situation was the commoner; and we can of course say if we choose that Catherine and Frederick the Great partitioned Poland because Poland was weak and might grow anarchical. That is what they said themselves.

Even with respect to areas like Nigeria, depreciation of commercial ambitions may have been pushed a good deal too far in this book.[5] Still, that particular territories were taken largely or even exclusively for strategic instead of directly economic reasons is very likely, indeed certain. By stressing this point, and corroborating it with copious use of unpublished official papers, the book performs a useful service, besides

[5] Both Stengers and Newbury (see n. 3) are convinced that the partition of tropical Africa would have come about in any case through commercial pressures, and was *not* a consequence of the occupation of Egypt. *Cf.* J. S. Keltie, *The Partition of Africa* (London, 1893); he was reasonably though not wildly hopeful about commercial prospects.

being very readable. What is to be regretted is that so much more is bundled and stuffed into the theory than it has any room for. To spin strategic hypotheses out to this length, while overlooking or denying the great tidal force of capitalism, leads to the kind of dilemma that the philosophic Lord Monboddo landed himself in when, rejecting Newton's force of gravity, he had to station celestial intelligences on each planet to keep it on its course.

The title of the book is greatly at variance with its sub-title, *The Official Mind of Imperialism*. It is the latter that forms the real subject; which implies a marked narrowing-down, and an assumption implausible on the face of it that the official mind was the true source of policy. This is to invite Seeley's comment on the type of historian who 'seems always to watch proceedings from the reporter's gallery in the House of Commons,' instead of opening his eyes to the grand march of events.[6] For the enquiring student of the partition, our authors hold, 'all roads lead ineluctably to Downing Street' (p. 19). Lenin thought they all led to Lombard Street. It is in any case a delusion of archive-searchers, who inhale a subtly intoxicating atmosphere and need its stimulus to keep them going, to suppose that ministers and under-secretaries are careful to leave behind them all the documents required for a verdict on their actions. They are at least as likely to be careful not to do so. That no record of discussions be put on paper was the strictest rule of cabinet meetings. Even if all such discussions had been written down, a great deal that we need to know would still be missing.

A kindred fallacy is the treatment of the governing class as a separate caste of mandarins, aloof from the vulgar pre-occupations of mere businessmen and absorbed in their 'high calling' (p. 20). They were usually aristocrats, it is true, with inherited reflexes or 'codes of honour' of their own. Chamberlain on the other hand emphatically was not, and the latitude allowed to him as Colonial Secretary by his Tory colleagues is recognized (p. 425). What mattered more, and what the book fails to reckon with, just as it turns a blind eye to the transformation of capitalism in that epoch, was the development of a consolidated plutocracy in Britain and in Europe: a social stratum within which Scottish earls and Prussian junkers

[6] J. R. Seeley, *The Expansion of England* (1883), Chap. 8.

married Jewish heiresses, and politicians collected director-
ships in the City, and old-fashioned notions of gentility
survived with less and less distinct meaning. William II in 1914
was *wery fierce* about his honour and that of his senile ally at
Vienna, but when the smoke cleared away in 1918 he was
discovered in Holland in the comfortable enjoyment of a
fortune that he had been up to date enough, with the advice
of his banking friends, to salt away abroad. Without reference
to this process of fusion at the top of society, this mixing of the
cream, the new imperialism cannot be comprehended.

Ministers mostly belonged to the plutocracy, and the func-
tionaries who mostly formulated their opinions for them lived
on its fringes and were steadily impregnated with its mentality.
The changing outlook would not be reflected at all adequately
in Whitehall minutes and memoranda. A department of
State, as a collective brain, does not exist for the sake of
thinking, but of directing action, and it exhibits still more than
an individual mind the blockages that allow new volitions to
gain access only along well-worn tracks, by translating themselves into terms already familiar. Time-honoured phrases,
clichés, maxims continued to be repeated in that epoch, while
their substance altered; novel ambitions expressed themselves
to conservative minds like Gladstone's or Salisbury's in old
symbols like the route to India, which those who wished to
influence such men had to know how to manipulate. Talk of
'a hardening of arteries and a hardening of hearts' in high
quarters (p. 470) is no substitute for recognition of all this.

The narrative constructed here, from official sources, of
ministerial shufflings and wafflings before the occupation of
Egypt is in many ways illuminating; its fatal drawback is that
ministers are treated purely as political computers, and the
influence on policy of the bondholders is left out. The assertion
that the British Government did not desire to occupy Egypt
only amounts to saying that it would have preferred to go on
with the cheaper and discreeter method of letting Egypt be
exploited through a native puppet; just as U.S. marines are
only sent into a banana-republic when the local dictator fails
to deliver the bananas. Business interests wanting intervention
could always provoke a situation, or help a situation to take
shape, where ministers would have no choice about inter-

vening, and could do so with a good or at least a brave conscience. In 1882 it was provided by the riots at Alexandria,
which came about much in the same way as the Boxer rebellion
in China in 1900, likewise provoked by a long course of
meddling and bullying by Western hucksters and likewise
followed by Western military action and improved business
prospects.[7]

By the time of the British bombardment of Alexandria,
wrote Lord Cromer, 'the question of protecting European
financial interests in Egypt had fallen completely into the background.'[8] That was just where the financial interests wanted
it to be, well hidden under official jargon about 'pacifying'
Egypt and protecting the Canal. True, as Robinson and
Gallagher admit, Bright's objection that to intervene was
precisely the way to endanger the Canal was 'sane and simple'
(pp. 110–11), and it was verified by events. Lord Randolph
Churchill showed equal perspicacity (being then in opposition,
instead of at the India Office) in a speech at Edinburgh the
following year. 'You will be told that Egypt is the high-road
to India, and that Britain must hold it at all costs. This is a
terrible and a widespread illusion. . . . The Suez Canal is a
commercial route to India . . . but it never was, and never
could be, a military route for Great Britain in time of war.'[9] A
few years later Robinson and Gallagher show us Chamberlain
taking this for granted and using it to defend his forward policy
in South Africa as necessary to keep the Cape route open (p.
416 n.). Here is a good sample of the versatility with which
imperialists could jump from one rationalization of whatever
they wanted to an opposite one.

In short this study of ministerial head-scratchings is more
significant psychologically than politically. W. S. Blunt (whose
indispensable *Secret History* is barely mentioned) had a talk with
Gladstone before the crisis and found him willing to take an
interest 'as far as a man can who is totally ignorant of the ABC
of a question,' but concluded: 'He has evidently made up his
mind about nothing, and will let himself drift on till the smash

[7] See on this an important recent work by V. Purcell, *The Boxer Uprising*
(Cambridge, 1963).
[8] *Modern Egypt* (London, 1908), Vol 1, p. 282.
[9] W. S. Churchill, *Lord Randolph Churchill* (new edn., London, 1951), pp.
219–20.

comes.'[10] Robinson and Gallagher unwittingly supply a neat confirmation when they sum up their narrative by saying that the Cabinet 'muddled and drifted with events' (p. 120). It could hardly have been otherwise when the trio chiefly involved were Gladstone, old and preoccupied with Ireland; Granville at the Foreign Office, old and deaf, idle and amiable; and Hartington at the India Office, a stable-boy in ermine. 'They say there's but five upon this isle; we are three of them; if the other two be brained like us, the State totters.' The State did totter.

In southern Africa credulity is strained even more than in Egypt by the assertion that policies were 'inspired by concepts peculiar to the official mind,' not by money pressures (pp. 73–4). Wavering between objective and subjective—between what ministers were really doing or allowing to be done, and what they liked to think, or wanted others to think, they were doing—grows more pronounced. Conquest of the Sudan and the Transvaal 'at first sight,' it is allowed, 'might suggest a full-blooded drive for empire': but our gift of second-sight rescues us from any such misapprehension; 'this was not how ministers saw their onslaughts' (p. 410). Finally we see another old premier, sick and sorry, brought face to face with realization that the jingo party had rigged things in such a way that he and Britain *must* go to war—'and all for people whom we despise, and for territory which will bring no profit and no power to England' (pp. 453–4). In other words Lord Salisbury simply did not know why the Boer War was about to be fought. Historians content to look through his spectacles will know as little as he did.

Of how things were really happening in those years a great deal may be gleaned from the diaries of W. S. Blunt, who knew the presiding figures as they were off-stage. One day in 1893 Harcourt, then Chancellor, was grumbling to him about 'the brutality of the British public,' 'the slaughter of the Matabeles' for the sake of new markets, the Press in the hands of the financiers. Blunt asked why he did not make a stand against it all. '"Oh," he said, "we are all burglars now,"' and relapsed into his cigar.[11] No government or ruling class is likely to acknowl-

[10] *Secret History of the English Occupation of Egypt* (London, 1907), p. 89.
[11] *My Diaries, 1888–1914* (2nd edn., London, 1932), p. 115 (9 November 1893).

edge such things in public documents. We may be sure that the imperialists of Athens did not actually say, even if they thought, what they are made by Thucydides to say in the Melian dialogue. If Lenin deals out too summary a drumhead justice to capitalism, Robinson and Gallagher go to the opposite extreme. On their rules of evidence no conviction could ever be secured against any business lobby. Capitalism to be found guilty would have to be caught *in flagrante delicto* with a signed confession in its pocket properly witnessed by three ministers of the Crown.

For some years now a *New Cambridge Modern History* has been heaping itself up on library shelves. By a gradual filtration of ideas through school and college teaching, it will exert a widespread influence. It was to be expected that a compendium on this massive scale, in Britain of all countries, would be planned with very special attention to the subject of imperialism. Instead it suffers on exactly this subject from a vast lapse of vision or memory. This applies generally to the three concluding volumes, X to XII. No. XII has some excuse in having to cope hurriedly with everything from 1898 to 1945. It tends to show more awareness of French or Dutch than of British colonial short-comings; and its conception of British imperialism fading away through self-criticism or change of heart—of the public having grown 'anxious' to give up India (pp. 532, 554)—is an over-indulgent one. It took the hammer-blows of the Second World War to loosen the imperial grasp. But it is in Vol. XI, last of the three to appear (1962), that sins of omission are most glaring, for this deals with the climactic period 1870–98. The editor's introduction notices imperialism in a perfunctory page or so (pp. 45–6). In later chapters there is too little about Ireland, too little about Burma, Malaya, and other British colonies, and about other empires altogether. Of the causes of imperialism there is far too little discussion; of the evolution of capitalism in relation to seizure of colonies, practically none. Hobson is not mentioned; Lenin's *Imperialism* only to be brushed aside.

A. P. Thornton reappears in this volume, with a chapter on Mediterranean and middle-eastern rivalries; but on the empire question it is Messrs Robinson and Gallagher who are called on to do most of the bowling for Cambridge. As before, they bowl very fast, and with great subtlety of flight and spin, but so wide of the wicket that they are bound to give away a lot of byes. In fact their Chapter XXII on 'The Partition of Africa,' the longest in the volume apart from the introduction and the only one buttressed with references to original sources, is essentially a synopsis of their book. Forty out of the forty-eight pages are devoted to northern and tropical Africa, six to the south; then at the end come a number of sweeping statements (p. 640) offered as though logical deductions from the evidence. The new imperialisms of that age, 'the gaudy empires spatchcocked together in Asia and Africa,' are held up to derision. But we need not trouble about them; they had no organic connection with Britain or the British economy; they were mere freakish echoes or imitations of the true empire-building, in Canada or New Zealand, that had gone before. Only the 'gullible' could mistake them either for 'necessary functions of the balance of power,' or for Lenin's 'highest stage of capitalism'.

To have these empires so forcibly censured is most welcome, even if the censure comes on p. 639 of the volume instead of in its proper place on page 1. It is quite true also that imperialism was in one aspect a vast Gilbertian extravaganza, or soap-bubble Ruritania, or mad-hatter's tea-party. Still, it was a frolic into which a grand army of politicians, parsons and professors threw themselves heart and soul, in full bark and cry; and if some were, in Lenin's phrase, 'hired coolies of the pen,'[12] many others really believed what they said, or a good part of it. Imperialism in England became as a French observer said an obsession.[13] Colonial governors, like the field-marshals of 1914–18, really existed, with all the preposterous plumes on their hats. They were not bad dreams ready to vanish at cockcrow.

And if investigation in Africa yields only such negative results, why does Volume XI devote fifty pages to it, to the neglect of so many other colonial regions? That much of Africa was sand or swamp, unlikely to set bankers' mouths watering, is as true as it is obvious. But why does Cambridge

[12] *Imperialism*, preface to French and German editions.
[13] V. Bérard, *British Imperialism and Commercial Supremacy* (English edn., London, 1906), p. 44.

have it so much at heart to impress the point on us? The explanation can only lie in that unconscious conservatism, that predisposition to give bankers the benefit of the doubt, that scholars in our snugger academies suck in with their alma mater's port. It is easier to acquit nineteenth-century bankers of unlawful desires in the Sahara than anywhere else except at the North and South Pole. And one acquittal leads easily to another. Capitalism did not really covet its neighbour's sand. Therefore capitalism cannot really have coveted its neighbour's oil, or his coal, or his rubber, or his ox, or his ass, or his man-servant, or his maid-servant, or anything that was his. Henry VIII did not chop off the head of his last wife. Therefore Henry VIII cannot have chopped off the heads of any of his wives. Twice two is not five. Therefore twice three cannot be six.

A price has to be paid for this reassuring triumph over Lenin, whose bones are thus left bleaching in the Sahara. Before the last war the 'jolly old empire' was very much a part of Cambridge orthodoxy, and students who declined to take it at its face value were regarded by their seniors as very abandoned characters. (This fact of modern history is recorded here because it has failed to find its way into Volume XII of the New C.M.H.) Now all that has to be written off. But capitalism, or jolly old free enterprise, is still very much a part of orthodoxy, and its youthful wild oats, its unsavoury connections of former days, are best forgotten. Imperialism was bad, but capitalism had nothing to do with it. This quiet disengagement, or British compromise, has a not very distant relative in West Germany, where it is agreed that Hitler was a bad man, but that Krupp and the rest only joined him in a fit of absence of mind.

In Volume XI the strategic interpretation is endorsed and expanded. What brought Mr Gladstone into Egypt, an incongruous Mark Antony, *to tumble on the bed of Ptolemy*? The Canal. Why was the Canal so electrical? Because of India. *Salus Indiae suprema lex*: here Cambridge finds its guiding thread through the whole diplomatic labyrinth. What it overlooks is that the cry of 'India in danger' was a convenient one for financiers and concession-hunters, as well as historians; for anyone with an eye on Burmese timber, Yunnan railways,

Malayan rubber, or Persian oil. It was a plausible excuse for all businessmen found in compromising situations, an unanswerable claim for official backing. If there had been space-travellers in those days India would have been a compulsory reason for Britain to take part in the race to the moon—which after all is actually within sight of Simla. It was a plausible excuse besides for charging the cost of military operations up and down Asia and Africa to the Indian taxpayer. The hard-up Indian Government itself, to do it justice, regularly protested against the fraud, and pointed out that the benefit to Indian security from most of these campaigns abroad was nil.[14]

British Africa was not much more than 'a gigantic footnote to the Indian empire,' Robinson and Gallagher repeat (p. 616). Whatever truth the epigram may possess, it merely throws the question of the real motives of empire one stage further back. And obviously, by adopting the thesis of these two writers and giving it a startling prominence, Cambridge History assumes the obligation to answer the question at this further remove. The duty stares it in the face to explain *why* India was of such enormous consequence to Britain. Undoubtedly most British statesmen did believe that it was; the word 'India' might have been found engraven on their hearts. Some of their enemies believed it equally. 'If we are to bleed to death,' the Kaiser wrote in his most hysterical note of July 1914, 'England shall at least lose India.'[15] But how much was the Indian empire really worth, and how were its dividends appropriated? In *Africa and the Victorians* two or three very instructive pages (pp. 10–13) are devoted to the problem, and economic as well as other assets are noticed. Cambridge on the contrary does not try to answer the question; it does not raise the question; it does not perceive the question. This inmost *arcanum imperii* remains an official secret.

Chapter XV on India, by P. Spear, covers 1840–1905, in twenty-eight pages: India in other words is given four or five times less coverage than despised Africa. It is not backward in recognizing Indian aspirations, and some Indian grievances,

---

[14] See Hira Lal Singh, *Problems and Policies of the British in India, 1885–1898* (Bombay, 1963), pp. 191 ff.
[15] See K. Kautsky, *The Guilt of William Hohenzollern* (English edn., London, 1920), p. 178.

even if here and there a more archaic stratum of thought peeps out. The accepted or acceptable point of view about all this has changed a great deal in Cambridge since before the last war, when India was still struggling for independence. But no real consideration is given to the poverty of India and the extent to which it was man-made. Famines are treated as random acts of God, owing nothing to excessive rents and land-taxes and the usury that went with them. Anti-famine measures, belatedly developed, are given somewhat more credit than they deserve, and we are told on p. 428 (also on p. 22) that there were no deaths from starvation after 1880. The unregenerate *Cambridge History of India* of thirty years ago recorded an 'excess mortality' in 1900 of 750,000, including deaths from epidemics aided by hunger, in British India alone.[16] And while this chapter includes a short passage on British economic interests in India (pp. 428–30), it asks no more than the old *Cambridge India* asked whether there was a link between the comparative prosperity of Britain and the abysmal misery of India; how far the relationship between Dives and Lazarus was one of parasitism, like the vampire colonial rule of old Spain or of Portugal today. Dadabhai Naoroji was expressing a growing conviction of many Indians when he maintained that India was paying annually to Britain, through all kinds of direct or devious channels, a ruinously heavy tribute. He estimated that by 1870 it had risen to over £27 million, and that altogether Britain had used its political power to drain India of something like £500 million.[17]

Atrocities committed on both sides during the Indian Mutiny are only fleetingly mentioned. Imperial history altogether was a vastly more painful business than a reader would gain any inkling of from New Cambridge. The atrocities in the Belgian Congo, which even Abdul the Damned of Turkey humorously joined in a protest against, are passed over with the same reticence. So are the brutalities of the American conquest of the Philippines, the death-rate in the British concentration-camps for Boer women and children, and the savagery of the intervention in north China after the Boxer rising.[18] How this

---

[16] Vol. VI, p. 308.
[17] *Poverty and Un-British Rule in India* (London, 1901), p. 34.
[18] Vol. XII, pp. 228–9, makes some amends as to this.

is remembered by the Chinese the reader may discover by turning to pp. 270–1 of the *Outline History of China* published at Peking in 1958; and it might be prudence as well as virtue in the West to remember its misdeeds at least as long as their victims do. More philosophically, it may be unwisdom for us all to put too easily out of our minds those high crimes and misdemeanours that *call heaven and earth to record them* against mankind and its rulers, whether Cambridge History records them or not; they are part of what has made our world and the human race what they are. In this volume our attention is guided rather towards pleasanter topics like the increased use of soap in England.[19] History itself is being given a good wash, or undergoing a process of saponification; now and then as the reader turns the pages he may seem to catch a glimpse of Soapy Sam, the well-known Bishop of Oxford of those days, or even of Lady Macbeth washing her hands.

John Strachey was one of the few theoreticians of empire who have been involved in the business of running one, as his Anglo-Indian ancestors, all the way back to Clive's time, had been. It may be regretted of him, as of John Morley before him, that imperial office subdued him more than he succeeded in subduing it. He had the ill-luck to be Secretary for War in the first stages of the guerrilla campaign in Malaya, and during the Persian oil crisis. In *The End of Empire* (1961) he defends the Malayan repression on much the same ground that Tories argued for keeping India: it was not our duty to hand over power to a small active minority (p. 256). About the Persian affair, which ended so gruesomely for the Persian patriots, his only remark is that he and his Labour colleagues were very badly informed by their expert advisers (p. 161). He was more at home in the theory of empire than in its operation, and this last book of his deserves careful study as his last word on a subject he had thought about all his life.

Imperialism is not of merely historical interest, Strachey

---

[19] P. 4. The editor, F. H. Hinsley, has since published a work called *Power and the Pursuit of Peace* (Cambridge, 1963). One of John Strachey's last writings was a review of it in the *Observer*, 23 June 1963, which ended: 'I am frankly aghast at the complacency of Mr. Hinsley . . . . Humanity will miss its last chance if it listens to the Dr. Panglosses, such as Mr. Hinsley, who tell it that all is for the best in the best possible of nuclear worlds.'

D

emphasizes; over the past four and a half centuries it has largely moulded world conditions (p. 11). But he views Britain today (Lenin needless to say would not) as having 'suddenly' become 'a post-imperial society' (p. 7), and he asks the country to recognize and accept this novel position and set about facing life without colonial flannel next to its skin. His contention is that the empire was at no time really vital to Britain, though it was often highly profitable to sectional interests. He produces a table showing annual changes in export-import prices from 1854 onwards, and argues from it that imperial power conferred no ability to dictate the terms of trade, which have been more favourable to Britain since 1945 than they ever were in the heyday of imperialism, and were never better than in the dismal year 1933 (pp. 148–52). This is a weighty argument; it does not, all the same, rule out the possibility that imperialism was at various stages vital to Britain's continued advance along its own peculiar road towards its own peculiar form of capitalist democracy.

Strachey reviews the Hobson-Lenin theory sympathetically though critically in chapters VI and VII. Hobson's book he takes as 'the starting-point of any rational explanation' of imperialism (p. 98); and it fits in well with his own line of thought. He praises Hobson for seeing that there was an alternative to imperialism, in social reform and redistribution of income at home, to prevent the piling up of masses of surplus capital that could only be put to use by being exported (p. 115). Conversely he feels that Lenin's basic error was to dismiss this alternative as a mere mirage. Holding strictly to the doctrine of the increasing misery of the workers under capitalism, Lenin 'overlooked the economic consequences of democracy,' the effect on social injustice of 'an all-pervasive democratic political environment' (pp. 109–12).

Here is one of the passages where Strachey—as a good (or fairly good) Labour Party man—may be suspected of taking democracy too much for granted. Certainly he is stressing a primary truth when he says that capitalism is not, as its uncritical admirers have always supposed, a self-righting mechanism, which will always find the best way to function if left to itself (pp. 113–14). It will only work better, or less badly, under vigorous pressure from outside. There had to be enough 'democracy' to allow of organized pressure from labour. But again, this would have been necessary for any concessions to be extracted, whatever funds they were to come out of. An employer rich enough to raise wages because he enjoyed an unearned income from the Kaffir Circus would not raise wages unless he was forced to. Strachey may be brushing Lenin's crumbs off the table too hastily when he maintains that during the days when Britain had an empire a real redistribution of income was taking place, and not a hand-out of colonial surplus profit.

To the other (or capital-export) side of the classical theory, in broad outline, Strachey remains faithful. Even if Lenin failed to see that the capitalist leopard could have some of its spots scrubbed off by the democratic brush, he was right in much of his analysis of his own epoch. His approach was 'by no means unrealistic for the Britain of 1900–14' (p. 117); and Strachey considers that but for imperialism there might have been a capitalist collapse in 1900 similar to that of 1929 (p. 112). He shares Lenin's common-sense conviction that the vast scale of overseas investment is proof by itself of some link between it and imperialism: to refuse to recognize such a 'prime mover' as the leading force of an epoch is to reduce history to 'an unaccountable jumble of facts and dates' (p. 123).

Strachey's ancestry lends a special interest to what he has to say about India, and his two opening chapters, a factual study of the conquest of Bengal, give the book a refreshingly realistic start. Chapter IV is an interesting re-examination of the old question of whether, or how far, the plunder of Bengal assisted the industrial revolution in England. Plundering a colony is a wasteful way of exploiting it, as he points out, and the profit that reached England from the ruination of Bengal seems to have been 'modest, though not insignificant' (p. 63). His conclusion may be as fair a one as the problem admits of: that this profit was far from being the prime cause of the industrial revolution, but played a real part none the less in helping it to get 'off the ground,' or 'over the hump' (p. 68). He does not fail to notice Britain's inherited obligation today to give far more help than it has done so far towards getting an industrial revolution launched in India.

On the British Raj, after its infamous beginnings, his

summing-up could scarcely be bettered. It was 'selfish and selfless, ruinous and constructive, glorious and monstrous' (p. 13). Urging how much the old India stood in need of a drastic shake-up, which it had no energy to achieve for itself, he is in step with Karl Marx as much as with Sir Richard Strachey. But as he comes closer to the present he is apt to overstate the civilizing influence of democracy on imperial rule as well as on capitalism at home, and to view the Raj with a somewhat too indulgent eye; he is too ready to see it floating smoothly towards its splendid harbour, and the Labour Party's finest hour, the grant of Indian independence. Thus he sees the Morley–Minto reforms of 1909 as a 'genuinely voluntary' first step towards 'democracy and independence' (p. 130).[20] And he goes much too far when he says that no one can accuse England in the twentieth century, as in earlier days, of direct, barefaced exploitation of India by the exercise of political power (p. 147). He thinks of economic relations between the two countries as governed by the terms of trade, which were outside the authority of the Raj. These mysterious entities scarcely explain such items as the charging of British military expenditure outside India to the Indian revenue, a matter on which the Whitehall attitude was, an Indian historian has lately written, 'most arbitrary and unsympathetic' and revealed 'a pettifogging and huckstering mentality.'[21] An English historian has lately said of another item, the handicapping of Indian cloth manufacture for the benefit of Lancashire: 'A more unsympathetic and selfish act of policy it would be hard to imagine.'[22]

Strachey finds some good words to say of British administration in Egypt also. Cromer, greatest of the proconsuls, made the country at least semi-modern, reduced taxes, abolished the corvée (pp. 86–9). If in spite of this the fellah showed few signs of growing prosperity, Strachey blames over-growth of population: as in all such cases, an inadequate excuse by itself. As to the reasons for the occupation in 1882, he rightly puts the pressure of the bondholding interests first, and all other

---

[20] Here the *New C.M.H.*, Vol. XII, pp. 214–15, is more realistic.

[21] Hira Lal Singh, *op. cit.*, p. 197.

[22] S. B. Saul, *Studies in British Overseas Trade 1870–1914* (Liverpool, 1960), p. 198. Chap. VIII of this work, on trade with India, supplies much material for an estimate of India's value to Britain, though it is not concerned to explore the imperial relationship.

motivations well behind (pp. 81 ff.). He gives strategic factors their due weight in particular contexts; he makes room also, as it is indispensable to do, for motives of an irrational or psychological order, including eagerness to take part in colony-hunting simply because others are hunting for colonies (pp. 89–90, 96–7). Similar instincts can be seen at work on the world stage today, and in the nursery among any set of children; imperialists were in many ways child-like, if not childish. Strachey points out how contradictory, even muddle-headed, imperial thinking in men like Milner was (pp. 94–6). All these other incentives could come into play once economic rivalries created a congenial environment for them; in themselves they were all, as Strachey sees clearly, secondary.

He describes the Boer War accordingly as a struggle to decide whether the cheap labour of conquered Africans was to be exploited on farms, for the benefit of Boer settlers, or in mines, for the benefit of British capitalists (pp. 91–2). One might add that the final outcome was a compromise by which cheap African labour would be exploited both on farms and in mines. Oddly, Strachey thinks this settlement the best then possible, on the ground that the evils of *apartheid* could not be foreseen by the Liberals of 1906 (p. 95). South Africa's future ought really to have been easy enough to foresee without recourse to any patent double million magnifyin' gas micro-scopes of hextra power.

One need not share all M. Barratt Brown's opinions, or the robust philanthropy that allows him to contemplate a rise of world population to 10,000 million as a prospect to 'en-courage the humanist' (p. 1), in order to be edified by his *After Imperialism* (1963). It is a big book that brings in many of our biggest problems, and has important things to say about them. Despite its title the first two-fifths of the book, which concern us here, are devoted to the part that imperialism has played in the past century or so. An initial sketch of its pre-history is necessarily rapid, and there are patches of slippery ground got over with a hop, skip and jump; but it is always suggestive, and has the great merit of linking the origins of modern imperialism firmly with those of modern capitalism. It thus serves to introduce the book's main theme: the series of relationships set up by capitalism, reaching out from western Europe, between the developed and undeveloped regions of the world, and what is likely to take their place in the coming epoch.

Like Hobson and Strachey, Brown believes that since at any rate the early nineteenth century Britain's prosperity, as distinct from that of sectional interests, has not been built on the profits of empire. His grand tenet is that prosperity is indivisible; no country can expect to advantage itself in the long run by retarding or depressing any other. In the long run what is good for our neighbour is good for us. Foreign tariffs in the later nineteenth century impeded British exports, but by enabling other lands to industrialize they raised up better, because richer, customers for Britain later on (p. 81).

In his laudable desire to satisfy us that we can face the future without colonies, Brown like Strachey may sometimes make too little of the advantages of imperialism in the past, notably its political or 'psychological' advantages.[23] He does well to remind us, as Strachey does over Bengal, that a colony may suffer catastrophically from exploitation only marginally profitable to the metropolis (p. 158). And undeniably the philosophy of do-it-yourself is the one that pays best in the end. Even the Netherlands, which may have been drawing a sixth of its national income from Indonesia (p. 173), has grown more prosperous, because more energetic, since losing its ill-gotten gains. The trouble is that in ordinary circumstances a country is not in a position to turn over a clean sheet and choose a mode of life rationally and dispassionately. 'National' and 'sectional' interests are therefore easier to separate in theory than in the hurly-burly of existence. Without empire Britain might have evolved along healthier lines, like Norway; or along more morbid lines, like Spain after the loss of empire; but in either case it would not have been growing into the Britain whose actual structure and character we are confronted with.

Brown never loses sight of the special significance of India. He too considers the economic effect on England of the plunder of Bengal, which he thinks may have done rather more to accelerate the agricultural revolution than the industrial. Later,

[23] Barratt Brown has expressed himself 'happy to accept' this comment; see the long and valuable Preface to the new edition of his book (1970), p. ix.

in the nineteenth century, he allows the value of India to British investors and exporters of capital goods, but attributes the chief development, the railway programme, to 'a succession of rather exceptional events' (pp. 64–5). Among these was the Mutiny; but strategic railways for the control of India and movement of troops to the frontiers would surely have been required before long even without the Mutiny. It belongs to Brown's case to maintain that India never became indispensable to British capitalism as a whole. Nevertheless, with the emphasis he lays on India's vast importance to the British balance of payments, we come at last to a realistic view of why the British ruling classes were so passionate about the 'defence of India'. He differs too from both Strachey and Cambridge in refusing any special praise to Britain for 'giving up' India in the end. There was no longer a choice. In Malaya, where there was still a choice, Britain was prepared to fight 'a major colonial war' (p. 191).

Brown's picture of the effects of British rule on India forms a good corrective to the bedside cheeriness of the C.M.H. He is aware for instance of the connection between the recurrent famines and the growth of the area devoted to cash crops for export, which, along with the crippling of native handicrafts, worsened pressure on the land (e.g. p. 59). In some details outside the economic sphere his picture may be too gloomy, or not factually accurate. He may underrate the good that imperialism did to India and other colonies (as Napoleon's army did to Italy and Germany) by jerking them, however rudely and painfully, out of stagnation into change. British rule did play upon communal division between Hindu and Muslim, but the charge that it conjured up communal bitterness in a land where this had been 'almost non-existent' (p. 181) can be too easily challenged. No landlords were set up by Britain in the eighteenth-century Punjab; and the Muslim League was not primarily 'landlord-based,' but urban and petty-bourgeois (p. 209).

Brown's specific criticisms of Hobson (pp. 92–5) and Lenin (pp. 95–101) are rational, if unavoidably too brief to take up many of the controversial points. He finds it over-simple to explain British imperial growth in terms of protection of investors, but he seems less on his guard in some other directions.

Thus he says 'it is clear from Cromer's account' that Egypt was occupied for strategic, not pecuniary reasons (p. 88). It is really far from clear, even taking Cromer's evidence without the plentiful pinch of salt it calls for. Curiously, Blunt's evidence is not referred to. Brown rejects the idea of men like Rhodes genuinely believing in new colonies as the antidote to social revolt at home; yet he admits that the fear of population growth, and the need for new markets, were genuine enough (pp. 90–1). His conclusion that the real utility of empire lay in 'the strategic position it conferred in world power-politics' (p. 107) is a little indefinite.

Writing in 1902 at the end of the Boer War, Hobson was he thinks 'blinded by the single glaring case of Rhodes and South Africa to make a general analysis that did not apply elsewhere' (p. 95). Comparatively little of the massive overseas investment was going into newly annexed colonies, while two-thirds, between 1900 and 1913, went into the Americas (pp. 92–5). He reckons that in 1913 nearly one-tenth of Britain's national income came from abroad, but only one-sixth of this from India and the other non-white dependencies (pp. 98–9). Still, even though 1·5 per cent of the national income may not sound much, one-sixth of an overseas income vital to the balance of payments and, in many ways, to the comforts of the ruling classes in particular, was not a trifle. Be all this as it may, Brown has good ground for stressing the factor of chauvinism, of the tradition of imperial power among all Britons including the workers, and for saying that with this, and a general economic improvement assisted by cheaper food imports, 'it was hardly necessary to offer bribes' (pp. 100–1); Lenin's theory of crumbs, in the special application he was making of it, was redundant.

If Brown does anything less than justice to Lenin's work as a commentary on Europe before 1914, he treats it as a brilliant prophecy of Europe as it was to become after 1918. Lenin was reasoning very largely, he points out, from a German economy concentrated and monopolistic in a degree that British industry was far from having reached, but was destined to reach in the following decades (p. 97). In the 1920s the dividing up of the world among giant corporations went on exactly as Lenin had predicted (pp. 125–6). In the 'thirties possession of empire assisted Britain's recovery from the Slump (p. 135). Brown has an interesting discussion of the balance of advantages and disadvantages at this date of imperial tribute, and the relevance of the 'crumbs' (pp. 142–7). The balance is not easy to strike, but evidently the biggest gain went to the monopolies, whose strength was reinforced, while whatever gains any one else made were far more than outweighed by the economic stagnation that empire helped to prolong.

Colonial profits to big business were so lavish that Brown is willing to take seriously Hitler's complaints on behalf of German monopoly capitalism of its being cut off from raw materials by lack of colonies; and to blame 'the narrow and restrictive policies' of the 'Haves' for driving German, Italian and Japanese capitalists—the 'Have-Nots'—into fascism and then into war (pp. 129–31, 148). Here he may be accused of following Lenin (rather than Marx, who made very full allowance for the 'political' elements in any situation) almost too closely. It is salutary for us to be reminded in season and out of season that Krupp and the rest were at any rate eager accessories after the fact, willing receivers of stolen property. But to see the Second World War, as Lenin saw the first, as springing from a simple clash of rival monopolists, is to forget the whole business of appeasement, the climax of a long Western diplomatic effort beginning long before Hitler to keep Germany solidly in the capitalist camp against the U.S.S.R. Appeasement failed, Lord Home said not long ago, because Hitler turned out to be a madman. So, from the standpoint of world capitalism, he was. Brown himself assumes that the great cartels on both sides in 1938–39 were working for peace. Also questionable is the view that fascism originated 'in the outward pressures of monopoly capitalism' (p. 150). Fascism might be said to originate, most visibly in Japan, in those older tracts of national life and emotion that capitalism had only half assimilated. It was taken up by capitalism primarily from fear of internal collapse. For Mammon, after all, survival must come before expansion.

As between Hobson, who saw in imperialism a defect of capitalism that could in principle be corrected, and Lenin, who saw in it the revelation of capitalism's total and incorrigible depravity, the conclusions of our two recent socialist critics tend to agree with the former more than the latter. The world has not yet moved far enough or decisively enough away from imperialism for experience to have demonstrated which opinion is nearer the truth. As between the whole trend of thought represented by these two critics and their forerunners, and that represented by the non-socialists who see in the empires no evidence at all as to the nature of capitalism, the weight of argument and probability is heavily in favour of the former. It is to be hoped that the controversy will not end here. Too often before now a great historical question has been quietly buried in an empty coffin, and forgotten.

3
Imperialism, American and European
Some historical contrasts

'American imperialism' is a thing we hear about continually. To conservatives, with their blind eye staunchly to the telescope, it is only a pair of words, a nonentity, as unreal as the unicorn. To liberals it is a chronic embarrassment; to many further left it is—to borrow the title of Felix Greene's new book —*The Enemy*,[1] the adversary of the human race. We see it stirring in Latin America, in the Middle East, in the Far East; we guess at its secret burrowings in other regions, including the British Isles. Its character and direction are of vital concern to the whole world, yet to see them in a clear focus is puzzlingly difficult. A frequent allegation is that American prosperity has come to be dependent on huge armaments production and the aggressive policies required to justify it. Many Americans have their own motives for encouraging such a belief; left-wing critics who endorse it may be unwittingly playing into their opponents' hands. A less irrational look is given to aggressive policies by the contention that the U.S. must increasingly get raw materials from outside, and must have access to them, and for secure access and cheaper procurement must have political control, and without this the economy and the living standards of the people will crumble. Here too critics eager to convict the U.S. of economic imperialism may show a perilous readiness to accept the assertions of the monopolists. Capitalists over the years, we may recall, have assured us that national prosperity must collapse if child labour is stopped, or trade unions started, or tariffs reduced, or wages raised, or India lost.

Even the inhabitants of Utopia sent out colonists to seize

[1] F. Greene, *The Enemy. Notes on Imperialism and Revolution* (N.Y., 1970).

land from their neighbours. Imperialism of one sort or another has run through all world history; but we have no general theory capable of embracing or classifying its multifarious doings. Marxists have curiously seldom tried to look outside the framework of Lenin's theory. It may be of some use then to look back over the story of American expansionism, comparing its motive forces and lines of development with modern Europe's, and noticing that at every stage there have been analogies but also significant divergences which call for explanation in terms of contrasting social and mental patterns. An enquiry into them cannot by itself answer the question of what American imperialism is today, or what can be expected from it tomorrow. But besides offering something towards the general theory of imperialism that we lack, it may in some degree help us to form a clearer view of America as the biggest practical problem of our time.

By the late nineteenth century Europe and the U.S. were both ruled by plutocracies, but in one case with tenacious survivals from an older feudal society, in the other with a still active leaven of democracy. In Europe empire and war, before becoming useful to influence the working class, were of essential service in bringing together aristocracy and bourgeoisie. Tory and Liberal in Britain, royalist and republican in France, Junker and chimney-baron in Germany, all found in expansionism and militarism a common ground that allowed them to combine into solid modern ruling classes. Blue-blooded landowners and their younger sons were to the fore in all the Continental (and Japanese) armies and the British navy, and in the running of colonies, particularly the British: Radicals could allege with some reason that the colonies existed largely to provide them with employment. To a nobleman accustomed to the management—sometimes intelligent, sometimes even benevolent—of large estates, that of an Indian province came naturally. To the son of a Lincolnshire squire, accustomed to run his own parish and jail his own poachers, it came naturally to run a district in Ceylon, where the natives could not be much further beneath him on the human ladder then the degraded race of farm-labourers at home. Empire and war gave these men moreover a sense of function, of being needed by their countries, such as any upper class requires to keep it in good heart. The rich cannot live by cake alone, any more than the poor by bread.

In Europe higher government service was a dignified calling, being in form or in fact service to the Sovereign, most markedly in the departments reserved for 'good' families, the diplomatic and military and imperial. America had no notion of official employment being more reputable than commerce, and it was unquestionably less lucrative. There was no old landowning class conditioned to prefer such employment. There were no ready-made colonial administrators, eager for colonies to manage, or officers to the manner born, eager for an army. Nothing has so clearly marked America off from Europe, or revealed the tenacity of its early ways of thinking, as its lack of interest in the glorious trappings of war. Even Britain, in this as in many things the stepping-stone between the two continents, loved to admire uniforms, if not to wear them, and loved its navy, if not its army. America inherited from it the old Whig conviction that a standing army was dangerous to liberty; and in spite of periodic fits of alarm it suffered far less from the corroding anxiety about social anarchy that did so much to reconcile middle-class Europe to its aristocratic armies. Only one war has ever faced Americans with what a European would think a real casualty-list, and that was a civil war, less likely than any other to kindle a taste for martial glory. At the end of it the victorious army went quietly home, instead of marching off to conquest abroad like the army of the French Revolution.

To Europe with its numberless battlefields, where every State was forged by ages of war, expansion has meant first and foremost conquest by the sword. To America it has meant profit, influence, even power, to be acquired by trade and technology, with war only as a last resort and then fought if possible with machines in place of flesh and blood. Even the gadgetry of war America, today loaded down with it like the medieval knight in his cumbrous armour, was remarkably slow to accumulate. Navy as well as army grew sluggishly until well on in this century. A steel magnate like Carnegie was all against warships, when his compeers across the Atlantic were clamouring for them to fill order-books. To them this 'staunch pacifist'[2] must have sounded like Lucifer denouncing sulphur.

Many European countries came by colonies long before modern political consciousness dawned, and Demos took them over as he took much else from the past. In Britain most of all he grew up familiar with the romantic trappings of empire, the governors in plumed hats or princes in jewelled turbans wending their way to Buckingham Palace, regimental banners inscribed with names of battles far away, echoes of bugles from the Khyber Pass. Misgivings about whether this was doing any good, on either side, were slow to stir, and down to the end seldom if ever seriously troubled the working classes of western Europe. By contrast the U.S. came into existence through rebellion against an empire, and started with a disposition— which has never been consciously cast off—to regard all empires as wicked, like the depraved monarchies that begot them.

At the outset the instinct of the State in Europe, as in Asia, was to expand within its own continent, to stretch its frontiers to include adjacent areas. Such growth has more chance of permanence than seizure of colonies far away. It is thanks to geography as well as to socialism that of all Europe's empires (except Portugal's) only the Russian has, much transformed, survived. Russia had next door to it the vast vacancies of Siberia, readily occupied though not readily developed. America combined this asset of immense contiguous territory with the British asset of advanced political institutions for colonists to carry with them. Like the settlement of the white British Dominions its westward march was at the same time a 'people's imperialism'[3] of free settlers and an operation of modern capitalism. If the U.S. was born in revolt against British control, this very revolt was partly inspired by a nascent expansionism of its own. Franklin and Washington were, besides high-souled patriots, participants in companies formed to grab new lands to the west, beyond the line drawn by London, from their native owners.[4] One is reminded of how two centuries earlier the Dutch, heroically fighting for their

[2] O. J. Clinard, *Japan's Influence on American Naval Power 1897–1917* (University of California, 1947), p. 145.

[3] A phrase used by W. Kolarz, *Russia and her Colonies* (London, 1952), p. 3.

[4] J. Hardy, *The First American Revolution* (London, 1937), p. 37.

independence from Spain, simultaneously embarked on their long career of rapine in Indonesia.

On a map, Massachusetts is a tiny dot, and the whole of New England northward from Virginia, the nucleus of the entire trans-continental expansion, is a mere strip some 750 miles long, scarcely bigger than Old England. The opening of the prairies by pioneers and homesteaders was followed up and taken toll of by the big-scale capitalism growing concurrently in New England, by means of loans, investments, railway concessions. Plundering of the public domain and its resources went on in a style that must be supposed to have given some hints to European financiers on the prowl for concessions in Turkey or China. All this represented for American capitalism its stage of primitive accumulation. Westerners often grumbled about the behaviour of Eastern bankers, and might go through moods of something very close to anti-imperialism. Bryan's words about mankind being crucified upon a cross of gold would serve very well today to describe U.S. capitalism in Asia or Latin America. But within the U.S. the framework of a democratic constitution and State rights kept such tensions from going too far, and brought about a commonwealth instead of an empire, with a capitalism of a new, buoyant kind such as Europe with its social and mental rigidities could never have hit upon for itself; a signal example of how economic systems are modified as they evolve by their social and economic environments. Without America, Marx's forecast of the future of capitalism would have been much more nearly accurate.

Most of the European States that colonized outside Europe were, like Japan, small countries with resources too limited to support their ambitions. America by contrast was rather a Common Market than a single nation, big and varied enough to go on enriching itself without much need to suck nourishment out of colonies. If a certain commodity was lacking, its absence would be felt by one industry or group of interests rather than by the entire economy. In any case the old simple urge of a Portugal or a Holland to get hold of the sources of commodities like silver, spices, sugar, and monopolize the profit of retailing them to the rest of Europe—an urge with which national feeling was quick to identify itself—was out of date by now. True, the old situation might recur with the discovery of new materials, notably oil, which British capitalism after the first World War had a brief rosy dream of cornering. In general, by the time the U.S. came of age the business of tapping colonial products and bringing them into a world market had been done: many of them could be found inside the U.S., the rest it could easily buy.

Curiously free as it was from the sabre-rattling jingoism of Europe, the U.S. in the course of its gigantic growth was bound to come by a national conceit of its own. For any country the sensation of being in the van of progress, of having something to teach all the rest, is likely to prove a strong intoxicant. The Melville of *White Jacket*, even cooped up in the beastliness of an American man-o'-war, was heartened by a glowing conviction of belonging to a new civilization, whose advent was a stride forward in human history. Bret Harte saw the 'bland, indolent autumn of Spanish rule' in California followed by 'the wintry storms of Mexican independence' and then by 'the reviving spring of American conquest'.[5] Walt Whitman felt the West wind prevailing over the East, American might overflowing across the Pacific, when he wrote, on the arrival of the first envoy from Japan,

> 'I chant the new empire . . .
> 'I chant America the new mistress. . . .'[6]

These may seem literary daydreams. But empires must first have a mould of ideas or conditioned reflexes to flow into, and youthful nations dream of a great place in the world as young men dream of fame and fortune. In our day it is the unquestioning assumption of a diplomatic historian like Kennan, one of the most enlightened of his kind, that his country may often have been foolish, but is incapable of wickedness, because Democracy, virtuous itself, only wants all mankind to be virtuous. He complains of a 'mystical, Messianic' streak in Soviet Russia, and in the same breath speaks of the unmistakable summons of 'history' to America.[7]

The planting of the new civilization across the prairies

[5] 'The Right Eye of the Commander', in *The Luck of Roaring Camp* (1868).

[6] 'A Broadway Pageant' (c. 1860). I owe this reference to my colleague Dr. R. Jeffreys-Jones.

[7] G. F. Kennan, *American Diplomacy 1900–1950* (N.Y., 1951), pp. 120–21 (Mentor Books edn.).

included the pushing out (or *flushing* out, as operators in Vietnam would call it nowadays) of their scanty Red Indian population. This could be set down as part of the necessary cost of progress, and to Americans did not feel at all like the brutal aggression that Europeans overseas were always committing. Like Australians cleansing the territory God had given them of its blackfellows, they kept a good conscience, but were none the less imbibing a belief that this was how all creatures recalcitrant to the American way of life must if necessary be dealt with. Protests were occasionally heard, as they were in European countries, about such treatment of natives; but one fact that stands out is America's inability to produce a decent type of public servant for handling native questions. It was misconduct by Indian Agents that provoked the Apache trouble in 1882. 'As one reads of the outrages perpetrated by these savages', says an American army historian, 'one can hardly believe them to be the work of white men.'[8] He was poorly informed about white men and their history, to be sure; but there is a striking hint in this record (or in that of the occupation of the South after the Civil War) of what the administration of an American colonial empire would have been like.

Red Indians could be killed, but not turned into helots. A worse incitement to moods favourable to imperialism came from the South. New England's linkage with the slave-owning South was as if Old England and South Africa had been joined together geographically as well as politically. In economic terms the South, like the West, was in some degree a colony of the North-east, which drew profit from loans to the plantations.[9] But the Southern States before the Civil War had (like the South Africa of Cecil Rhodes) a private imperialism of their own. With their soil-exhausting agriculture they needed more land, and looked greedily towards the Caribbean. Their ambitions descended directly from the eighteenth-century wars of European merchant-capital over West Indian islands and slave-plantations; a 'Southern' empire would have been regressive and barbarous even by comparison with the not too

---

[8] Col. W. A. Ganoe, *The History of the United States Army* (revised edn., N.Y., 1943), p. 358.

[9] J. E. Cairns, *The Slave Power* (London, 1863), p. 76.

elevated standards that European colonialism was now attaining.

But Southern society had closer affinities than the North with that of Europe, and would have found it easier to provide administrative cadres, if at a very low level; also to provide an army of conquest and occupation, out of the mass of poor whites who were to provide the Confederate soldiery, men with resemblances to the dispossessed Irish and Highland peasantry that provided Britain with a great part of its colonial army. There were dreams of a Latin-American empire, including all Mexico.[10] Walker's 'government' in Nicaragua in the 1850s was an unofficial experiment; it was recognized by Washington, where Southern politicians and wirepullers were always active. Cuba was the grand objective. Devious methods and contradictory aims have been characteristic all along of America, that large, variegated, changeful country and elastic government; they showed themselves freakishly in the doings of Soulé as U.S. envoy at Madrid in 1854, and in the 'Ostend Conference' of U.S. representatives in western Europe in October of the same year, in furtherance of 'the "Young America" programme of Cuban annexation through revolutionary machinations in Europe.'[11]

Washington rejected this scheme, and the defeat of the South in the Civil War scotched its ambitions, though not without some germs surviving to infect the national life. Southern police brutalism against Negroes finds a counterpart in the violence that has marked many American interventions in other countries, very much as massacres of workers in Paris in 1848 or 1871 went with similar treatment of rebels in French colonies. Ideas such as were current by the end of the nineteenth century of an 'Anglo-Saxon' or a British-German-American bloc, and pointed forward to later Herrenvolk theories, could find nourishment in Southern racialism. One Southerner talked of 'the noble Gothic race' destined to rule America and the whole earth.[12] When the Filipinos, America's first victims in Asia, were being conquered in 1899 they complained that

[10] J. E. Cairns, *The Slave Power* (1863), p. 204.
[11] A. A. Ettinger, *The Mission to Spain of Pierre Soulé (1853–1855)* (London, 1932), p. 335; and see Ch. X generally.
[12] Quoted by J. M. McPherson, *The Struggle for Equality* (Princeton, 1964), p. 423.

even the highly educated among them were called, by their not very well educated assailants, 'niggers'.[13] Kipling's call to America to take up its share of the white man's burden was falling on sympathetic ears.

It was also unhealthy for the U.S. that (apart from Canada) it had no neighbours on anything like its own level. European nations often fought, but they were always aware of one another as sharers of common standards. In the New World the Latin countries, which had started their independent lives not long after the U.S., lagged very far behind it, and the contrast between their prevailing backwardness and its own dizzy advance was bound to stimulate a Yankee vanity already too cockahoop. German aggressiveness in the modern world has rested on similar foundations laid long ago, before the first industrial capitalist was born, in the predominance of German feudalists over Slav peoples and primitive tribes south and east, and of German traders over Scandinavia and the Baltic.

To a U.S. infected with racialism the Amerindian and African infusions in nearly all the Latin-American States—some of them like Ecuador with scarcely any 'pure' white blood—were likely to deepen other unfavourable impressions. But even without this, a country worshipping efficiency was sure to feel impatient at their sloth and shiftlessness. English businessmen, who were first in the field, felt the same impatience; and in lands where even a tourist is almost compelled to grease official palms or brandish a stick, a foreign corporation will soon slide into the same practices. Righteous indignation in the U.S. today about communism in Latin America has been superimposed on an older feeling of much the same kind about muddle or anarchy there.

Little as the Monroe Doctrine might often seem to mean in practice, it did at least mean that from early days the U.S. saw its interests and rights not as confined to its own territories, themselves ill-defined, but as spreading out in some nebulous fashion over an entire continent. European meddlings helped to foster the hazy feeling of a 'special relationship' between the U.S. and its 'sister-republics'; and it has been a constant part of the pattern of U.S. expansionism to be drawn into regions where older empires have misgoverned or interfered. In 1815

[13] R. B. Sheridan, *The Filipino Martyrs* (London, 1900), p. 153.

a patriot argued that the U.S. ought to assist the cause of
emancipation from Spain, and make an alliance with Mexico,
thus striking a blow at Britain which battened on the wealth
of Spain and Spanish America and meant to use it for an
onslaught on its own lost colonies.[14] Three decades later the
U.S. was fighting Mexico instead of allying with it. But this
early piece of jingoism was, very typically, seen by most
Americans as liberation of worthy settlers in Texas oppressed
by a barbarous government, very much as Britons tried to see
their South Africa war half a century later as a deliverance of
Uitlanders or settlers from oppression by the Boers. When
Napoleon III and his Hapsburg puppet threatened Mexican
independence not much later the American army, formidable
at the close of the Civil War, provided a strong deterrent.

Had Europe secured Mexico it might have gone on to spread
its tentacles into other parts of southern America. That U.S.
protection was sometimes genuinely needed there made it
insidiously easy for thoughts of U.S. domination to sprout.
After Chile's victory over Bolivia and Peru in the War of the
Pacific in 1879, which many saw as really a victory for Britain,
the U.S. representative at Lima suggested a protectorate over
Peru. He thought the downtrodden masses would be happy to
be governed from Washington, and within ten years Peru
could be thoroughly Americanized and then become a member-
state of the Union and ensure for it a commanding position in
all South America.[15] About this time Blaine as State Secretary
was emphasizing earlier loose claims to a 'paramount interest'
in the New World, which sound as if they may have owed
something to the precedent of British claims to paramountcy
in India and its borderlands; the Pan-American ideals that he
sponsored lent it a more inoffensive colouring. In 1879 President
Hayes confided to his diary that it must be part of the nation's
destiny, though not one to be unduly hastened, to annex all
the neighbouring lands, including Canada.[16] In 1880 he talked
of control over a future Canal in 'language which implies the
reduction of the Central American republics to a position of

[14] W. D. Robertson, *A Cursory View of South America* (Georgetown, 1815).
[15] Christiancy to Blaine, 4 May 1881, Conf.
[16] Cited in P. Belmont, *An American Democrat* (2nd edn., N.Y., 1941),
p. 378.

virtual vassalage to the United States.'[17] In Europe no Great
Power talked openly in this style about its smaller neighbours,
even in the Balkans. One reason for this difference was that the
U.S. had no diplomatic service worth the name, again partly
because it had no aristocracy. It could be friendly or un-
friendly, but found it hard to be civil.

To these vaulting ambitions, all the same, public feeling
remained apathetic, as it had been during the 'shoddy episode'
of Grant's scheme to grab the Dominican Republic in 1869–
70;[18] and this at a time when Europe was moving towards its
noisiest frenzy of imperial expansion. Private American enterprise, it is true, was pioneering the routes that Dollar Diplomacy
would follow along. Until national resistance began to be
provoked, individual adventurers could get their way as a rule
by bribing local bosses as they were accustomed to do at home.
Henry Meiggs building railways and a financial empire in
Peru and Chile during the 1860s and 1870s was a buccaneer of
this sort, but American also in having a genuine passion for
construction.[19] C. R. Flint, international dealer in guns and
warships, was another.[20] Railway speculations and plunderings
in the U.S. spilled over into Mexico;[21] and struggles for control
of railways at home fought out among men like Gould and Fisk
with the aid of armed gangs were a realistic rehearsal for
Caribbean operations by the Marines.

American mercenaries in China took part in the suppression
of the great Taiping Rebellion, and were suspected of wanting
to carve out a principality for themselves. About 1853 a notion
was afloat that America had designs on Burma, and this served
as a further pretext for the British war on Burma in that year
and the annexation of Pegu. Karl Marx, who welcomed signs
of American interest in the Old World because America was
'the youngest and most vigorous representative of the West',
derided the notion.[22] If there really was any inclination about

[17] J. L. Latané, The Diplomatic Relations of the United States and South
America (Baltimore, 1900), p. 177.
[18] D. Perkins, The Monroe Doctrine 1867–1907 (Baltimore, 1937), pp. 15–19.
[19] See W. Stewart, Henry Meiggs—Yankee Pizarro (Duke Univ., 1946).
[20] See C. R. Flint, Memories of an Active Life (N.Y., 1923).
[21] L. Corey, The House of Morgan (N.Y., 1930), p. 223.
[22] The Eastern Question, ed. Eleanor Marx and E. Aveling (London, 1897),
pp. 80–81 (12 Aug. 1853); Marx and Engels On Colonialism (Moscow
anthology, 1960), p. 70 (30 July 1853).

this time to join in the European game in Further Asia, its one distinct emergence was Commodore Perry's arrival in Japan in 1853 to demand a trading treaty. Americans and Victorian Britons shared the same mystic faith in the life-giving virtues of commerce. But it was typical of the ambiguous processes of American official thought that while Perry was sent with a squadron, and was himself convinced that it would be an error to be 'over-conciliatory',[23] he was forbidden to use it; and Townsend Harris, the first American envoy, got his treaty by telling the Japanese (truthfully enough) that if they did not give way the British would bombard them. On his way out he had been instructed to impress on the Siamese the contrast between British greed and American disinterestedness; his gifts to the royal family included electrical gadgets and other novelties, symbolic of the new era that America was ushering in.[24]

From the Far East as from the Caribbean energy was diverted by the Civil War and then the great industrial leap forward. For the most part America was content to straggle behind European Powers, critical of their high-handed methods but happy to share in resulting gains to trade. How this ambivalent attitude was developing can be gauged from decade to decade by the way Americans reacted to the grand empire of the age, the British. Decadent and vicious as Europeans were, Asia's ruling classes were undeniably far worse; and to Americans—insular and shut up in their own habits and opinions even by comparison with Britons—all Asiatics looked mysterious and unprepossessing. When the zoologist Hornaday visited Singapore and Malaya in the 1870s the snobbery of British colonial society struck him as contemptible, its harddrinking habits as appalling. Yet some good was coming out of it. 'It takes the British Government to rule such places and make them habitable for producers, and worth something to the world.'[25] Americans being too civilized to do this rough work themselves, ought in other words to welcome its being done by others. When ex-President Grant toured Asia and hobnobbed with its monarchs, whose descendants were to be the campfollowers of his successors, he also was in two minds about

[23] A. L. Sadler, *A Short History of Japan* (Sydney, 1963) p. 239.
[24] C. Crow, *Harris of Japan* (London, 1939), pp. 60–61, 95, 247–8.
[25] W. T. Hornaday, *Two Years in the Jungle* (London, 1885), pp. 295–6, 330.

imperialism. He told the Mikado that he considered British rule in India a good thing on the whole, but was indignant at the way Europeans were behaving in many other parts of Asia.[26]

Europeans frequently felt the same irritation at American sermonizing and moralizing as Charles Surface at his brother Joseph's fine sentiments. The average American out in the East was less pernickety, being there frankly, like other mortals, to make money. In early days in China he was often an opium-dealer. At Canton, Hickey tells us, Americans were known to the Chinese by 'the expressive title of second chop Englishmen.'[27] 'The presence of foreigners is a protection and a blessing to the people', the American community in Shanghai declared in 1869. '... The withdrawal of pressure would be dangerous to native and foreign interests.' The English community added that the policy being adopted by both their governments of treating China as an equal was a huge blunder. The Hon. J. Ross Browne, retiring U.S. minister, perfectly agreed.[28] Practical attitudes towards China went on converging, until in 1900 American troops were fighting side by side with Europeans and Japanese, under a German commander, to put down the Boxer rebellion.

In the uncharted Pacific the advance-guard of American civilization was more unsavoury than in either Latin America or Asia. It was made up of men like the whaling-crews who, as R. L. Stevenson learned when he lived in the Pacific, stopped at the Marquesan Islands to carry off by force a stock of their beautiful women.[29] Perry had been sent to Japan primarily to secure a better footing for American ships and crews, whose chief concern there was to obtain supplies of women and liquor, by fair means or foul.

At the end of the century Captain Mahan could speak of an 'extraordinary change of sentiment on the subject of expansion', a 'revolution' in American opinion.[30] This burst of im-

[26] J. R. Young, *Around the World with General Grant* (N.Y., 1880), Vol. 2, pp. 543-6.

[27] *Memoirs of William Hickey*, ed. A. Spencer (9th edn., London, n.d.), Vol. I, p. 202.

[28] Addresses to the retiring U.S. envoy, and his reply, June 1869.

[29] R. L. Stevenson, *In the South Seas* (1896), p. 50.

[30] Capt. A. T. Mahan, *Lessons of the War with Spain* (2nd edn., London, 1899), p. ix.

perial enthusiasm, not quite so sudden or unheralded as he
thought it, was evidently in many ways an echo of Europe's.
It was the climax of a phase in America's evolution—the
epoch, among other phenomena, of Henry James—that
brought it closer in various ways to Europe and European ideas
than ever before or since. In economic history it was the time
when the U.S. established itself as the world's biggest industrial
State. By 1890 it was overtaking Britain in iron and steel
production; in the 1890s it was going on to pile up a very large
export surplus. With this came a novel sensation of dependence
on foreign markets; a fever of high tariffs on both sides of the
Atlantic was erupting in trade wars, and the U.S. had a fit of
alarm about a shortage of customers. It was an irrational fear,
in view of the bounding population that supplied a growing
internal market. But capitalists are often as irrational as other
folk, and many Americans had too little purchasing power as
yet to be of much value to them as customers: Negroes, in
particular, and the mass of recent immigrants.

Immigration was bringing fresh problems with it. The new-
comers pouring across the Atlantic were Europeanizing their
new home at least as fast as it was Americanizing them. Their
numbers were swelling, and most of them were now coming
from less developed parts of Europe: more than three millions
from eastern Europe, the same total from Italy and Iberia, and
so on. An influx of old-fashioned peasants on this scale,
together with the growth and concentration of capital that
their labour made possible, could not but mean a heavy
dilution, over a fairly long period, of America's hopeful new
way of life. There was of course no ingrained inferiority in
them, and they had talents and qualities of their own to enrich
their adopted land. But they were for the time being ignorant
of many things, hampered by difficulties of language, often
superstitious and priest-ridden, sometimes demoralized by
suffering. They provided therefore a mass of labour easily
exploited by employers, and of voters easily duped by politicians.
It was an irresistible temptation to the voracious elements of
the older American society, and brought these forward rapidly
at the expense of the more idealistic. Already in 1847 when
Sarmiento the exiled democrat from Argentina visited the
promised land he was painfully struck by symptoms of degen-

eracy.[31] The great experiment in democracy was beginning to
sink (never quite completely or finally) into Tammany Hall
demagogy, the labyrinth of corruption and manipulation that
Ostrogorski described in 1902.[32] By 1871 even Whitman's faith
was being staggered by the 'hollowness of heart' all round him,
despite the 'hectic glow and these melo-dramatic screamings'
(essential ingredients of imperialism, he might have added)—
by the 'depravity of the business classes', by public life 'saturated
in corruption, bribery, falsehood', by the 'almost maniacal
appetite for wealth.'[33]

These business classes for their part were soon as deeply
alarmed, in a different way. With the strikes of 1885 the reality
of class struggle, the possibility of social explosion, broke on
them suddenly and frighteningly—to the delight of Engels,
who visited America and kept a watchful eye on it.[34] In the
following decade troops were called out on 328 occasions to
deal with disturbances in forty-nine States or Territories. 1893
was a particularly bad year. Fear of socialism, or of social
disorder, could be expected to inspire, as in Europe, thoughts
of adventure abroad to distract popular attention, and also to
weld a heterogeneous population into an American nation.
Hearst and his yellow press combined demagogic agitation
with jingoism, and did much in 1898 to whip up feeling against
Spain. Behind this was the calculation which the English
observer E. Dicey read correctly when the Spanish war came:
America was going in for expansionism for the same reason as
Britain, recognition that 'democratic institutions are no longer
a panacea for the cure of social discontents'.[35] Meanwhile the
long struggle of respectable America to lick masses of raw
immigrants into shape—with the Gatling-gun as one instrument—was itself a sort of domestic experiment in colonial
administration.

One trait that immigrants were likely to pick up quickly and

[31] See D. F. Sarmiento, *Viajes por Europa, Africa, i América* (1849), pp. 411,
484, 504–5 (Paris edn., 1909).
[32] M. Ostrogorski, *Democracy and the Organization of Political Parties* (London,
1902), Vol. 2.
[33] *Democratic Vistas, and Other Papers* (London edn., 1888), pp. 11–12, 29 n.
[34] Marx and Engels, *Letters to Americans 1848–1895*, ed. A. Trachtenberg
(1953), p. 286.
[35] See R. H. Heindel, *The American Impact on Great Britain 1898–1914*
(University of Pennsylvania, 1940), p. 69.

to deepen was the racialism already in the air of America. To poor whites from Europe, as to poor whites in Alabama, it was a consolation to find someone to look down on, and against whom they could feel at one with the respectable folk who looked down on *them*. A common prejudice against the black man helped the melting-pot of white nations to do its work; American nationalism itself was thus tinged with racial arrogance. Asians were another element too alien to be absorbed.[36] They were coming to undercut the white man and steal his job; and it it not hard to trace an emotional connection between the massacre of Chinese at Wyoming in 1885, and the more wholesale massacre of Vietnamese eighty years later for the crime of wanting to steal Asia from free enterprise.

From the time when America's westward-facing frontier reached the Pacific a mood could be felt like Alexander's, pining for fresh worlds. An expanding territory had come to be part of American life, an end in itself, difficult to renounce. Born with more of an instinct of progress than Europe possessed, the country wavered between progress in terms of quality or of mere size, as it still wavers today between the choice of being a 'Great Society' or the Greatest Power. There may have been a lurking wish to put off the day when America, having reached its natural frontiers, would have to stop walking and sit down to look at itself, to take stock of what had become of its soul.

As the largest of oceans the Pacific had a fascination of its own for the richest of nations. On its further shores were some of the few materials America lacked, among them tungsten and manganese, in demand because of the growth of steel production.[37] On those shores lay also, dragons guarding a golden fleece, two peoples who were taking shape in American imagination as two grand forces of evil. Tsarist Russia was an unrepentant despotism, as loudly condemned as Soviet Russia later. A Russian ascendancy would inaugurate a new Dark Age, ten times worse than the old one, wrote an alarmist.[38] Japan

[36] See I. Black, 'American Labour and Chinese Immigration', in *Past and Present*, No. 25 (1963).

[37] Clinard, *op. cit.*, p. 6.

[38] W. D. Foulke, *Slav or Saxon* (2nd edn., N.Y., 1899), p. 139. There is a note of Social Darwinism in the book; Russia is 'semi-barbarous', but survival of the *fittest* may not be that of the *highest* (pp. 2–3).

was 'yellow', and Japanese settlement in California was a chronic cause of irritation. Fears of Japan striding across the Pacific by way of Hawaii were easily conjured up, and ensured official backing for the settlers and traders in Hawaii who were taking over power step by step from the native government, until in 1893 Queen Liliuokalani was deposed, and in 1898 the islands annexed.

When the Senate Foreign Committee, approving the annexation, talked of Japan affronting the 'national honour', it was falling into one of the clichés that Europe had inherited from its old monarchies and their dynastic squabbles. In the mind of this fledgeling nation a crowd of antiquated ideas jostled, as Engels again noticed.[39] It was a blend of atavism or nostalgia with a groping effort to express new sensations in old images, in a land whose religion, philosophy, literature, had nearly all grown in alien soil under far-off skies. American trade unionists called themselves 'Knights of Labour', mothers christened their urchins 'Marquis' or 'Duke'.

In the Old World that America was still tied to, the fresh outburst of imperialism beginning about 1880 may have received further stimulus from fear of America's industrial supremacy, every year more unchallengeable. In turn it incited Americans to follow suit—as earlier when Perry crossed the Pacific—by arousing an uneasy sense of being left out of something good, a kind of new gold rush, or of something grand, that a high-principled nation ought not to stand aside from. All imperialism in history has been largely imitative; it has seldom or never grown spontaneously out of the needs or impulsions of a single State. Greece caught the contagion from Persia, Rome from Carthage, Islam from Byzantium, Holland and England from Spain and Portugal. European States themselves were now to a great extent rushing after one another in search of colonies because they saw their neighbours doing so. Witte observed that the Russian generals who were so anxious to lay hands on Manchuria were quite unable to explain what they wanted to do with it. He was struck also, when in America, by the dense ignorance of the world displayed even by responsible men.[40]

[39] Marx and Engels, *Letters to Americans*, p. 269.
[40] *The Memoirs of Count Witte* (English edn., London, 1921), pp. 107, 162.

A special factor was that among the old colonial Powers one, and that one Britain, was eager to draw America into the stampede.[41] It would be a splendid vindication of British colonialism to be emulated by the great Democracy: this would go far to disarm the protests inside Britain that had never ceased to be heard. British investors in America could look for a share in any profits that might accrue. Most important, Britain's strength was over-extended, it was isolated, its rivals were clamorous and pressing. It was time to bring in the New World again to redress the balance of the Old, like Canning in 1823. America's advent on the scene was 'the most hopeful and the most surprising feature of the Far East problem', wrote a traveller in 1899.[42] It was heartening in the Boer War which began that year that America had just fought a war of empire under cover of very similar watchwords. During these contests the two countries were each other's only sympathizers—and Germany was the most hostile critic of both.

In American eyes British colonialism usually appeared less disreputable than others, and as a French cynic pointed out Liberal scholars like Froude and Seeley had been making it look so progressive that 'Imperialism became the latest philosophy of history and almost the last dogma of religion.'[43] Mahan, the apostle of American sea-power, was also a very uncritical admirer of the British empire. It had taken to heart, he believed, the lessons of the American Revolution and the Indian Mutiny, and given its allegiance thenceforward to the purest ideals of enlightenment.[44] Tempered by justice and conscience 'and the loving voice of charity', the British sword had done wonders for India.[45] Englishmen frequently felt themselves to be doing the Roman empire's work over again, with improvements; to Americans like Mahan the British empire offered similar inspiration. Another thought sedulously

[41] See Heindel, *op. cit.*, Ch. IV, on the Anglo-American rapprochement of 1898, and its greater warmth on the British side. On European attitudes to the war of 1898 cf. L. Y. Slëzkin, *Ispano-Amerikanskaya voina 1898 goda* (1956), Ch. 3.

[42] A. Reid, *From Peking to Petersburg* (London, 1899), Ch. 21.

[43] V. Bérard, *British Imperialism and Commercial Supremacy* (English edn., 1906), p. 44.

[44] Mahan, *op. cit.*, pp. 243, 250, etc.

[45] *Ibid.*, p. 231.

encouraged by Britons was that if the crown of India ever fell from Britannia's head it would be picked up by the Tsar.[46]

When Kipling was crossing the Pacific in 1888 his American companions were full of laments over the sad state of their country, its rotten politics and so on, and one of them wound up with the remark that what they needed was a war. 'A war outside our borders would make us all pull together.'[47] Britons all pulled together, and Bismarck had shown how blood and iron could unite Germans. America had only fought a civil war, whose morbid echoes still lingered, and uneasiness about the nation's solidarity was being worsened by the undigested mass of immigrants and the spectacle of foreign Powers with restless ambitions and new designs of warships. There was too an undercurrent of an impulse to show the world that America knew how to fight. Europe had been impressed more by the bungling of the Civil War, on the winning side especially, than by its heroism. In this land without an army many an ordinary citizen owned a gun as a sort of badge of free citizenship, much as Europeans had worn swords as a badge of gentility. Again an antique convention was perpetuating itself in a novel social and material context. Warlike prowess was Europe's loudest boast, soon to be put, in 1914, to its supreme test. Japan won genuine recognition at last by defeating China in 1895. Only through the same ordeal could America shake off the reproach of being a mere nation of shopkeepers, preferring filthy lucre to 'honour'.

The war of 1898 with Spain, conducted with the dash of a Wild West film, satisfied these cravings; it yielded, like any of the small colonial campaigns that Queen Victoria and her subjects delighted in, a crop of what could pass for 'glory'. Among its immediate motives economic aims played only a secondary or indirect part. Norman Angell, arguing his life-long thesis that capitalism has nothing to gain by war, would be able to portray not unconvincingly a reluctant U.S. government pushed into war by popular frenzy, against the inclinations of big business.[48] Unlike the Transvaal with its gold, Cuba con-

[46] See e.g. Foulke, *op. cit.*, pp. 41, 53.

[47] R. Kipling, *From Sea to Sea* (London, 1900), Vol. 1, p. 469, and Ch. XXII in general.

[48] Sir N. Angell, *From Chaos to Control* (London, 1933), pp. 121-2.

tained little but sugar, and over this American interests were divided: the 'Sugar Trust' or big refiners were ready to welcome an extra source of supply, the growers of cane-sugar or beet at home wanted no extra competition from outside. Planters and settlers in Cuba who wanted to get things into their own hands made the most, as in Hawaii, of its alleged importance to strategic security. This chimed in with a spirit of national self-assertiveness, made up of diverse elements. Jingoism was most rampant in the South, and in the West where Indian skirmishes and Buffalo Bill had engendered something of the same mentality as Negro-baiting and Jim Crow. From these two regions also came the bulk of the volunteers, many of whom must have been poor whites with visions of high pay or plunder.

Paradoxically the rallying-cry that brought Americans of very different sorts together was sympathy for the unfortunate Cubans, in revolt as they had often been before against a senile and vicious Spanish rule. That the struggle would be against one of the reprobate European monarchies, a contest between New World and Old, lent it a further appeal, and might be expected to impress immigrants with memories of heartless treatment in their native lands. This unconventional republic was breaking into one of the old colonial empires, towards which, as towards that of Portugal, the greedy Powers of Europe had exercised a curious self-restraint, as if from respect for the sacred rights of property. In the nineteenth century indeed, in strong contrast with the seventeenth or eighteenth, Europeans never directly fought one another over colonies, even if they frequently quarrelled.

At opposite poles in so many ways, America and Russia yet had moral as well as physical resemblances. For both of them, with their huge resources, any new enlargement was in a special sense irrational, and in need of the camouflage of irrational sentiment. Among Russians it was always the summons to march into the Balkans and liberate fellow-Slavs and Christians from Turkey's barbarous grasp that stirred popular enthusiasm; and while material interests were not lacking, increasingly the chief end in view was to refurbish the Tsar by giving his discontented subjects something to admire him for. Likewise in 1899 it was 'borne in upon the moral consciousness of a mighty nation'—as Mahan put it—that Cuba was lying at its door like

Lazarus at the door of Dives.[49] It is noticeable that Mahan repeatedly drew an analogy between the compulsion of conscience that good Americans used to feel to aid runaway slaves, and the compulsion they ought now to feel to aid downtrodden peoples.[50] Because America had lately emancipated its slaves, Russia its serfs, each felt morally fitter to emancipate other nations. Perhaps each felt all the more ardour because they had to smother an uneasy recognition that their work of liberation at home had been done very imperfectly, that neither moujik nor Negro was much better off than he had been before.

Puerto Rico was annexed: it was small enough to be viewed as, like Hawaii, a strategic outpost rather than a colony. Since competition from its sugar was not wanted it could not be given equal status within the Union, and an exercise in casuistry by the Supreme Court was required to square democratic principles with 'the doctrine of inferior races'.[51] But thanks to its Negro minority the U.S. was already familiar in practice if not in theory with the distinction between first- and second-class citizenship, which in European empires was as obvious and natural as, until recently, restriction of voting rights to men of property had been. In America in other words race-consciousness was in some ways the equivalent of class-consciousness in Europe.

As to Cuba, whatever patriots there might feel, the U.S. felt entitled to stand astonished, like Clive, at its own moderation. By the Platt Amendment of 1901 it insisted on no more than naval bases and (like Austria in its treaty of 1815 with the Bourbons after helping to restore them in Naples) on a right of intervention whenever dissatisfied with the way the country was managing its affairs; and Cuba's affairs included those of American planters, bankers, and merchants. This amounted to a stranglehold on Cuban independence; but the dismal record of most independent Latin American countries could make it seem good for Cuba as well as for the U.S., and European practice outside Europe supplied ready models: the Capitulations imposed on Turkey or Morocco, extraterritorial rights in

---

[49] Mahan, *op. cit.*, p. 226.   [50] *Ibid.*, p. 227, etc.
[51] J. H. Latané, *America as a World Power 1897–1907* (N.Y., 1907), pp. 151–2.

China, the Unequal Treaties with Japan. 'Neo-colonialism' of
this kind might just as well in fact be called 'proto-colonialism':
it had grown up side by side with full occupation of colonies
from the beginning. The novelty was that the U.S. was doing
spontaneously what Europeans had done where a country's
size or remoteness, or their own mutual jealousies, prevented
them from taking it over completely.

Besides Puerto Rico the Philippines were annexed, also at
some expense of moral and verbal jugglery. Thoughts of keeping
these islands only came uppermost after war broke out, and
were again very mixed. So were the imperial motives trumpeted
in jingo newspapers in Europe: the difference was merely that
American statesmen, to the amusement of educated Europe,
solemnly repeated the rhapsodies that elsewhere were left to
journalists. It was a fresh manifestation of America's more
democratic spirit. President McKinley's reasons for taking the
Philippines sounded as if some malicious caricaturist had made
them up. 'The march of events rules and overrules human
action', imposing fresh duties on 'a great nation on whose
growth and career from the beginning the Ruler of Nations
has plainly written the high command and pledge of civilization. Incidental to our tenure in the Philippines is the
commercial opportunity to which American statesmanship
cannot be indifferent. . . .'[52]

Boswell was always seeking scriptural warrant for polygamy,
and his Bible was always falling open at the history of King
Solomon. But America could truthfully deny cupidity about
the Philippines themselves. Commercial opportunity meant
China; the islands were only a convenient *pied à terre* close by.
America's presence might be reckoned good for China as well.
In 1898 the other Powers were closing in on it, and a partition
was threatening. America with its superior competitive power,
like Britain with its established position in all Far Eastern
markets, felt no need of a private share of China, and only
wanted an Open Door.

Yet though America was not being led into temptation by
Filipino sugar, it found itself immediately committed in these
islands to a naked war of conquest; an abrupt transition
prefiguring on a small scale the course of American imperialism

[52] Instructions to the U.S. peace commissioners, Sept. 1898.

after 1945. Ostensibly it had come here to assist another revolt against Spain, but it was easy to argue that the Philippines were not a nation like Cuba. Rather they could be looked upon as a miniature India, illiterate in fifty languages, where American sway could promise the same beneficial results as British sway in India. America in short was coming as liberator and remaining as master, like Prospero releasing Ariel from the cleft tree-trunk and keeping him as a bond-servant. But it was embarking on empire in an Asia where, thanks to what its predecessors had done, colonial nationalism was already smouldering. Faced with mass resistance Americans sank at once to the same level as Europeans before them or Japanese after them. No ideology, anti-Communist or any other, is needed to brutalize soldiers fighting such a war. Spain's attempt to break the resistance of the Cubans by herding them into concentration-areas, which America had denounced, was now repeated against the Filipinos, as in later days against the Vietnamese; it made a good symbol of the chaining up of colonial peoples by their white conquerors. Memories of Red Indian wars stirred again; Filipino guerrillas seemed 'even more perfidious' than the redmen of Arizona,[53] and General MacArthur like many commanders on the Western frontier quickly grasped 'the profitlessness of treating the captured insurgents with consideration'. His methods yielded results, even if they 'did not please some American ethicists 6000 miles away'.[54]

It was, a British businessman on the spot wrote, a scene of chaos and massacre, 'one of the blackest records which has ever stained the pages of history'.[55] There is another reminder of the Vietnam war in the gloomy words of an American officer to another Englishman—'We know we have got into a dreadful mess, but how are we to get out of it?'[56] Then as now it was not every Englishman that welcomed America's plunge into imperialism; this one wrote of what was happening, as a friend and admirer, in sorrow more than in anger. America's own 'ethicists' agreed with him, and three thousand pages of an

[53] Ganoe, *op. cit.*, p. 406.
[54] *Ibid.*, p. 411.
[55] J. D. Ross, *Sixty Years in the Far East* (London, 1911), Vol. 2, Ch. 37.
[56] Sheridan, *op. cit.*, pp. 143–4; cf. p. 103: most of the Volunteers were 'men from the Western states, without character and without principle'.

E

enquiry into the army's behaviour piled up. It must have done something to turn America away from such adventures for a long time, like the revulsion of feeling in Britain after the Boer War with its 'methods of barbarism'.

In the 1900 election a remarkable number of parties took the field, some of them anti-imperialistic, and some more or less socialist. Home politics and foreign policy were both at the same time in a state of flux. Yet the outcome in both was anti-climax: the old two-party system reasserted itself, imperialism—in the sense of a popular cult of the establishment of direct American rule abroad—went off the boil. Once the war with Spain was over there was a precipitate retreat from glory: volunteers were eager to be home again, war-fever was forgotten like any other craze, the later craze of sending Americans to the moon for instance. Mahan saw with regret a public 'gorged and surfeited with war literature' swept back into indifference by 'an immense wave of national prosperity'.[57] More philosophically Dr Johnson might have said of nations, as of individuals, that they are never more harmlessly employed than when they are making money. This little war had been a tonic to national unity and self-respect, easily translated into a mood of business confidence. Negatively this was strengthened by a gradual discovery that polyglot immigrant masses were a handicap to socialism more than a menace to law and order. But a more positive development was under way. Under pressure of a vigorous labour movement American capitalists, reluctantly but less so on the whole than their European rivals, were learning the lesson that higher wages mean better customers and bigger profits. They learned it more willingly because they had no alternative customers in the shape of a big army and navy. Capitalism was taking on a qualitatively new character; God, the Great Salesman, was revealing America as his chosen land.

There were still ups and downs, as always: employment sagged in 1904, 1908, 1912. But the general trend was of rapid expansion, and conditions of life acceptable especially to new-comers from Europe helped to quench any desire for radical change. Correspondingly the ruling groups were less tempted than those of Europe to look for further diversions in the style

[57] Mahan, op. cit., p. 19.

of 1898. One leading attraction of empire to crowded Europe was in any case missing here. Britons found room in their Dominions to make new homes; Frenchmen could settle in Algeria; Germans and Italians were at least tutored to think of colonies as areas where surplus population could be settled under the national flag. Export of men and women, irrelevant as it might be to capitalist interests, was as important to imperialism, by strengthening its popular appeal, as export of capital. Still half empty and receiving millions of foreigners— whose loss European nationalism increasingly grudged— America could not think of it as a passport to prosperity.

It was from the Philippines, America's new base in the Far East, that troops were sent to China in 1900 to take part in the bloodthirsty suppression of the Boxers. But in 1900, as again in the intervention in Russia two decades later, for which it provided a rehearsal, there is some substance in the contention that America was going in with the others in order to restrain them. Unable to restrain them from further pressure on China, it was soon drawing back. It was turning away too from the cordial relationship with Britain that an American had seen as 'the protection of our common civilization',[58] and that the French cynic saw (like De Gaulle in our day) as threatening the world with a hegemony of 'Pan-britainism'.[59] Nothing is more striking than the divergent paths taken by the two 'Anglo-Saxon' countries from this point: the U.S. returning on the whole to industrial expansion, or contenting itself with unadventurous sallies into its own Caribbean backyard, Britain by comparison neglecting its industry and reposing on its imperial couch.

After 1900 the next event in the Far East was the Russo-Japanese war of 1904–05, the first serious war for many years and the first of a new and warlike century. It gave a vivid demonstration of the price in blood to be paid for power in this climactic epoch of mass armies and mass slaughter; a price America was sensibly reluctant to pay. When it was over the belligerents soon came together, drawing with them their allies, France and Britain. In face of this combination any active American policy beyond the Pacific was impossible, a fact which healthily reinforced the tendency to give priority to

[58] Foulke, *op. cit.*, Pref.   [59] Bérard, *op. cit.*, p. 42.

development at home. The Great War split the Old World, but along lines little desired by the U.S., which would have preferred a European grouping against tsarist Russia and Japan, as a quarter-century later it would have preferred one against Soviet Russia. Powerful American interests came it is true, for adventitious reasons, to favour entry into the war; all the same, the government drifted into it very hesitantly, and the country took only a trivial share in the fighting, at a time when the romantic glow of 1914 had long since faded in the morass of the western front. Still more disillusioning, the war ended with a Bolshevik revolution and Japan poised for further conquest. Economically and financially, it is again true, America came out on top. But the next twenty years were to show how little economic strength not backed by military strength could guarantee political influence in a militarized world.

'Few Americans have ever taken any interest in their insular possessions', one of them wrote in 1921.[60] Englishmen took equally little interest in their colonies, so far as any intelligent knowledge of them went, but were immensely conscious of possessing them, as a Victorian husband was of his wife and children. If there was in 1898 a touch of impatience to prove that whatever the European could do, even running colonies, the Yankee could do better, as soon as he had his Philippine toy he was tired of it. As a basis of power in the Far East the islands were soon coming to seem futile. Their sugar was not wanted; immigrants from them still less. An exodus of Negroes from the South into the big cities was already causing grave race riots in the early years of the century: the prospect of another coloured influx was another reason for not wanting colonies. Remarkably soon there was talk of giving the Philippines complete independence.

In Europe the prime function of government, inherited from a feudal past, was to discipline the rude masses; similarly in colonies the grand gift it professed to bring was Order. In British or French colonies, as compared with Portuguese or Russian, this came to be tinged with the newer ideal of Progress. America was in duty bound to put Progress first. But the

[60] S. Greenbie, *The Pacific Triangle* (London, 1921), p. 316. Cf. p. 319: 'We have recently been on the very verge of granting independence, but unfortunately, oil has been discovered by the Standard Oil Company. . . .'

medley of peoples and languages in the Philippines was a formidable obstacle, and there was a very wide gap, material and cultural, between Americans and the mass of any 'native' race. They stood at the opposite pole from the Spanish and Portuguese pioneers who set out from Europe with a material equipment little more elaborate than that of some of the peoples they subdued. And America, lacking a true civil service even at home, had no administrators to take the place of the Spanish friars in whose lethargically greedy hands the running of the islands had always largely been. On the other hand it found it natural—as Britain did by comparison with France, Spain, or Russia—to allow a good deal of local autonomy. Its businessmen were accustomed to control their own city governments and State legislatures through local bosses and lobby influence; to control a colony through its own politicians would be a logical extension of this.

Older and more static empires too were making use of puppet rulers, always men of feudal stamp, relics of a moribund past: Indian princes, Javanese rajas, Emirs of Bokhara. In the Philippines after three centuries of Spanish rule no such genuine feudal antiques survived. A partner more congenial to American taste was ready to hand in the form of an upper class long semi-Europeanized and now willing enough to adopt American ways, especially of making money. Its better element had come to the front in the revolt against Spain, but was easily split off from the rebel peasantry; there was no socialism yet in Asia to lend ballast to nationalism. At bottom the mass rising against Spain was an agrarian rising,[61] as all later anti-imperialist movements in S.E. Asia were to be (and as most Balkan risings against the Turks had been). To the extent that American policy steered investment away from land, into sugar mills as against sugar plantations,[62] it represented evolution along bourgeois lines instead of feudal stagnation.

But the relationship corrupted the colonial élite very much as big business had corrupted American politics; it turned it into something very much like the *comprador* bourgeoisie of China, out of which was to come the Kuomintang and America's most disastrous alliance in Asia. Even more than the British

[61] E. H. Jacoby, *Agrarian Unrest in Southeast Asia* (N.Y., 1949), p. 192.
[62] *Ibid.*, Ch. 6.

or Dutch, the Americans made contact only with the upper
stratum they worked through, and knew nothing of the masses
below. When the Philippines were finally granted independence
after the Second World War they were a country tied to U.S.
capitalism and run by the class of collaborators who had
battened on 'an economy in which the rich grew richer and the
poor poorer'.[63]

Virtually shut out for many years from the big world beyond
the Pacific, the U.S. was the more disposed to make itself felt
in Latin America. It could still believe that it was acting
defensively, to ensure its own security, or protectively, to save
its weaker neighbours from molestation. During the Spanish
war there was some panic fear of enemy warships bombarding
America's open coasts, and this lent colour to defence arguments which to foreigners might appear disingenuous. In 1903
came the seizure of the Panama Canal zone from Colombia. It
was the kind of coup that the Goulds and Rockefellers had
practised inside the U.S., and that public opinion on the whole
acquiesced in as a short cut to material progress, with the
impatience of a nation of technicians. Theodore Roosevelt was
anxious to follow this up by getting the Danish West Indies.
'They were, he said, the key to the Panama Canal.'[64] Every
'key' in this game requires another key to make it safe. But
though the Canal Zone might come to be part of an empire's
infrastructure, its seizure contrasted with Britain's conduct two
decades earlier in making the security of the Suez Canal the
pretext for occupying all Egypt and turning it into a lucrative
colony. And newspaper prophecies in England after the
Spanish War that the U.S. would go on to annex Mexico and
Nicaragua[65] were not being fulfilled. It was intervening forcibly
only in civil broils, or what could be made to appear such, as
in Colombia in 1903, or in San Domingo in 1904 when debts
to Europe might have invited European meddling, or in Cuba,
under treaty right, in 1906. When General Pershing—a
graduate of both Red Indian and Philippines campaigns—was
sent into Mexico in 1916 the invasion was a reprisal for what all

---

[63] W. M. Ball, *Nationalism and Communism in East Asia* (Melbourne, 1952),
p. 85.
[64] M. F. Egan, *Recollections of a Happy Life* (N.Y., 1924), p. 224.
[65] Heindel, *op. cit.*, p. 81.

foreign interests agreed in regarding as outrageous conduct by revolutionaries. It was reminiscent of the Austrian reprisal two years before against Serbia, but very unlike this it amounted in the end to little more than a gesture. Mexico was one of the bigger countries, where intervention could not be passed off as a mere police action; more important, it was united against the intruder as Latin American countries seldom were. 'The whole Mexican nation was actively hostile to our troops.'[66]

However, while British Toryism had failed to inveigle the U.S. into adopting its own type of imperialism, the U.S. was fast developing another of its own, less extreme but often highly irritating to both victims and rivals. British Liberals who hoped to see it setting a new standard of international conduct were disappointed. Lord Bryce was exhorting Washington to treat the other American nations with great tact, to be 'the disinterested, absolutely disinterested and unselfish advocate of peace and good will'.[67] Instead it was giving more and more backing to businessmen who had an instinctive sense of being entitled to something better than fair play anywhere in the New World. A British competitor complained of being squeezed out of Colombia by 'that economic penetration which is thought in the United States to be the proper accompaniment of the Monroe doctrine'.[68] A traveller more concerned with Latin American feelings reported them in the 1910s to be embittered by 'high-handed aggression, disguised under the name of progress and regard for liberty'.[69] 'To save themselves from Yankee imperialism', wrote a Peruvian, 'the American democracies would almost accept a German alliance or the aid of Japanese arms. . . .'[70] As now interpreted, the Monroe Doctrine was defeating its own ostensible purpose. 'Dollar Diplomacy', that Caribbean forerunner of American world policy after 1945, was by this time a familiar phenomenon. Yet even at this stage it marks a significant difference, not of

---

[66] Ganoe, op. cit., p. 455.

[67] Lord Bryce, South America. Observations and Impressions . . . (London, 1912), p. 509.

[68] J. A. Spender, Weetman Pearson, First Viscount Cowdray 1850–1927 (London, 1930), p. 210; cf. Perkins, op. cit., pp. 102–3.

[69] R. B. Cunninghame-Graham, José Antonio Páez (London, 1929), p. 293.

[70] F. García Calderón, in A. Alvarez, The Monroe Doctrine (Washington, 1924), pp. 257 ff.

psychology alone, from European precedent, that such interventions were hole-and-corner affairs, furtively carried on at
the bidding of one lobby or another, not in the open with fire
and enthusiasm.

In the rest of the world, still largely composed of empires,
the unique industrial strength of the U.S. allowed it to buy
whatever it wanted from them, and in some ways become a
participant in their habits of mind as well as their profits.
South-east Asia was producing tin and rubber very largely for
the British, French and Dutch to sell to America, in return for
American goods for their own consumption in Europe.[71] Here
was a trade triangle not unlike the older one of Indian opium
paying for China tea to be drunk in Britain, in which too the
U.S. had come to be involved. In a sense it was employing the
old empire-builders as managers, to spare itself the embarrassing task of running colonies on its own. Even if the price of raw
materials from Asia had to include the commission paid to them,
it was still low, because they helped to keep Asian earnings low.
Altogether the situation lent some meaning to Kautsky's
prediction of a 'super-imperialism' uniting all capitalist
interests. An idealized version of this may be detected in Colonel
House's scheme of early 1914 to avert a European war by
getting all the big States to cooperate in a grandiose development of the backward world.[72]

American feelings about the old empires still wavered.
Increasing investment in the countries owning them gave U.S.
capital a sort of sleeping partnership. It was an ill omen that
the first big American investment in Europe consisted of loans
to Britain for the Boer War.[73] Liberal objections to imperialism
were still alive, on the other hand, and some unflattering pictures
of colonial conditions were drawn. One observer in the 1920s
described an Indochina run by bored Frenchmen only longing
to get home to Paris, while behind a civilized façade oriental
oppression still flourished.[74] Britons in India were frequently

[71] Jacoby, *op. cit.*, p. 6.
[72] *The Intimate Papers of Colonel House*, ed. C. Seymour (London, 1926),
Vol. 1, pp. 247-9, 253, 271. The U.S. was able to export capital before 1914
because still getting capital from Europe: C. K. Hobson, *The Export of
Capital* (London, 1914), p. 29.
[73] Corey, *op. cit.*, op. 227.
[74] H. A. Frank, *East of Siam* (1926), pp. 223, 83.

nettled by American failure to appreciate their work. A book like *Mother India* made amends. It depicted India as incapable of looking after itself, an attitude clearly linked with the racialism in American thinking; it was full of indignation (often well warranted) about the way Hindus treated their women, and full of admiration for British efforts to improve things.[75] These efforts could be put in the same category with America's periodical descent on some disorderly Central American republic under colour of straightening out its affairs.

On balance the U.S. was moving towards a solidarity of feeling with the old empires, at any rate the British which it heard most about. Much of the style and matter of American apologetics of world power today can be traced back to British imperialism in its later, defensive days; to such windy rhetoric as Younghusband's, with an *obbligato* accompaniment of religious phrases, about the high moral purposes of the British invasion of Tibet in 1904,[76]—or Zimmern's eulogy of British imperial history with the navy invariably 'the champion of common human rights', almost too eager to go 'crusading' in defence of right against wrong.[77] Britannia must rule the waves, not for any selfish ends but for the good of all. In the same vein an American expert on China wrote a book in 1904 to convince his countrymen that they must secure the mastery of the Pacific;[78] 'mastery', he explained, not implying ill will to anyone else. If British imperialism failed after 1900 to secure the U.S. as partner, it was destined to have the U.S. as heir. In recent years indeed America has looked like a provincial actor jumping on the stage to repeat the same catch-phrases and claptrap that Britain won applause with, now when they have grown stale and silly; an illustration of Marx's dictum about history doing things twice, the second time as a farce.

Only in the past twenty years has opportunity come to America to add political power to economic. In the interwar years, when Red peril and Yellow peril were so evenly balanced, nothing could be done beyond the Pacific (in the Manchurian crisis, for instance) without worsening one or the other. The

[75] Katherine Mayo, *Mother India* (1927).
[76] Sir F. E. Younghusband, *India and Tibet* (1910).
[77] A. Zimmern, *The Third British Empire* (1926), pp. 80, 102.
[78] T. R. Jernigan, *China's Business Methods and Policy* (1904), p. 298.

Slump, which turned Germany and Italy back to imperialism, pushed America further into withdrawal. While Europeans had alternatives to look to, socialist or fascist, America had none, and the breakdown of the 'way of life' that all classes had come to identify themselves with had all the more prostrating an effect. Even Dollar Diplomacy in the Caribbean flagged during the 1930s, as much from this paralysis of the nation's belief in itself as from New Deal enlightenment. This was the gloom from which the public was rescued, psychologically as well as materially, by Pearl Harbour. Victory over Japan, and possession of the atom bomb, raised relief to exaltation. It was the first, and the only, clear-cut victory in a big war that America has ever won; everyone else was crippled; an 'American century' seemed to be dawning.

It was America's turn to be carried up to the mountain-top and shown the kingdoms of the earth. Yet it could not, without loss of faith in itself as well as of others' faith in it, annex any of them, even a Guatemala. Instead it wanted to play once more, on the grandest scale, what history and national character had made its favourite rôle, that of Perseus or St. George slaying monsters and throwing a shield over life, liberty, and the pursuit of profit. Hollywood has reflected this fantasy among the rest of America's daydreams. Just as all the Kaiser's army manoeuvres ended with a triumphant cavalry charge, every American adventure-film had to end with a hero galloping or driving at full speed to rescue some unfortunate in the nick of time; in Griffith's classic *Intolerance*, for example, made in 1916 just before the U.S. sprang (or more accurately, shuffled) to the rescue of European democracy.

Japan between 1941 and 1945 professed, not altogether groundlessly, to be liberating South-east Asia from its Western oppressors. America in turn, in its grand irruption into Asia, was coming to liberate it from Japan, as in 1898 it came to save the Philippines from Spain. And however much it had been already flowing, financially and spiritually, into the mould of the European empires, taking their shape and ready to replace them when they crumbled, its outlook and tactics were still, until a few years ago, more modern and adaptable than theirs. It was Europe's obstinate clinging to power after 1945 that drew America on, creating situations that it could scarcely help taking advantage of or, as in Vietnam, being sucked into. Thus in Iran the U.S. stepped in to assist a royalist counter-revolution and win a big share in the oil-fields when Britain's foolish obstinacy had pushed one wing of a divided ruling class into a programme of nationalization. By and large America in contrast with its predecessors was buying its way into the Middle East by offering higher royalties. Its 'imperialistic' backing of Zionism has only hampered it, and helped Russia. But every onward step in regions where colonialist practices had long been habitual made them more a part of American habit too, and enabled a hydra-headed CIA to multiply its activities.

One legacy from the old empires was a besetting fear of Red plots up and down the planet. Britain, France, Holland, from 1917 on were anxious to make it appear that all nationalist movements against their rule were instigated by agents of Moscow. To some extent their governments really believed this, being now shaky and uncertain, and not wanting to admit to themselves that they were really disliked by their subjects; but they had in addition to disarm liberal criticism at home, and also in America where there was for instance an 'American League for India's Freedom'. Japan's profession of defending Asia against communism, as well as Western greed, and Hitler's of defending Europe, was something else that America could take over from its defeated opponents. It was shouldering now the responsibility that haunted Wilson when he tried to keep out of the Great War because only a U.S. with intact strength could shore up '"white civilization" and its domination over the world'.[79] His academic phrase meant, in the vernacular, defence of capitalism. But this could still masquerade as defence of freedom against its arch-enemies, communist Russia and China. Unhappily the character of the Stalinist régime made it easier for old American dislike of European monarchies and their colonialism to be turned into condemnation of Stalin and his 'Soviet empire', or Mao the 'Red emperor'. It was helpful too, so far as Western opinion was concerned, that China was the old 'Yellow peril' in new guise, neatly filling the blank left by Japan, while the U.S.S.R. could be viewed as a half-Asian country under a barbarous Asiatic despotism.

Instead of a Doctrine protecting the New World against the

[79] Clinard, *op. cit.*, p. 171.

Old, we now have one to protect all the old world of class society against socialism. In effect the Platt Amendment imposed on Cuba has been generalized to cover all countries under the American umbrella, with even the small fry being left under their own, however dubiously independent governments. There was a precedent in the Mandate system invented as a concession to the spirit of the age by the victorious Allies in 1919, and operated in countries like Iraq through client rulers who remained clients when the Mandate nominally ended. A working model was provided by the Philippines, where a reliable governing class had been successfully fostered, and was tied to America by common interests and by fear of its own discontented poor. The islands could now be given independence, and were a showpiece highly attractive to other propertied groups in eastern Asia.

King George had plenty of friends in America, and President Nixon has plenty of friends in Asia. The more fiercely nationalism flares up in Asia, becoming at the same time a mass movement for social reform, the more class interests it necessarily antagonizes, and all these are eager allies of America. It does not take much shrewdness for them to see that the way to get money or guns is to discover a Red plot, as Titus Oates discovered Popish plots, or as a quack doctor might scare a rich old patient. In America itself there are always interested parties to lend them a hand, and to palm off the most unsavoury characters as so many William Tells resolved to sell their lives dearly against communist aggression. In the meantime they sell their services dearly to America. Tory England after all had no difficulty in seeing Southern Secessionists as men rightly struggling to be free, and even had thoughts of intervening in the Civil War on their side.

It is an instance of the fine distinctions that a national conscience often draws that the U.S. even now feels a little uncomfortable with monarchs, but is quite at home with dictators, military or civilian. Bao Dai was less congenial to it than the much more tyrannical Ngo Dinh Diem. An implicit assumption is indulged in—a capitalist version of the withering away of the State—that authoritarian government backed by an American-trained army and police will establish conditions for 'free enterprise' to flourish in: a modern middle class will then grow up, and the country will become safe for something like America's own mode of guided democracy. In most social contexts this prospect is quite chimerical; and from the point of view of mass welfare indirect rule may be even worse than actual colonialism. It has occurred to visitors in Latin America that if Washington were directly responsible for things there, roads and hospitals and schools could not be quite so scarce.

It is America now that sets out to police the world, while European and Japanese capitalism calmly looks on and shares in the proceeds. Yet America is in various ways less well equipped for the task. In Latin America and some parts of Asia it has had on the whole a deceptively easy time in asserting its suzerainty. It is the Far East that has proved baffling. Militarily the old empires, set up before Asian nationalism took form, relied heavily on native troops. America has endeavoured to follow suit. Eisenhower talked hopefully of 'setting Asians to fight Asians', and may have thought with Pompey that he had only to stamp his foot and the legions would spring up. In South Korea it would seem for the time being that a useful recruiting-ground has been discovered. Elsewhere, and especially in South Vietnam, things have not gone so well. One awkwardness is that for the sake of appearances local troops have to be left to fight, or run away, under their own leaders. In any case there is nothing in their make-up to qualify Americans to officer native armies as Europeans used to do, any more than to administer colonies themselves.

They have it may be said a species of 'native troops' of their own, Negroes whom army service has offered some opportunities denied to them in other fields.[80] But after years of war the American people at large seems—to its credit—scarcely less un-military than it was before. No officer-caste has grown up in the image of the Junker or the Samurai; even now 'officership is a low-status profession'.[81] A Vietnam war has no cavalry charges and little glamour. Instead we see increased reliance on scientific methods of destruction, that can lead to nothing better than a grotesque future of government from the air, of peoples condemned to live a nocturnal existence while in the

[80] M. Janowitz and Lt. Col. R. Little, *Sociology and the Military Establishment* (revised edn., N.Y., 1965), pp. 51–52.
[81] *Ibid.*, p. 39.

daytime American planes fly about distributing good-will leaflets and napalm. We see, too, increased reliance in client countries like Brazil on scientific methods of police terror, borrowed by the CIA from the Gestapo and the SS.

The CIA would look the most un-American of all things, were it not able to claim ancestry in the private detective agencies like Pinkerton's that throve by supplying employers with spies and gunmen to keep their workers down. Today the morbid police mentality that it embodies, with its doctrinaire ban on any popular change anywhere in the world, suggests an ideology stiffened into dogma, floating free of any base in rational calculation. Something like this may have occurred towards the end of other epochs, as in the last phase of the Holy Alliance when the Tsar Nicholas I was the policeman of the continent, wielding his power in some ways quixotically, in a spirit of infatuated devotion to an order of things that no one else any longer took so literally for gospel. It is only Russia and America, the two nations which could be seen more than a century ago as the two great ones of the earth,[82] born alike to extraordinary if conflicting destinies, that have been able in modern times to preside by turns over the last stand of an epoch or the inauguration of a new one. They have been the two extensions or amplifiers of western Europe, inventor of almost everything that has made the modern world, but too small and too divided to work out its conceptions on a grand scale, or doing so only in botched forms by fighting wars and making empires. In the ancient world Greece lay in something like the same position between Persia to the east and Rome to the west.

Whatever its bosses may desire, America is the last country to be easily kept immobile for very long. More than any other it has been a bundle of contradictions, jungle economics and Puritan conscience, generosity and greed, jostling together, and has swung to and fro more widely. It lost interest overnight in its first flutter in colonialism, in a volatile fashion impossible to a Europe rancid with hereditary ambitions and vendettas. Ability to forget is one part of learning. Engels thought of America as likely to 'travel in tremendous zigzags',[83]

---

[82] Pierre Soulé, quoted in Ettinger, *op. cit.*, p. 216.
[83] Marx and Engels, *op. cit.*, p. 190.

but to progress towards socialism faster than Europe once it began.[84] There is more than mere hypochondria in the nervous anxiety of conservatives ever since 1917 to seal it off hermetically against socialism, to keep 'dangerous thoughts' out of its head. American imperialism, by origin a *racket*, an outgrowth of big-business racketeering at home, now has this obsession added to it. In eastern Asia it has landed the country in 'one of those dreadful, tragic, hopeless situations which seem to mark the decline or exhaustion of a colonial relationship':[85]—the words are Kennan's, describing Spain's final efforts to hold Cuba, and written a few years before America's efforts to hold South Vietnam began. Vietnam may turn out to have saved not only itself but also America, by tearing the web of deception and self-deception that Americans have been weaving round themselves.

The hopeful view that they are still economically and morally capable of changing course, and prospering without either arms-race or colonialism, was stated again not long ago, with due caution, by the American Marxist Perlo.[86] Progress has always been halting and imperfect, and whatever its shortcomings a country can only be measured by comparison with others. Peace and fraternity, America's early watchwords, have never lost all their virtue. If they do, if there is to be an ultimate failure of democracy in its first homeland, it will be a misfortune for the world only less great than an ultimate failure of the first homeland of socialism.

[84] *Ibid.*, pp. 225, 237, 243.
[85] Kennan, *op. cit.*, p. 13.
[86] V. Perlo, in *Morning Star* (London), 7 June 1968. I have benefited by discussion of this point with Dr David Horowitz, and by his trenchant criticisms of the first draft of this article throughout.

4
The Peasant Revolution
Some Questions

A few years ago there began to be great hopes of a new wind of change blowing through the Third World, a fresh impetus to socialism from the backlands. They were inspired by the Cuban success, following on the Chinese, and by Maoist revolutionary preaching; together these seemed to constitute a still more potent version, a New Testament, of Marxism, which having lost its way in Europe was having a rebirth outside.

But no Marxism can work magic; and in some hopes of these last few years there was a flavouring of the miraculous. Many western socialists were the more easily impressed by these prospects because of frustration in their own countries, where labour movements have fallen into narrow parochialism and the left wing has been as much in a blind alley politically as the backward lands economically. It has at times, as a result, seemed inclined to wait for political salvation to come from the wilderness, from eruption of volcanoes that in the West seem extinct. It was almost a new stirring of the old European dream of the noble savage: humanity uncorrupted by the fleshpots of Egypt was to arise from the Andes or the Mountains of the Moon (even, it appeared at times, from Harlem) to accomplish what a degenerate western working class no longer cared to attempt. Blueprints could be got from China for revolution in any social conditions from Stone Age onward. Wishfulness of this kind had shown itself, in fact, even before Maoist doctrine came to endorse it. One foretaste can be recognized in the counsel of despair that made the Indian Communists defeated in 1948 in their strongholds look to border hillmen for new recruits. Today the Naxalite sect of the fragmented CPI is reported to be, with a stiffening now of advice from Peking, seeking support afresh in remote tribal fringes.

Revolution was made in China, and is being made in Vietnam, by a peasantry in the true sense, a solid, settled, close-packed mass of cultivators; a peasantry which is not so often met with outside Asia. Border hillmen, tribal minorities, are as different from it as peasants are from townsmen (and often, as in Vietnam before socialism came, on as bad terms with it), and there has been too much tendency to lump them all together in a common primitiveness. The day of the true primitive, the Mongol or Berber nomad who used to overturn effete kingdoms, has long gone by. In remote jungles of the Amazon or Congo it may be fairly easy to start a fight which could smoulder for years without presenting any serious challenge to a government. Elsewhere there is every gradation between the 'true' or Asian peasantry and the primitive tribe. But most peasants of all sorts are miserably poor, and there are vastly more of them than there were industrial workers in the West when these could be thought of as the grand revolutionary force. Daydreams and extravagances apart, many found it easy to believe that the tale of the civil war in China was going to be repeated in the whole backward world: revolution infiltrating and then inundating the countryside, until the towns and industrial centres were isolated and at last swallowed up in the flood.

Yet tangible results have been meagre. Here and there, in Tanzania for instance, there has been modest progress of a less explosive character. Actual peasant revolt, like working-class revolt before it, has often not come when it might have been expected, and when it has come has most often failed, as the Hukbalahap rising in the Philippines did. Much of the globe, including large areas of Africa and Latin America, has remained as barren of general progress as the developed countries—those of Communist Europe among them—of political progress.

A glance back at earlier history shows us the peasantry of some European and Asian countries, like France or Russia or China, in a state of insurrection against monarchy and land-owners for centuries on end: that is, there was nearly always an outbreak bigger or smaller in one province or another. None of these was successful by itself; the biggest, like the German peasant war of 1524–25 or the Taiping rebellion in China in the mid-nineteenth century, had some urban affiliations, though they too failed. Real success came when peasant revolt coincided with (and did not collide with) movements of other class forces, which did not exist outside Europe before our day. Bourgeois revolution was scarcely possible without peasant backing as in France in 1789. It might be said that the German peasants failed in 1524–25 because the middle class in the field at the same time was too weak; and, conversely, that the German middle class failed in 1848 because the peasant movement then in the field was too weak. It might further be conjectured that socialist revolution, in turn, failed to come about in the western countries for lack of a big, mutinous peasantry to reinforce the working class; in Germany for example in 1919. At any rate there has been no successful socialist revolution without a massive peasant revolution running alongside working-class militancy, as in Russia in 1917 (just as in 1789 it ran parallel with bourgeois ambitions). In China, peasant revolt guided by socialist ideas and cadres actually superseded the working class. But there was a very special combination of factors in China, too easily overlooked: a peasantry accustomed for ages to anti-feudal revolt, a national spirit, a foreign invasion, and finally a world war that brought the revolution to the brink of success. The Russian revolution had been made possible by the First World War, and the Cuban almost caused a third.

A mass outbreak must either propel the mass forward, or push it mentally, historically, back; and in the past the effect was oftener retrograde than not. Resistance to revolutionary France and Napoleon pushed the peasants of south Italy and Spain further back towards the middle ages; the great Indian uprising against European domination, the Mutiny of the peasant soldiery in 1857, was in many ways atavistic, and so was its Chinese parallel, the Boxer Rebellion of 1900. Like the Boxers, Burmese peasant rebels three decades later pinned their faith to magic charms and bullet-proof talismans,[1] and some of the Mau-mau insurgents in Kenya even more recently must

[1] See M. Collis, *Trials in Burma* (London, 1938), Chap. 7, Section 7.

have belonged equally to the past. This mental blindness has gone with the style of peasant fighting, which has not often been a modern guerrilla style. The Spanish peasants of 1808–14, who fought on guerrilla lines, only fought in their own districts, and were effective chiefly as auxiliaries to a foreign regular army, Wellington's. Rustics fighting on their own in small bands have been apt to deteriorate and become hardly distinguishable from brigands, which some of their members may indeed have been. But as a rule, the instinct of peasants defying authority has been either to make a sudden brief local tumult, as in France in 1789 or Russia in 1905, or else flock together in unwieldy masses, imitation armies, as in Germany in 1524 or China in 1900. Numbers promoted confidence, a delusive confidence that expressed itself aptly enough in faith in divine protection or magic charms. Small groups need more positive ideas, to keep on fighting and not lose sight of their purpose, as much as they need adequate weapons. Not only political ideas, but proper organization and tactics, must be brought from outside to a peasantry, by men with a better knowledge of the enemy's strength and how it can be combated. True guerrilla warfare is a quite recent and sophisticated development, dovetailing old feeling with new thinking. Recent history shows that the combination is possible, but very far from easy.

A complicating factor is that peasant populations have normally been stratified, in one degree or another, and in many areas, notably in parts of India, this is now deepening. Under older feudal conditions the better-off peasant was often the most rebellious, as in England in 1381, Germany in 1524, France in 1789. Long after hatred grew between richer and poorer peasant, as in tsarist Russia, the countryside as a whole might continue rebellious. But most old-time outbreaks were fairly brief, sudden flockings together of rioters into bands that any peasant might join in, with one motive or another, including plunder.[2] A modern guerrilla struggle, carefully organized and long sustained, is a very different thing, and may require more united sympathy than can be expected from a peasantry divided into strata or classes, the richer ones well aware of the menace of communism to them as well as to the

[2] See S. M. Dubrovsky, *Krest'yanskoe dvizhenie v revoliutsii 1905–1907 gg.* (Moscow, 1956).

rulers. It was a vital factor in China and Yugoslavia that there was foreign invasion to draw them together.

In the theory of peasant revolution Latin America has had a prominent place. Cuba's leaders have seemed at times to value their own achievement only as the spark to kindle a continental blaze; like Lenin making his seizure of power in 1917 with Europe, rather than Russia, as his hoped-for prize. Wide areas of Latin America may well be thought as incapable as any in the world of any peaceful reform, because of the semi-feudal modes of exploitation that have come down from the past, no longer historically 'necessary' or rational, but very hard to shake off. Their vested interests are part and parcel of a ramshackle social structure that its custodians, including those in Wall Street and the White House, are afraid of tampering with for fear of the whole thing collapsing. On the other hand the same state of affairs may have the same paralysing effect on socialist reform or revolution.

As against any more cautious forecasts, the revolutionary thesis, or messianic vision, has been that devoted bands of volunteers should start armed struggle at once, in the backlands where authority is feeblest, confident that once the fight begins and the sound of guns is heard the population will be drawn in, first the few and then the many, until the people's army becomes irresistible. Impatience with anything less bold is understandable after caution has so often ended in failure, an abrupt snuffing out of reform either by the local army with its equipment from the U.S. or by the U.S. itself, the policeman of the New World as the tsars once were of Europe. It was to prove this vision that Guevara made his heroic but tragic attempt in Bolivia.

Guevara seems to have thought in terms of a Cuban situation repeated everywhere, a people nearly unanimous against a discredited dictatorship and only waiting for a bold lead. But every revolution is likely to hinder repetition of itself elsewhere by putting the other side on its guard. Besides, Cuba was a very special case, like China, as in fact every country capable of revolutionary pioneering must be. It was small and compact; a plantation economy had produced a semi-proletarianized peasantry; and there were old ingrained habits of resistance.

Except in the superficial form of upper-class faction-fighting, these habits have never had much hold on Latin America either on the national or on the agrarian level. Under Spanish and Portuguese rule the continent was curiously quiescent, thanks partly to the conquered and conquering races each serving as a check on the other. It got its independence in the end too easily. Against Spain indeed sanguinary wars had to be fought, but mostly by a landowning élite making use of a cannon-fodder of half-wild *gauchos* and *llaneros*, half-Indian horsemen of the plains, to which they then returned. The U.S. had to do its own fighting for independence, and it was the British who employed alien—German—soldiery against it. Of later times it must be said that there has been more grumbling and oratory about Yankee overlordship than real effort to throw it off. Cuba had the great, if painful, advantage of being kept under Spanish rule to the end of the nineteenth century, and going through a long series of slave revolts and then of battles for independence; altogether a toughening education.

On the agrarian plane likewise Latin America's record is not striking; and other things being equal, villages like nations are likelier to be ready for revolt today if they have been long familiar with revolt in the past—as Russian or Chinese peasants were, German peasants after 1525 were not. One grand cause of rustic passivity in Latin America has been, again, the mixture of discordant races. In many regions, particularly some of those like Bolivia where hill and jungle favour guerrilla operations, the peasantry is closer historically to the African level than the European. It is still mainly or largely Indian, of many diverse stocks, with the addition of mixed groups that may be on bad terms with both the 'pure' races. In the stagnation of most of the South American interior racial blending or integration has gone on slowly, as in India where millennia after the Aryan occupation there are still big pockets of unassimilated aborigines, as well as the vast number of those whose ancestors were turned into 'untouchable' helots.

A kind of passive resistance by the Amerindians to plantation and urban labour led to their replacement in the developing coastal areas by African, Chinese, East Indian coolies; active struggle by such a population, sullenly withdrawn or relegated (again as in India) to the wilds, is another matter. Its forefathers had little share in the wars of independence, except to some extent in Mexico where their involvement was the starting-point of a long-drawn social revolution that has put Mexico ahead of most of the other republics. In other countries they were often drawn, or rather dragged, into inter-state wars, and displayed, in Paraguay above all, some of the military virtues in an astonishing degree. But they were only conscripts, made use of by ruling élites as *gauchos* and *llaneros* had been; and it may be questioned whether 'martial races' moulded by organized, disciplined warfare, like the Germans or modern Turks, are (whether as peasants or as workers) good material for rebellion. The well-drilled serf conscript of the old Prussian army had qualities the opposite, except for courage, of what guerrilla warfare calls for.

Compared with most Africans it is a handicap of the Amerindians that they have been for centuries under White domination, physical and—through the Church, so far as it reached them—mental. By contrast with the Cubans, face to face with a foreign-backed ruling clique before their revolution, these Amerindians, whose linguistic boundaries do not coincide with existing political frontiers, have no country, and only form the bottom layer of a society meaningless to them. They can neither strike out a path of their own nor identify themselves with any 'national' feelings, even with the anti-U.S. feeling so strong in the towns. Bolivia has been through innumerable 'revolutions', that Indians did well to keep clear of for fear of being—quite literally—roped in to fight for one faction or the other. To this day a backwoods Indian seeing a white man firing his gun, even if it happens to be a Guevara, must be expected to react in the same way. One may, in short, be left wondering whether the leaders Amerindia needs today are not men of the school of Gandhi, or Ambedkar, or Danilo Dolce, instead of the school of Guevara.

How explosive peasant discontents may be depends a good deal on the political cauldron that holds them. In the old imperial territories this has grown in recent years much less rigid, and its elasticity has helped to reduce the internal pressures. Except in a few African areas direct colonial rule has almost disappeared; imperialism has handed over administration to the most conservative local leadership available. Nothing need be lost by such handing over except the salaries of colonial administrators, formerly in British India and French Africa and so on a very important consideration, and to the Portuguese middle class, it may be, even now, but in general nowadays a triviality. In return for this small sacrifice the foreign capitalist is able to withdraw safely out of sight, and the most tangible incentive to unrest is removed. Rebels, un-lettered ones especially, need a vivid, personal image of what they are to fight against. To rise against an invisible overlord might be like rebelling against the law of gravity.

To depict the change as merely formal, or a mere conjuring trick, as communists[3] and nationalists have often done, is too simple. Easy optimism about the capitalist leopard changing its spots is wrong, but so is the dogma of Lenin or Mao that it can never change, except in outward disguise. Socialists underrated for too long after the last World War the immense resilience of capitalism, when faced by stiff competition from socialism, as a productive system; and it would be another mistake to ignore its mental or political adaptability—no doubt much smaller, but still appreciable. It has changed, and under sufficient prodding and pushing can change further. 'Neo-colonialism', its present phase in relation to the undevel-oped regions, has all kinds of shades, depending on the energy of local leaders, the extent of foreign interest in local resources, and other factors. At the lowest it must be regarded as an advance on the old colonial methods; it loosens things up, makes further advance possible, though far from certain. It might be compared with the emancipation of the serfs in Russia in 1861, which solved nothing permanently, but did signalize a new epoch in Russian history; most obviously it brought a lull of some decades in agrarian conflict.

Portugal is a very backward corner of western Europe, and its empire an anachronism, a clinging to methods that others have been leaving behind. It was the first western empire to begin, premature and therefore more parasitical than most, and it is the last to end. In its early years it sprinkled Africans with baptismal water, in its last it sprinkles them with napalm;

[3] This is a blemish in the otherwise valuable *Introduction to Neo-Colonialism* by J. Woddis (London, 1967); see e.g. p. 50.

in between it has bestowed very little else on them. By keeping them backward and illiterate it avoided any serious opposition from them until a few years ago; and at home it has been strengthened by a dictatorship of many years' standing, which has prevented any loud criticism such as all the other colonial powers, and now the U.S., have had to face. The dictatorship has made life worse for its subjects both at home and in Africa. Yet without some outside agency to serve as a link, any combination of the two against it is hard to foresee. No such combination ever emerged effectively in any of the other empires, even where, as in Britain or France, there was freedom of speech in the ruling country. It is enough to recall the lamentable record of the British Labour Party on India. The British people had been for too long tutored into a belief that its prosperity depended on India; the Portuguese people has been taught that its prosperity (such as it is) depends on the African possessions being kept.

There is also, as influential and less vulnerable to calculations of profit and loss, national pride. Portugal's explorations and conquests of bygone days were remarkable, even if their results fell before long into miserable decay; Portuguese ships were harvesting the wealth of Asia when English seamen were content to haul a few fish out of the North Sea. Memories of that past have been cherished, and remnants of empire hung on to, because in modern times Portugal has had too little to feed its self-respect. Spain hung on to Cuba and the Philippines to the last gasp for the same reason, as well as for the revenue they brought in. France fought to keep its empire after 1945 partly to wipe out the ignominy of German occupation, while victorious Britain could afford to show more sense and liberality.

Cuba as the first American country to reach socialism owes much to its having been the last to escape from European imperialism; one of the last African countries to escape from it may prove the first to reach full socialism. This is Portuguese Guinea, a mere dot on the atlas, but one that deserves very close attention because it concentrates in its narrow limits many problems to be seen elsewhere on a bigger, more amorphous scale. It deserves attention also because its struggle is led by one of the most remarkable men that modern Africa has produced; and because there is a remarkable book about it, written from first-hand knowledge gained by painful tramping and canoeing through jungle and swamp, and in the light of wide knowledge of Africa's past and present and its place in the world: *The Liberation of Guiné*, by Basil Davidson.[4]

'Violence is the essential means of imperialist domination', writes Cabral, and therefore any serious resistance to it must include willingness to resort to force.[5] Guerrilla fighting has been going on since 1962, and a large proportion of the interior has been cleared, or nearly cleared, of the Portuguese. This has been accomplished with means as scanty, from a starting-point as humble, as could be found almost anywhere in today's Dark Continents. Guiné has under a million inhabitants, with no genuinely urban element, half a dozen languages, and a range of social systems from the primitive democracy of the village to a semi-feudalism that some areas (typical it may be of Africa as a whole) have been moving into in recent times. Some of the Fula tribal chiefs or petty feudalists aided the Portuguese conquest, while the free villages resisted it; and today it is these villages that supply the readiest recruits for the struggle, while the chiefs are again on the Portuguese side, as the Indian princes were on the British, and try to hold their people back. It was only in the late nineteenth century that most of the interior was conquered, and it would be instructive to know how many stories of the resistance have lingered in popular memory, and helped to inspire that of today.[6]

Davidson's account makes it clear, and this is one of its most important points, that the rebellion was anything but spontaneous. Resentment and hatred of the foreigner were strong, but they were not dry tinder to blaze up into revolt as soon as a single spark fell on it. 'The terrors of guerrilla warfare can be accepted, can be justified', Davidson writes, 'only when they are suffered as part of a *necessary* self-defence. This is a hard lesson that has nothing to do with revolutionary verbalism.'[7] That resistance *was* a necessity was something that villagers

---

[4] Penguin African Library, 1969.

[5] A. Cabral, Foreword to B. Davidson, *The Liberation of Guiné*.

[6] A Nigerian writer has stressed the continuing psychological importance of the fact that Africa did resist conquest; see B. Davidson, *Which Way Africa?* (revised edn., Penguin African Library, 1967), p. 50.

[7] *The Liberation of Guiné*, pp. 20-1.

could only be convinced of, first in one district, then in another, by slow, patient political preparation, long discussion carried on through supporters native to each area. The guiding party (PAIGC) was founded in 1959 by Cabral and five others; it was three years before it felt able to start armed action. In this sense the Portuguese might well repeat the stock complaint of conservatives, that all the trouble has been due to a few 'agitators', the handful of educated Africans who took the lead.

Between a man like Cabral and his peasant followers the cultural gap must be about the same as between Guevara and an Aymará Indian of Bolivia. Cabral had, as Davidson says, to re-Africanize himself before he could comprehend and be comprehended by the villagers. Guevara could scarcely Indianize himself; and that revolutionaries of his school have failed even to grasp the need to get inside the skin of the peasant, especially the Indian, in order to win his confidence, is a criticism that Cabral (who has visited Cuba and talked with Cubans in Africa) seems inclined to stress. There is indeed a startling contrast between the years of patient preparation in Guiné and the Guevarist vision of South American peasants flocking to the sound of guns in the hands of liberators whose language, even, they might not understand. A shade of difference may be perceptible even in Cabral's and Guevara's conception of the proper relation between guerrilla bands and peasantry. Cuba had from the first some non-peasant elements ready to begin a fight and carry it on, seeking and winning peasant recruits but retaining a certain separateness from the peasant mass, as of Crusaders from ordinary Christians.[8] Guiné had scarcely anything to count on except its peasantry; guerrilla bands could emerge only from within it, and have remained an organic part of it, responsible to democratic criticism.[9]

There could be no clearer demonstration than Guiné provides of the importance of the idea. In such a situation also the man who brings the idea has exceptional freedom to lead in one direction or another. Instead of seeking reassurance from old-world magic, like so many peasant rebels before them, these in Guiné, to all appearances as deeply buried in the past as any

[8] See Che Guevara, *Guerrilla Warfare* (Penguin edn., 1969).
[9] *The Liberation of Guiné*, p. 113.

of them, are being guided by civilized leadership towards
modernity and rationality. Given this orientation, stress of
conflict makes the process a rapid one. Davidson quotes a
remark of Cabral that the villagers are losing their old dread
of the forests, those haunts of demons and evil spirits, because
today these forests are their shelter from Portuguese bombing
raids.[10] Guerrilla warfare—of the modern species—means
continual movement, as Davidson says, 'movement in the
mind even when you are sitting still'.[11]

In all this the question arises of whether Guiné must be
looked on as a brilliant exception, or whether it can serve as
a model for other regions in or outside Africa; beginning
naturally with the other Portuguese colonies where revolts
are going on, Angola and Mozambique. The most obvious
discrepancy is of size. It remains to be seen whether a movement like Guiné's, based on very close-knit, intimate contact
between leaders and local cadres and ordinary men and
women, can be reproduced in a territory of much greater
extent. A similar question is whether Guiné may be better able
than the other two colonies (and many other African countries)
to acquire a sense of national unity, as the PAIGC leadership
hopes it will. Hitherto Guiné has never been anything remotely
like a nation, that odd entity which, with all its defects, was
indispensable to modern Europe's progress and seems indispensable to progress in newly-developing regions now. All the
triumphs of socialism have been nourished and sustained by
patriotism. Bolshevik power was consolidated by the Allied
intervention; the Chinese revolution drew as much on anti-
Japanese as on anti-Kuomintang or anti-landlord feeling;
Yugoslavia came to socialism by fighting Nazi invasion, Cuba
came to it more quickly under threat of Yankee invasion;
Vietnam is continuing a millennium of struggle for independence.

For Guiné to dream of nationhood might seem preposterous,
even by comparison with some other African countries. Still,
it has never been easy to say precisely what a nation is, except
by reference to what it does. If most African countries have
come by their frontiers accidentally, there has been more
accident and less destiny in the history of all nations than their

[10] *Ibid.*, p. 13.　　　　[11] *Ibid.*, p. 17.

historians like to admit; and history may now, aided by conscious intention, be able to recapitulate in a few decades what
formerly took centuries of blind evolution. To fuse Guiné's
peoples there is the presence of the white man, the foreign
enemy, on their soil. They may be supposed to share a common
philosophy of life, and mode of living, as those of India did
before they became a nation. Guiné like India got from foreign
rule a small intelligentsia of modern outlook, and a lingua
franca, though Guiné got not much else. Like Cuba it is small
enough to see itself easily in the mirror of today's events.

Its first national institution is a party, its second a miniature
army. It was a landmark in the struggle when the leadership
was able to form a mobile force willing to fight anywhere, as
distinct from the local militias willing to defend their own
homes. This has been a difficult stage in other revolutions too.
The parliamentary army in the English civil war was such a
mobile force, detached from local allegiances; a fact that must
have assisted its later drift into a professional army divorced
from, and disliked by, the public. There must be some risk of
this happening in any rising now; it may have happened in
some measure in Algeria. China has taken precautions against
it, part of Mao's all-round purpose of keeping the revolution,
and making the nation, totally democratic (or, what may not
be quite the same thing, egalitarian). Guiné too is making a
democratic society its goal, the virtues of the old rural fraternity
combined with those of modernity. Its leaders are aiming, in
other words, at something very different from the condition of
those many other African lands where there was no long,
transforming struggle for freedom, and power was transferred
to a small élite class. Here again no doubt vigilance will be
required, and the principles of the 'cultural revolution' in China
will be relevant. Yugoslavia is a warning that even a wartime
leadership of the most genuinely popular origin can to some
extent harden in peacetime into an élite.

If this can be avoided, so simple a society, purged by the war
of its feudal ingredients, should be free to organize itself almost
as if making a social contract in the style of the old philosophers.
Cabral and his friends, already thinking of problems of reconstruction, view agricultural growth as the chief objective, with
radical decentralization to release local initiative, even

abolition of anything like central ministries.[12] Ministries and their sweets of office are the honeypots in which once progressive politicians in many new countries have stuck fast; and real democracy may be impossible without real decentralization. Sheltered by friendly neighbours, Guiné might actually be said to be embarking on a direct transition from primitivism not only to socialism, but to anarchism, or the withering away of the State—or rather, it will never have known the State, except as an alien imposition. Even as a nation, it will have been formed by consent, instead of by the slow work of time, and should be able to avoid the excessive nationalism so dangerously mixed with the socialism of Russia or China.

Orthodox Marxism would query whether such a community, a federation of hamlets, could properly be called socialist, when it would have no heavy industry, no big towns, little of a working class. It might also ask whether rural communes left to their own devices will not stagnate, as they are apt to in India under the plan of leaving many things to the *panchayats* or local councils. Guiné will be relying on momentum gained in the war, and on the activity of individuals thrown up everywhere by it. With these assets, and luck, it may not be too sanguine to think of Guiné growing into an African Denmark, instead of a new Liberia, with a more strongly cooperative economy, profiting from agricultural science and making arrangements with other African countries for some of its industrial needs. Iceland lives well, with nothing to sell but fish. Aldous Huxley speculated years ago about a Utopia where every household would have a gadget on the roof to provide solar power, and all the Birminghams and Pittsburgs would have faded into bad dreams. Big industry is, after all, increasingly engaged in producing useless or noxious things that nations and private consumers have to be hypnotized into thinking they want.

Here we stray into the realm of fancy, and it may be well to recall that Guiné is not yet fully liberated: further, that it is not clear how it can be expected to complete its liberation, by its own efforts alone. Portugal is a relatively weak opponent; but any occupying force with modern weapons may be able to hold on to positions like the coastal settlements of Guiné

[12] *The Liberation of Guiné*, p. 137.

indefinitely. The Vietnamese can raid big American bases, but scarcely capture them; in Saigon the population has not risen against the occupying forces, and it does not seem to be antici-pated that the population of Bissau, the Guiné capital, will. Anachronistic rule like Portugal's infects, rather than trans-forms, the urban section of a subject people, the one most in contact with it; and every long conflict corrupts and demoralizes some sections, while it purifies others. Guerrillas have seemed at times—often in Algeria, occasionally in south Vietnam—to be resorting to indiscriminate terrorism against towns, as if indulging peasant rancour against townsmen, or trying to coerce the town into joining the countryside. That townsman and rustic have been natural enemies all through history is a fact with an important bearing on all peasant-revolution prospects. Guevara condemned indiscriminate terrorism, restricting it to punishment of prominent enemies of the people, and Cabral's principle seems to be the same.[13] But this leaves the Portuguese still in Bissau.

In Guiné Davidson saw 'Soviet artillery, Czechoslovak auto-matics, Cuban-made uniforms of Chinese cotton.'[14] Britain could have been helping the cause of freedom there in other ways, and ought to help, but has not helped. It is not for want of asking: Cabral came to London in 1960 and 1965 to put his country's case, and his party asks for political support from any country, African or other. He complains with good reason of a *'wall of silence* built around our peoples by Portuguese colonialism',[15] which has close links with other western capitalist interests, and whose forces are free to use NATO military supplies in Africa. Morally its African wars are a joint west-European and American responsibility. Britain has had the closest and oldest links with Portugal, and by its conduct over Rhodesia it has incurred lately a fresh debt to Africa.

Contrary to all socialist prophecy, the capitalist world camp has come to be more united and harmonious than the socialist camp. It confronts the backward regions in the shape of vast corporations, acquiring a steadily more 'multi-national charac-

[13] Guevara, *op. cit.*, pp. 26, 97; *The Liberation of Guiné*, pp. 60–1, 133.
[14] *Ibid.*, p. 88.
[15] *Ibid.*, Foreword.

ter';[16] it has arrived, in other words, at a stage not unlike the 'ultra-imperialism' that Kautsky foretold long ago, and Lenin ruled out. Further expansion of socialism in either the advanced or the undeveloped regions seems to depend on the emergence of a combination of forces, an intercontinental united front to challenge that of capitalism. It does not seem likely to be brought about by the peasantry alone, any more than by the working class alone, to say nothing of any of the lesser forces that have been hopefully thought of, like the intelligentsia or the student movement. Any single class by itself has limited horizons and ambitions. Progress in Europe was always brought about by a combination of classes. But today, thanks to the world market and its division of labour, some regions have a working class with hardly any peasantry, others a peasantry with hardly any working class; while various groups, like the Negroes in the U.S., stand outside the main class structure of their countries.

For progressive forces to join hands round the globe is harder than for coupon-clippers. Intransigent Maoism rejects any cooperation, either with Russia or with Western progressive opinion. And this opinion, in relation to the obscure wrestlings in the backlands, often seems scarcely to exist, except as a figure of speech. It has done about as little for the black inhabitants of southern Africa as the white man's liberalism for Negroes in the U.S. By contrast aid from the socialist countries looks prompt and vigorous.

The comparison is not in reality altogether so much in favour of the socialist countries, quite apart from the deplorable dissensions among them. It is an unlucky fact that socialism could only gain a foothold in the world, and survive, by winning control of one or two States big enough to defend themselves against capitalist aggression; but any big State is compelled to think of its frontiers and strategic concerns in ways that have nothing to do with any ideology. This is as true of China as of Russia. Maoist revolutionism, besides defects due to Peking's ignorance of the outside world, has been blended all along with Chinese interests, real or imaginary

[16] G. Arrighi and J. S. Saul, 'Nationalism and Revolution in Sub-Saharan Africa', in *Socialist Register*, ed. R. Miliband and J. Saville (London, 1969), p. 145.

(great-power interests have always been a bizarre mixture of the two), the result being at times a foreign policy of transparent opportunism. A right-wing military government in Pakistan has received fraternal embraces, rebels in Guiné have been cold-shouldered because they were receiving help from Russia.[17]

It may be naïve to fancy that aid programmes enjoy much backing of public good will in any of the communist countries. Demonstrations in Peking of sympathy with suffering peoples far away are really anti-American demonstrations; it is, unfortunately, much easier to hate foreigners than to sympathize with them. Both in China and in Russia the sensation of being looked up to by weak peoples as patrons and protectors is liable to feed a national self-complacency already far too strong in each of them. Russia's satellite-states have not even this satisfaction, in return for what they have to spend. There cannot have been systematic debate in any of them about the principles at stake. But in Czechoslovakia, and no doubt in the rest, and probably in the U.S.S.R. itself, there have been two currents of dissent. One was a feeling among many Party intellectuals that it was wrong to supply aid, especially arms, to régimes like those of Egypt or Iraq which kept their own socialists in jail. The other was a general impatience among workers and ordinary men and women at being made to give so much, out of scanty resources, to far-away people whom they knew nothing about. If Yugoslavs of the industrial north grumble at their government for investing capital to develop the backward south, it is not surprising to find a joke current in Poland that the average Polish worker has five dependents to maintain: one wife, two children, one Arab, and one Vietnamese. Cynicism like this can hardly be good for the prospects of socialism in eastern Europe.

The alternative argument, that socialist countries can do most for socialism by building it successfully at home, looks egotistic, and is denounced by Peking as 'goulash socialism'. Building socialism however does not mean only providing more pudding, but a new civilization, a new kind of humanity. Police socialism can make no appeal to prosperous countries, and realists may be mistaken (as they so often are) in assuming

[17] *The Liberation of Guiné*, p. 88.

that poor countries do not care about such matters as civil rights. Russia may indeed have something to learn about grass-roots democracy from Africa. But as things are, with the working class reduced to the same political indifference by communist rule as by capitalist affluence, aid depends on government decision; it is one more aspect of communist bureaucracy, and gives it one more pretext for continuing, and for suppressing criticism. This applies above all to the most expensive form of aid, military supplies in large quantities not to rebels but to governments, such as Soekarno's in Indonesia, most of which has been either a dead loss, or worse.

Where rebels are in action arms are the prime requisite, and these can only come from the 'East', but they will seldom be enough by themselves. What progressive westerners can do to help is far less clear, even nebulous. Broad support can be gathered only for limited, reformist aims, which the all-or-nothing philosophy of Maoism repudiates; it has to be sought from a medley of liberals, wanting to bring capitalism under decent control, and socialists, wanting to get rid of it. But what they can do, although inadequate, has the merit of being voluntary instead of bureaucratic, inspired by true civic sense, by recognition that the world cannot be healthy while large parts of it, with which the advanced countries have multiple ties—economic, historical, moral—are left unhealthy.

Being voluntary it is harder to mobilize, as well as more heterogeneous. Even communists in the west have been inclined to think of colonial issues as marginal, and belonging to the sphere of philanthropy; whereas what has to be learned now is that they are vital to all our own chances of progress—that only by involvement in events and movements outside our own frontiers can we hope to get on the move once more, whether as socialists or as liberals, against the juggernaut of monopoly capitalism. In a way this is harder to grasp now than earlier, because of the abandonment by Britain and most others of direct colonial rule. By turning itself into an anonymous net-work of cosmopolitan corporations, exchanging the plumed helmet of the governor for the bowler hat of the stockbroker—by reverting, so to speak, from Empress of India to John Company—imperialism has lost its glamour, its romantic attraction; but it has also blunted the sense of responsibility for

F

colonial welfare that a minority formerly felt, while sales of
stocks and shares swell the number of its campfollowers.
Nevertheless, today's new generation has a strong bent towards
internationalism, and could find a better outlet for it outside
Europe than in the Common Market, which has made some
appeal to it. There is a growing intelligentsia that could find
many points of contact, more freely than any political party,
between the west and the 'third world'. There are smaller
countries apter to give a lead than unwieldy Britain; in Sweden
the Socialist Party has given money to rebels in Portuguese
Africa, and a long campaign has been waged to prevent a big
company from taking part in the construction of a dam for the
Portuguese in Mozambique.

Hitherto only sensational happenings, at Suez or in Vietnam
or Ulster, have been able to rouse the same widespread interest
that floods or earthquakes do. A dull steady grind of injustice
far away in South Africa or Bolivia, or even as close at hand as
northern Ireland, has touched only a few consciences. It
seems a necessary preliminary to any real change that some
heads should be broken, as in Ulster in 1969. By itself violence
may accomplish much, or little, or nothing, according to
circumstances; but it may have the effect, as we have seen
student demonstrations do, of galvanizing outside interests in
favour of reform, and frightening authority into accepting it.
General Booth's maxim was that sinners would not repent until
hell fire was flashed before their eyes, and it is much the same
with sinful governments and respectable newspaper-readers.
But a fright, by itself, is more likely to throw them into a fit
of reactionary hysteria. It is here that enlightened opinion can
play its vital part, by persuading the public at large to draw
the right moral, to move forward instead of back. The bigger
and more permanent the volume of opinion that can be
mobilized, the less violence will be needed as a spur to change.

It is in Africa that hopes of revolution and of more peaceful
progress confront each other most distinctly, and yet may prove
to be each necessary to the other's success. There are three
Africas, besides colonial territories; one of these, the Muslim
north, is likely to go its own way, increasingly preoccupied with
the Middle Eastern conflict and drifting in Egypt's wake

towards a military-bureaucratic socialism. All Islam has lived ever since it began under what might be called army rule; and the primacy of the soldier is bolstered today by the feuds with outsiders in which most Muslim countries are involved: Arabs with Israel, Pakistan with India, Turkey with Russia. At the opposite point of the compass South Africa has been taking shape as a State unique in the modern age, something like what the southern Confederation would have been if it had won the American civil war, but with far more modern dynamism, a capitalist edifice reared on a primitive base of racial domination. It is the 'black Africa' in between whose nature and future are most enigmatic. An impressive recent study depicts it as on the whole inert, now that the glow of independence has faded, and in danger of remaining stagnant and subservient to the West, because it lacks the driving force of any sufficient class division and tension, within the peasantry or between it and any other class.[18] To gain ground economically it needs joint planning; but this calls for a high measure of political agreement, still more elusive.

On this view, the sole force capable of setting black Africa in motion might be common hostility to South Africa. This was already strongly expressed in the 'Charter of Unity' signed at Addis Ababa in 1963 by thirty governments, with several northern ones as well;[19] fortunately we have an opposite alignment here from the one in Latin America, where nearly all governments fawn on the United States. Hitherto most of those of black Africa have been too busy with their own doings, or with doing nothing, to take very much notice of the freedom struggles against Portugal. They will all be faced with an inescapable challenge if, as many predict, South Africa moves further out from its own limits and draws Portugal and Rhodesia into an aggressive alliance.[20] Those who welcome the prospect will trust to a rallying against the white front to give a fresh, more urgent meaning to the old gospel of African unity. It would be a recapitulation on a vaster scale of the coming together of scattered tribes against the white man in Guiné.

[18] Arrighi and Saul, loc. cit., p. 172.
[19] Text of Charter in Davidson, Which Way Africa? pp. 185–201.
[20] Davidson and other speakers at the Anti-Apartheid movement conference in London, 6 July, 1969, dwelt on how the various liberation struggles in southern Africa were now converging.

Intelligent observers have for several years warned western conservatism of such a prospect, with the unwelcome addition of a great expansion of Chinese influence. 'The Chinese are gambling heavily on the correctness of their analysis that Africa is ripe for revolution', a journalist wrote in 1964, and he thought that before long they might be proved right.[21] Five years later another drew an alarming picture of guerrilla training by the Chinese, soon to be followed by an influx of munitions along the Tanzania-Zambia railway they are building, to feed a war against white rulers all over southern Africa.[22] Peking may be assumed to regard this confrontation as the best thing that could happen to speed Africa's slow evolution, and, of course, to strengthen its own position. One may wonder how far it would really achieve either of these results. There would be a situation, with China taking the place of Russia, like that of the Middle East, the Arab countries confronting Israel. This has gone on for a long time now, and while it has stirred up a vast amount of excitement among the Arabs, it might not be easy to say what good it has done them otherwise. The binding force of a common hatred can be stimulating, but, like other drugs, also stupefying. In Africa, where race would be the substitute for the shared language and religion of the Arabs, black racialism would be lamentably deepened, as religious fanaticism has been among the Arabs. Israelis and South African whites are both small intrusive elements, but both firmly established and far more efficiently organized than their opponents can be for a long time to come. Russia all this time has been making an immense investment in the Middle East in the form of arms, for very precarious political returns, and China might fare no better in Africa.

South Africa compared with Israel has the asset of a large territory, the drawback of a large hostile population within its own borders. The flashpoint might come with a rising of the black proletariat there; and this too is a thing that some progressives have looked forward to because of the absence of a big proletariat anywhere else in the continent.[23] It requires

---

[21] C. Legum, *The Observer*, 27 September, 1964.
[22] P. Keatley, *Guardian*, 16 July, 1969, in one of a series of articles on 'The Battle for Africa'.
[23] E.g. Arrighi and Saul, *loc. cit.*, pp. 174-5.

strong nerves to hope for a rising that the whites would meet
with all the courage, and all the ferocity, of the British suppressing the Indian Mutiny, or of the Nazi armies in eastern
Europe. There are degrees of brutality among reactionary
régimes and their troops, as Guevara observed;[24] racial in-
doctrination carries it to its worst extreme. If things do come
to this, enlightened opinion will not be altogether unprepared.
A consultation of the World Council of Churches on 24 May,
1969, endorsed economic sanctions against racialist rule, and
support for armed revolt when all else failed. But western
enlightenment is still very limited. In a full-scale war of race
the bulk of British and American sympathy would be with the
whites, and there would be reactions against coloured minorities
at home. It would be so all the more if there were any direct
Chinese participation. Without this it is hard to see the war
ending in victory; with it, hard to see how it could end without
destroying the country, and with it the continent's biggest
industrial base. After all, somehow it must be made possible
for both black and white to live in South Africa.

Slow, piecemeal reform of the prison-fortress of South
Africa is an unheroic choice compared with revolution, yet one
to be preferred if there is any ray of hope for it to be brought
about by gradual sapping and mining, by a combination of
pressures internal and external. In this theatre conservative
interests are not all united. For world capitalism the big settler
population makes South Africa a profitable but perilous salient;
Boer racialism is to it a silly nuisance, like the same aberration
in Alabama; the industries its investments are creating will
require markets all over Africa. In the sight of Mammon, as of
God, skin colour does not count. Inside South Africa there is a
pallidly liberalizing, conciliatory tendency, diverging from the
high and dry doctrine of the race maniacs.[25] World capitalism
can be induced to back and strengthen this faintly better
tendency; but not by the light of reason alone. There must be
something to scare it into a sense of urgency; this something
can only be an imminent danger to its large investments—a
realistic threat, if not the actuality, of revolution within and
war from without, assisted by foreign arms on a grand scale.

[24] *Op. cit.*, p. 80.
[25] See Arrighi and Saul, *loc. cit.*, pp. 149–51.

Already the threat is near enough to make some far-sighted westerners lament their governments' failure to offer Africa any alternative.[26]

Western progressives ought to be able to profit by this impending crisis to put much heavier pressure on these governments. Here would be a specimen of the only kind of collaboration now practicable between them and the 'East'— activity parallel but separate, uncoordinated, and perhaps the more effective for being so. Given a spreading sense of urgency, behaviour such as the sending of English cricket teams to South Africa, which give aid and comfort to the white diehards there, would come to be recognized as not merely callous or frivolous, but in the fullest sense criminal. We live in a world where sport is an important matter, and an initiative like that of the American Negro athletes in threatening to boycott competitions where British athletes appear, so long as they refuse to boycott South Africa, may lead quite far. In much wider ways, participation in these issues might have a significance for American Negroes in their own struggle, and be a fresh basis for cooperation between them and white liberals, which both may find easier at present abroad than at home. Brazil, under any less reactionary government than it has now, could be expected to take a hand in southern African affairs. India has a minority of its own in South Africa; and having entered various corners of the continent in former times as Britain's jackal, it owes Africa something, as some Indians are aware.

Even without race war as a tonic, it is open to us to take a less pessimistic view of possibilities of progress in the middle Africa between north and south. 'Everything of importance in Africa has changed', Davidson wrote not long ago, '. . . so far that everything now seems possible where little or nothing seemed possible before.'[27] In his more hopeful picture of the scene a ferment of ideas, a crescendo of discussion not only among the literate but in village and marketplace, takes a prominent place. This is a phenomenon of our modern world, where ideas can travel at a hundred times their former speed, like bullets outstripping arrows, and can overflow from one material level

[26] E.g. P. Keatley, in the last of the articles cited above, 21 July, 1969.
[27] *Which Way Africa?* p. 11.

to another. Labourers in Andalusia learn from the cinema to envy Americans with refrigerators, and to feel that they ought to have better wages, and if these are not forthcoming may go and work abroad, leaving their masters to get on without them. Educated Russians before the Revolution used to suffer from the contrast between their country and Europe, the sensation of being, or being thought by others, a 'dark people'. In our day awareness of such contrasts can spread far down.

Cabral is evidently interested in Marxist theory as well as practice, and one of his observations is that if we think of history in terms of class conflict, many parts of Africa must be said to have no history. He suggests that the driving force there, but not only there, has been 'the level of productive forces at any given place and time.'[28] It is a suggestion that calls for further elaboration. But, looking from Africa's present to its past, we can find many evidences of how lofty a superstructure of social organization or cultural achievement may rise upon a scanty material base. Davidson has remarked on its elevated philo-sophical-religious conceptions,[29] such as ancient India too produced out of very simple materials. Or one may recall the high praise bestowed by a contemporary European expert on the Zulu military organization, even though 'the Zulu weapons were those of savages'.[30] But if old Africa had a history with only an invertebrate class structure, new Africa may make history likewise. Decaying ideas have often kept their hold for ages after losing any real validity; what Mao and his revolution have shown is that, conversely, progressive ideas can take hold of men's minds even before the material situation is ripe for them. In Africa there should be fewer barriers to overcome, in the absence of rigid ideologies such as highly organized religions represent, and the complex social structures that have grown up with them, rather than give birth to them.

Clearly however the obstacles are many and great. One is that most of the mass media in the 'third world' are controlled

[28] *The Liberation of Guiné*, pp. 75–6.
[29] *Which Way Africa?* pp. 77–80.
[30] Col. C. E. Callwell, *Small Wars. Their Principles and Practice* (3rd edn., War Office, London, 1906), p. 30. Empire-builders were studying guerrilla warfare, and how to counter it, long before anyone on the other side did so. Engels, the military expert of Marxism, had thought of well-drilled regular armies as the only useful forces.

by anti-progressive interests, native or foreign.[31] Hence
Guiné's demonstration of how Marxism can lend guidance to
elemental discontents may have a significance far wider than
its own borders. As Davidson says, nearly all progressive movements nowadays in backward regions (or movements that want
to be thought progressive) label themselves 'Marxist', but their
Marxism acquires vitality only to the degree to which it can
adapt itself to new conditions and grapple with new problems.
In Guiné there has been a reshuffling of orthodox conceptions
of the classes and their rôles, with increased emphasis on those
that are, more than others, the bearers and propagators of
ideas. The party has owed much to what it calls a 'petty-
bourgeoisie' of literate, declassed individuals,[32]—precisely those
whom Marxism has been too apt to belittle, as 'waverers', by
contrast with the solid proletariat.

This party is well aware that peasants do not go to war for
the sake of ideas in any abstract sense. But the word *idea* has
manifold meanings; and the methods learned in Guiné of
arousing mass feeling, bringing it to consciousness, through
intensive village discussion and the forming of firm local
groups, ought to be more readily applicable to the politics of
reform and progress than to insurrection. It may be doubted
whether in the vast area of Africa already independent, insurrection can be the normal remedy for unsatisfactory
government. Single-minded Maoists sometimes appear to see
it as the cure for every political ailment, much as the old
Spanish doctor in *Gil Blas* treated every bodily ailment with
bleeding and hot water; or to welcome any and every breakdown of government, as giving socialist forces a chance to
seize power. But too frequent internal conflict would give the
world, and Africa itself, an image of Africa as incapable of
orderly self-rule. The troubles in Chad, leading to French
intervention, in 1969 are an example. Something similar might
be said of the problem of getting rid of an entrenched Communist bureaucracy without shaking things to pieces. In
Africa, where existing régimes are less deeply entrenched, it
may prove easier to get rid of unsatisfactory ones, by means of
new-style political parties with, as in Guiné, realistic pro-

[31] Woddis, *op. cit.*, p. 83.
[32] *The Liberation of Guiné*, pp. 32–3, 48–52.

grammes and close-knit local organizations. They are needed equally as props to progressive governments. For want of such a party to support him—and to criticize him—Nkrumah fell. The T.A.N.U. party in Tanzania may be learning to fulfil the need.

Maoism is biassed towards the same belief in an inevitably *increasing misery* of the world's peasants, as older Marxism had in that of the proletariat. One may tentatively ask whether the new belief may not in the long run prove as fallible as the old one has done; or whether, in areas where misery does increase, it may not be chiefly due to population increasing. It has often been a conservative subterfuge to say that peasants like India's are poor because they are foolish enough to have too many children; still, even Communist China has reluctantly had to recognize the force of the argument. Many conservative governments can now claim to be doing their best, by spreading birth-control, to rescue the poor from their own folly; whereas in past times ruling groups and their ideologists—Hindu, Confucian, and so on—recklessly egged the poor on to increase and multiply, and so supply the rich with cheap labour. Governments are not unaware that unchecked population growth can be a menace to order, largely because it leads to a drift from the countryside to the towns and the piling up there of a pauperized class difficult to control—though also difficult for any opposition to organize. This has been happening on a massive scale in South America, and tilting the ratio of numbers against the peasantry to an extent that casts one more doubt on the possibility of a seizure of power by a peasant movement alone.

With regard to poverty caused by exploitation, classes whose wealth is drawn increasingly from industrial investment may scarcely need to squeeze agricultural producers more than now, or as much as now. Old-time governments in Asia all rested primarily on land-tax, but this has been coming to represent, in India for instance, a diminishing section of a revenue drawn from diverse sources. Important groups still depend on owning land and squeezing peasants, and it is these groups that have done most to cause agrarian unrest in Asia and Latin America. But nowadays even landlords, of the brighter or bigger sort, are feeling the superior attractions of commercial investment, and governments like those of Pakistan or Iran have been helping to shepherd them away from share-cropping into stocks and shares. Even the Ranas and princes of Nepal have lately been bought out of their feudal estates, and are running luxury hotels in Katmandu for American tourists.[33] Foreign investment is largely relied on in these cases to get industry going. Paradoxically, a socialist régime trying to build industry quickly out of its own resources might have more need to squeeze its peasants, as happened in Russia, by way of primary accumulation. This would be unavoidable if there were a landslide to socialism over a large part of the 'third world', since it would be beyond the economic resources of the Communist countries to give adequate aid.

As for imperialism, it too, with efficient food production at home and synthetic substitutes for various raw materials, may have only a dwindling need to exploit backward villagers, to wring from the hard hands of peasants their vile trash. Politically, it has had plenty of time in places like Vietnam to discover what dubious allies feudal landlords make. In Japan the American occupation carried out from special motives a land reform, non-socialist but far from meaningless; it appears that something on the same lines may have been done in Taiwan. Modern capitalism has been learning to make life acceptable to its industrial workers and also to its own farmers; it may learn as time goes on to make life bearable for cultivators of the backlands as well, by promoting reformist measures, and selling or giving them the benefits of its formidable agricultural science, or by simply leaving them alone. For ideology, accompanied by welfare services, it can offer Christianity, as an army of American missionaries in Africa are doing.

Altogether, a competition has begun, and will spread further and further in the 'third world', for the peasant's allegiance. We have often heard of the 'two souls' of the peasantry, with its pre-bourgeois instincts of private property mixed in varying proportions with instincts of mutual aid and solidarity. This duality (which it shares with other groups of pre-industrial origin, notably youth) makes it a class that can be steered in

[33] I owe this information to my friend Dr Harka B. Gurung, a member of the National Planning Commission of Nepal.

either direction. Socialism can steer it, but to do so needs clearer thinking than it has often shown, about what the peasant wants, and what a socialist society wants from the peasant.

For both capitalism and socialism there is what may be called a maximal programme for the land, and also a range of compromise settlements where the two are less far apart. For capitalism the maximal programme is a fully capitalist agriculture. It was carried out only in a single country, the pioneer, Britain.[34] In later cases capitalism, recognizing it to be politically risky and economically not essential, was content in general to leave the cultivator with his own farm—or even give him one—while quietly using the mechanism of the market to make it a fief or appendage of big business. This strategy, which has a clear resemblance to the later one of neo-colonialism, may be said to have started in 1789. The French bourgeoisie then made use of the peasant as an auxiliary, promising him his land free from feudal exactions, with the tacit design of subsequently depriving him of it and turning him into a wage-labourer. But he proved so recalcitrant that this design was quickly dropped; the peasantry, or a great many peasants, were left with their holdings. Satisfied, though mostly still very poor, they turned abruptly into safe conservatives, clinging to patrimonial scraps of land, however harsh the toil or wretched the yield, with a tenacity rooted in old ancestral feeling and in ignorant fear of life anywhere outside the native village.

Socialism has approached peasants with the same ambiguity of purpose. As Che Guevara stressed, they fight in order to get land: he regarded this as the mainspring of 'third world' revolutionism.[35] (Yet the Bolivia that he chose to fight in was one of the few Latin American countries where a substantial land reform had already taken place.[36]) Having been aroused by this bait, they are then to be guided towards something

[34] The uniqueness of English capitalist farming is well brought out in 'Primitive Accumulation and Early Industrialization in Britain', by J. Saville, in *Socialist Register*, 1969.

[35] *Op. cit.*, p. 16, etc.

[36] As Guevara himself observed: *ibid.*, p. 130. See also on this A. Hennessy, 'Latin America', in *Populism*, ed. G. Ionescu and E. Gellner (London, 1969), p. 46. The whole essay is illuminating, e.g. on the Populist tendency to idealize the peasantry, as Maoism too has done.

quite different. Mao's revolution was, from this point of view, a gigantic feat of sleight of hand. With socialism the 'maximal programme' for agriculture is full collectivization. This again was applied in the pioneer country, Russia; unlike the capitalist model it has been repeated in others. Everywhere it has had some unfortunate consequences. In terms of production it has shown (in Europe, if not in China) only mediocre results, whereas capitalist farming in Britain has been progressive at least technically, though socially the reverse. In political terms, to collectivize a peasant requires about as severe pressure as to reduce him to a wage-labourer; either must rest for a long time on coercion, and rule out government by consent. Between cultivator and soil there is an altogether different relationship, psychologically if not economically, from that between worker and machine. One benefit that Maoism counts on from armed struggle in the countryside is that it will generate sufficient heat to fuse the stubborn individualism of the peasant into the mould of collectivism. But if twenty years of revolutionary war in Vietnam have not done this, nothing will. And it seems they have not done so completely. Resentment at forced collectivization caused a crisis in 1956; in 1969 the Party chiefs were debating once more whether socialism could survive if full collectivization was not restored, in place of the actual system of cooperatives.[37]

The argument of the extremists or maximalists presupposes that so long as the peasant is left with any vestige of his two souls, the egotistic one that affiliates him to capitalism will inevitably triumph over the good one that relates him to socialism. This means in effect that he can only be tricked or bullied into socialism; which in turn might be said to make nonsense of the whole idea of peasant revolution. But the assumption is surely too gloomy. Individualism is not identical with capitalism, whether in a cultivator or in an intellectual. In fact it has impelled the peasantry in western countries to strive, with more success than most groups of small producers or small businessmen, *against* capitalism—that is, against being steam-rollered by big business. The modern peasant, evolving into the farmer, grows aware of how he has been daily, invisibly, robbed by the market (as the undeveloped countries

[37] See articles by V. Zorza in *Guardian*, 10–11 September, 1969.

also are), and learns to protect himself and secure a share of the wealth that either capitalist or socialist industry can provide. He protects himself by organizing, as the workman does with his trade union, and by cooperative methods, or marketing and so on. How much real independence he can keep or win depends largely on his energy and his willingness to combine with his neighbours; much as an undeveloped country's freedom from neo-colonialism depends on its own determination to be free.

Of course the cultivator must be infected to a great extent by the mentality of a capitalist society round him. But he should be equally open to the influence of a socialist society, through education and diffusion of ideas, if it too is content with partial or indirect control over the land. Between the two systems there stretches a continuous band of possible forms, with greater or less emphasis on cooperation. Africa has often been thought of as ready to step straight into agrarian socialism. It would not be safe to trust too much to this; for if Africa has really been changing rapidly, whatever there was of primitive communism must also have changed, and may have become—as some tell us—a thing of the past.[38] Nonetheless it is reasonable to expect there and in other parts of the 'third world' a less rigidly individualistic temper than some European cultivators long since acquired, and fuller acceptance of cooperation.

Everything in Africa's future, where influences and interventions from outside must count heavily, looks highly speculative. 'The possible permutations and combinations of events and their likely timing are vast in number.'[39] Africa does not stand alone; the whole world outlook appears very obscure,

[38] J. Saul, 'Africa', in *Populism*, p. 146.
[39] Arrighi and Saul, *loc. cit.*, p. 177.

Reference may be made generally to three important works that have appeared since this essay was written: Amilcar Cabral, *Revolution in Guinea. An African People's Struggle* (London, 1969); D. M. Abshire and M. A. Samuels (editors), *Portuguese Africa. A Handbook* (London, 1969); Philip Mason, *Patterns of Dominance* (OUP., 1970).

To these may be added the articles in the *Socialist Register* (ed. R. Miliband and J. Saville) for 1970 by B. Davidson on 'The African Prospect', and by E. J. Hobsbawm on 'Guerillas in Latin America'; and the very interesting work by J. P. Harrison, *The Communists and Chinese Peasant Rebellions. A Study in the Rewriting of Chinese History* (London, 1970).

more than for a long time past, and Marxism, along with all other convictions that have given modern man a sense of being able to forecast and direct his future, has run into more complexities and perplexities than it bargained for. It is gazing into no crystal ball, but a muddy pool. One moral may be that it will be wise for some time to come to content itself with practical experiments here and there, like those of Cuba or Guiné, and not try to magnify any of them into universal programmes of action. In the meantime theory, analysis of past and present societies and their trends, which Marxism has largely neglected, may be able to catch up with experience.

We cannot put off trying to descry at least dimly the long-term prospects that may lie ahead, the lines of possibility of the coming decades. A great deal of active struggling against imperialism in one or other of its shapes remains to be done, and this cannot exclude struggle by force of arms. Acceptance of force as the last resort leaves it to be decided when this last resort has come, or in other words the speed with which action should be embarked on. Marx and Engels fixed their eyes on distant goals, and Lenin turned away from the short-cut tactics of Nihilism to those of gradual, long-term preparation. These men were not in a hurry, because they could think of socialism as bound to come, though not effortlessly, and were joining hands with a class they believed to have a natural, organic affinity with socialism.

Few can now think of anything as so certain to happen, and Maoism cannot think of its chosen ally, the peasantry, as naturally socialist. Consequently it is more apt to think in terms of the tactics of surprise, of forcing gates open by attacking weak points here or there, of gaining power first and talking of socialism afterwards. Some uncomfortable doubts may creep in here about whether socialism is being thought of for the sake of progress, or progress for the sake of socialism; both these ideals must suffer if they are too far detached from each other. Apart from this, it may be the case that the phase of modern history that made socialism through peasant revolution pure and simple a possibility, is a limited phase only, and confined to special areas—just as the period of possible working-class revolution pure and simple was a limited one. It may follow that whatever opportunity there is must be seized while it is still with us; that Maoism is right to advocate audacity, to gamble on any chance, because there may be no other chance. Maoism does not of course admit that the time for peasant revolution may be brief, any more than Leninism recognized that the time for proletarian revolution was brief; but it has often argued as if this fear were in its mind.

For a long time to come there is going to be a capitalist and a socialist camp in the world, and the hopeful eye must search for what benefits can be found in this division. Each must be said to need the stimulus of criticism and rivalry from the other. It may even be that the historical transition away from the worst of our present bad world will be brought about by their competition, more than by either one of them; though the opposite prospect of their rivalry blowing the world to pieces is at least equally obvious. In the undeveloped continents they have a vast field for competition, which may be peaceful or violent. In some areas, beginning with the Middle East, there might even be agreement on cooperation as an alternative to violence, on programmes of joint aid. Togliatti talked of some such possibility at the Italian Party congress in December 1962. It was, needless to say, denounced by the Chinese as a fresh disguise for neo-colonialism—all aid except from China is tainted; and Wall Street would be as prompt to see in it a new communist trick. Yet each camp genuinely believes in the superiority of its own social-economic system, and ought to be prepared to let new countries have the material means to make a choice for themselves, or to work out new amalgams of the two. It is any rate something that progressive opinion in the West might usefully advocate, on the ground that rich countries can grow richer by themselves, but the world can only grow more civilized—whether on a capitalist or a socialist foundation or on both—by moving forward together. Russia and America have not yet been able to agree even on a partnership to explore the moon. But that *may* come, and one kind of partnership *might* lead to the other.

Marx and Engels attached great importance to the solution of national problems like those of Italian or German unification, not because these had anything to do with socialism, but because they had to be got rid of in order to clear the way for socialism. Something like this might be said of many problems of the 'third world' and of the kind of solutions that can be envisaged for them. These will not always, or even often perhaps, be revolutionary. But revolution itself is a word of manifold meanings, as the 'cultural revolution' in China reminds us. Any historical process that rescues the peasant majority of mankind from ignorance and misery will be revolutionary. Its immediate outcome in the 'third world' might be more to the benefit of liberalism than of socialism; in the West too, for wide feeling can only be mobilized against imperialism (as exhibited in Latin America, or southern Africa) if it is shown to be *unnecessary*, and if it is unnecessary its abandonment will not (as Lenin could hope) bring capitalism to the end of its tether. But fresh possibilities will come in sight for socialists. In the backlands they will have more freedom of action, at home they will have helped to discredit capitalism by showing what it has been doing abroad. Both should have a better chance to lead their countries in the direction of a goal deserving the name of socialism, if the magnetic attraction of socialism—both its ideals and its performance—is strong enough. The broader the front of advance, the more likelihood of socialism being established by majority consent instead of by dictation, and growing truly into what the Webbs thought they recognized in Russia thirty years ago, a New Civilization.

5
Marx and India

The life-work of a genius like Marx is always unfinished, and for the most part unplanned, but no philosopher ever gave his system to the world in so unsystematic a fashion as he did. Much of his writing was governed by accidents of the historical tides swirling round him. Even his work on economics was left incomplete; on history and politics the bulk of his ideas are scattered about in his three or four pamphlets on contemporary events, in numberless letters, and most of all in the great mass of articles he wrote, primarily to earn his daily bread, for the *New York Tribune*. Marx complained of 'this wretched paper',[1] though no journal has ever deserved better of posterity, and of the 'very great interruption' to his studies caused by his journalistic work[2]; but if he had not been compelled to undertake it both he and we would have been much the poorer. Each main section arose from happenings somewhere abroad, which stimulated him to explore their historical background. It was for him a means of catching at ideas, indulging his insatiable curiosity, and working off nervous pressures in a flow of satire, wit, eloquence: Marx was one of the great Romantic writers, and a stylist to his finger-tips. For us, it is an immense chaotic contribution to a way of looking at the human universe which had begun taking shape before Marx, and is still taking shape. Only a man so phenomenally endowed could have afforded such magnificent prodigality. But every-

[1] Letter to Engels, 17.12.1858, cited in *Marx on China*, a collection of articles, ed. Dona Torr (London, 1951), p. 66 n.
[2] Preface to *Critique of Political Economy* (1859).

thing here is necessarily hasty, improvised, one-sided; at times the words even have an oddly un-Marxist ring. We know from his other writings how Marx looked at very broad ranges of history, and from his journalism we learn in microscopic detail his reactions to passing events. What we lack is a considered, all-round summing up of things of the middle order of magnitude: the English Civil Wars as a whole, the French Revolution, the Crimean War.

In his early years Marx was occupied with philosophy and the idea of socialism. In 1848 he and Engels wrote the *Communist Manifesto*, and felt that they and their friends were ready for the arena. Revolutions were just about to break out over much of Europe; but they ended in defeat, partial or temporary for the bourgeois liberals, more crushing for their unsolicited ally the working class. Subsequently old autocracies or ruling classes and new bourgeois groups drifted together, and against this combination Marx's hopes of a speedy overthrow of all ruling classes by the proletariat gradually dimmed. We can watch these hopes fixing themselves on upheavals, one after another, further and further away from the Lancashire where the world's biggest concentration of working-class strength lay. In 1854 a revolution in backward Spain fired Marx's mind and set him to studying Spanish history. In the same year the Crimean War started, and Marx caught avidly at the prospect of a serious defeat of the tsarist army that had helped to beat Europe down in 1849. His articles between 1853 and 1856 on the 'Eastern Question' fill a volume of over 600 pages, nearly as big as the first volume of *Capital*.[3]

This war ended in 1856 with tsarism weakened, but not decisively. Before the end of the year, British imperialism embarked on the second Opium War with China, and Marx had some hopes of crisis spreading from the Far East to Western Europe. A year later, Britain faced a more serious crisis, in the form of colonial revolution, or the Indian Mutiny. It was with a note of Isaiah as well as dialectic that Marx contemplated the revolt of the sepoy army. 'There is something in human history like retribution; and it is a rule of historical retribution that its instrument be forged not by the

[3] *The Eastern Question*, ed. Eleanor Marx and E. Aveling (London, 1897).

offended, but by the offender himself'⁴—just as, he may have reflected, capitalism was fated to be overthrown by its own creation the proletariat. But India was reconquered; in 1863 a new Polish rebellion against the Tsar was quelled; the Civil War in the U.S. from 1861 to 1865, presided over by an Abraham Lincoln perpetually afraid of frightening the enemy by showing too much sympathy with Negroes, brought them only a first instalment of freedom.

It was thus Marx's fate to have to put what faith he could, in default of the working-class seizure of power he had dreamed of, in a long series of dubious representatives of progress: a Spanish general, a Light Brigade, an octogenarian Mogul emperor, an American president. While disappointments multiplied, he took refuge in the grand task he had set himself of writing *Capital*, of tracking capitalism to the inmost recesses of its labyrinth. Strong emotional compulsions must have been required to keep him for so many years at his subterranean toil, like Shelley's trolls quaffing quicksilver at their labour—

Pledging the demons of the earthquake, who
Reply to them with lava—.

It was partly the scholar's impulse to sink the mineshaft of knowledge deeper and deeper from a hole in the British Museum reading-room towards the centre of the earth; partly an inveterate search for the only revenge that could be taken on a bourgeoisie equally repulsive in triumph, in England, or in capitulation, in Germany. There was too some lingering of a German academician's over-valuation of pure logical thought and its power to convince. Outside physical science no force of logic can be conclusive; and while learned argument has gone on and on, the plain workman has always known without aid of syllogisms that his employer lives by exploiting him; the Marxian mineshaft has meant little more to him than the Mohorovicic discontinuity.

In addition, the tangible effects and historical meaning whether of capitalism or of feudalism or slavery depend less

---

⁴ Article of 4.9.1857. See the collection of articles and letters by Marx and Engels, under the title *The First Indian War of Independence 1857–1859* (Moscow, 1959), p. 91. This is referred to below as *War of Independence*. Some other articles and letters on India are included in an anthology of Marx and Engels *On Colonialism* (Moscow, 1960).

on the common irreducible quintessence of each than on the range of variations that makes each of them so heterogeneous. For the zoologist, mouse and elephant are both mammalian quadrupeds, but for most purposes their diversities matter more. The mutant forms of capitalism that were taking their rise in Germany and the U.S. were to affect mankind differently in many ways from the earlier British species examined by Marx. His intellectual achievement as an economist was no doubt great; none the less the historian or sociologist may be forgiven for wishing that instead of grappling with other problems only here and there he had made the past and present of human society his chief field. He would then have enriched 'Marxism' with a greater wealth of more fully developed ideas, and have become even more unquestionably for our age what Aristotle was for Dante's, 'the master of them who know'.

Europe's closest neighbour and oldest acquaintance in Asia was Turkey, about which Marx was writing pretty often during the Crimean War years. He was inclined to generalize from Turkey to Islam as a whole, occasionally from Islam to Asia. India was comparatively well-known by the mid-nineteenth century; China far less so, Japan very little.[5] Marx not seldom offers generalizations about Asia that would be more convincing if restricted to India.

He came to be seriously interested in India about 1853; his first articles on it were concerned with the Parliamentary debates of that year on renewal of the East India Company charter. India was much in his mind when in 1857–58, the Mutiny years, he wrote the remarkable manuscript on *Pre-Capitalist Economic Formations*, where he sought tentatively to arrange world history in a series—logical rather than chronological, as his editor E. J. Hobsbawm points out[6]—of modes of production, or states of society, one of them the 'Asiatic'. This manuscript may be regarded as a part of the buried foundations

[5] Marx's notebooks on Indian history have been published in English as *Notes on Indian History (664–1858)* (Moscow, 1960). For a survey of his reading on Asia see E. J. Hobsbawm, Introduction to Marx, *Pre-Capitalist Economic Formations*, trans. J. Cohen (1964), pp. 20 ff. This work is referred to below as *Formations;* references to Hobsbawm are to his Introduction.

[6] *Ibid.*, pp. 19–20.

of *Capital*: Asia therefore as well as Europe made its contribution to the *magnum opus*.

At the outset Marx was disposed to classify Asian society as
one knowing no private property in land, on the hypothesis
(which appealed for obvious reasons to the British conquerors)
that all right to land was vested in the ruler.[7] This conjecture
he coupled with that of a special 'Asiatic State', whose primary
function was to provide for irrigation works on a scale beyond
the resources of private or local enterprise.[8] In point of fact,
water-control would seem to have played a bigger part in
China, where private ownership by peasant and landlord was
well-established, than in India; and in India a bigger part in
the south than in the north where political power always had
its strongest bases. In any case Marx did not speculate much
further about the Asiatic State, which was really not his own
idea but a suggestion borrowed from Engels.[9] Compared with
his solid German friend, Marx was more a citizen of the world,
and less interested by temperament in institutions such as
states and armies. It was the problem of ownership of land that
continued to preoccupy him, though by 1858 he had modified
his first impression. Events of the Mutiny revived controversy
about land-rights in India, and he leaned now towards the
opinion that any traditional ownership of all land by the
sovereign was, as in feudal Europe, no more than a legal fiction;
and that the true owner had been neither ruler nor landlord,
but 'village corporation'.[10]

From now on he was to use the term 'Asiatic' or 'oriental' as
a synonym for *primitive*, for some ancient and unchanging
social organization,[11] without much regard for what kind of
political superstructure this might support. His picture was of
a village whose households owned or occupied their plots by

[7] *On Colonialism*, p. 277. The idea came to him from Bernier, the
seventeenth-century French traveller in India.

[8] *War of Independence*, p. 16.

[9] The passage in Marx's article (n. 8) was taken more or less verbatim
from a letter just received from Engels (text in *On Colonialism*, p. 278).

[10] *War of Independence*, pp. 157–160; cf. *Formations*, p. 70. Modern opinion
broadly is that the village community possessed a territory occupied in
hereditary, unequal holdings by the members. Of actual collective ownership there is no sign; see Irfan Habib, *The Agrarian System of Mughalb
India* (Aligarh, 1963), Chap. V, e.g. pp. 118–19, 123.

[11] Hobsbawm, p. 58.

virtue of their membership of the commune; an entity isolated, self-perpetuating, and self-sufficient because based on a close integration of agriculture with handicrafts, especially weaving. It had to pay a land-tax, by handing over or selling a proportion of its harvest, but inside it a 'natural economy' prevailed, potter and blacksmith and leather-worker receiving their income in the form of a share of the crop.[12] So far, Marx's picture was realistic and valuable. It seems open to the objection that the village was a less homogeneous unit than he sometimes supposed: instead of a simple division of labour it was rather a small collective lordship, a microcosm of feudal India, a 'brotherhood' of land-holding peasants collectively employing a group of menials whose lowly caste sometimes marked them as descendants of an inferior race subjugated in past times. Caste itself implied an elaborate ideology. Again, the manor in Europe was in a great measure self-sufficient, and it too held its land in a semi-communal fashion. If it could evolve or disintegrate, why not the Indian village?

Altogether, Marx's scheme of a Robinson Crusoe village in a changeless countryside, above which dynasties rose and fell unmeaningly and unheeded, appears too stationary. Coherent evolution may have been impeded by too much movement, not too little. Beneath the level of political events can be glimpsed a great deal of restlessness, of tribes or clans moving about, pre-empting untaken territory or ousting occupants, and claiming superiority over weaker neighbours. It seems curious that while Marx repeatedly treats growth of population as the prime mover of, for instance, early Roman history, driving the simple clan community to war in quest of more land and of slaves,[13] he seems to neglect population as a factor in India. In all ages war and famine, besides, uprooted many; and in the final pre-British period Marx may have underestimated the disruptive effect of the eighteenth-century anarchy, even if British writers were apt to make too much of it.

Marx at any rate thought of the net result of the old order as stagnation: Asia had exhausted its capacity for progress. Of even the better features of any such vegetative state of existence Marx was, at this time of his life, intolerant. If he sometimes

---

[12] *War of Independence*, pp. 17–20; the same material reappears in a letter to Engels (*On Colonialism*, pp. 279–281), and in *Capital* (Kerr edn.), Vol. 1, pp. 392–4.   [13] *Formations*, e.g. pp. 92–3.

spoke with esteem of the craftsman's pride in his skilled work,[14] he also condemned the 'contented, slavish relationship' imposed on the craftsman by this very pride: the modern wage-earner, indifferent to his work, is free, though bored.[15] The rights of man included, for Marx, no right to be stupid. A passage on the barbarous torpor of the Indian countryside unites, like all his most dramatic outbursts, passion with acute reasoning: it links the tiny mindless insulated village with, as its opposite pole, the irresponsible Oriental despotism it supported.[16] Elsewhere he notes how the dualism of society was reflected in that of the Hindu religion, and luxury and misery in its medley of 'sensual exuberance' and 'self-torturing asceticism'.[17] Born in a Germany only lately beginning to emerge from two centuries of paralysis, and chafing at all Europe's slowness, he must have felt the vast immobility of Asia as a giant cloud-shadow of Europe's own. Marx's imagery has not been studied as it deserves to be; there might be found in it, as in Shakespeare's, a recurrent association between the bad old world he wanted to sweep away and dirt, stench, impurity. Only through revolution could the working class 'succeed in ridding itself of all the muck of ages'.[18] At times there is only one step between Marx's revulsion from the moral filth of class society and the obsessive longing of Pietist Germany and Bach's music to be liberated or cleansed from sin, to be washed clean in blood.

In Asia the hated Tsar himself could represent progress.[19] A modern Indian, or Uzbeg, reader may feel that Marx did less than justice to some Asian dynasties of bygone days, and their services to the arts, education, commerce. He may feel that Marx's horizon was too Eurocentric; just as within Europe, after the experiences of 1848–49, he seemed to deny any independent future for small nationalities like the Slavs.[20] But his

[14] Hobsbawm, p. 47 n.
[15] Marx and Engels, *The German Ideology*, 1845–6 (English edn. by R. Pascal, London, 1938), p. 47.   [16] *War of Independence*, p. 20.
[17] *Ibid.*, p. 15.   [18] *The German Ideology*, p. 69.
[19] *The Eastern Question*, p. 546. Cf. Engels, 23.5.1851, in Marx-Engels letters ed. Dona Torr, 1934, p. 37. Brian Pearce, who reminds me of this passage, has shown me an exchange of views between himself and Soviet historians in 1955 on their attitude to Russian imperialism in Asia.
[20] *The Eastern Question*, pp. 545 ff.

concern was not with one nation or continent or another, but with the uneven, straggling advance of humanity as a whole. Unlike his shimmeringly idealistic contemporary Mazzini, who had eyes for Europe alone, Marx envisaged a common destiny for West and East. The finest ideals of Greece or Rome, he wrote in an eloquent though unpolished passage in the manuscript of 1857–58, look 'childlike' in their narrow, limited perfection, today when mankind stands on the threshold of full self-realization for every individual.[21] Beside this shining vision of the future, every civilization of the past must pale its ineffectual fires. And if Marx felt little respect for Indian history, he had no contempt for Indians, believing them perfectly able to learn to run their own country, and finding in their character subtlety, courage, 'a certain calm nobility' or gentleness.[22] It was seldom indeed that he paid any such tribute to any Western people.

Britain's conquest of India had a twofold 'mission', destructive and constructive: 'the annihilation of old Asiatic society, and the laying of the material foundations of Western society in Asia'.[23] *Mission* may sound somewhat teleological; and there is an example here of Marx's readiness to jump from India to all Asia. So far there had been chiefly destruction; conquest, brutal and greedy, had made 'a heap of ruins'. British rule had inflicted more hardship on India than any previous domination.[24] Bankruptcy, chronic war, no public works, perversion of taxation and justice, were 'the five points of the East India Charter'.[25] Underlying all this was the subversion of the old village, painful yet necessary for future progress, in two ways: the ruin of hand-weaving by British machine competition, and the alterations in land-tenure. Of these two processes the ruin of handicrafts, though not the first to start, was the more purely destructive. Because it disrupted the village economy and its close-knit combination of agriculture with weaving, it represented 'the only *social* revolution ever heard of in Asia'.[26]

[21] *Formations*, pp. 84–5.
[22] *On Colonialism*, p. 68; *War of Independence*, p. 37.
[23] *Ibid.*, p. 33.   [24] *Ibid.*; cf. p. 15.   [25] *On Colonialism*, p. 57.
[26] *War of Independence*, p. 19. Cf. Rosa Luxemburg, *The Accumulation of Capital* (London edn., 1963), pp. 371 ff., on the disruption of the rural commune in British India and French Algeria.

It was crucial to all Marx's thinking that the new forces of production released by science were, in capitalist hands, for the most part destructive.[27] Machine industry carved out its market by eliminating handicrafts, and having accomplished this in Britain it was drawing the trail of devastation across Europe and Asia. It would be interesting, if it were possible, to determine whether machinery up to a certain date did indeed reduce by this cannibalism, instead of expanding, men's total of consumable wealth. But there is good ground for thinking that Marx overrated the impact of machine competition on handicrafts in India. It was habitual to him, with the impatience of genius, to pull out the thread of history faster than the Three Sisters were spinning it. Even before the unsuccessful revolutions of 1848 he was writing as if the bourgeoisie were already firmly in the saddle in Europe at large.[28] He remembered the blight that had fallen on the handweavers of England, he watched English manufactures creating a 'latent proletariat' in backward Germany,[29] and in his mind's eye, rather than in any statistical mirror, he saw the same process not merely at work, but completed, in India.

How could this have happened 'over the whole surface of Hindustan', as he wrote in 1853—much of it only occupied within the past few years? Marx's own figures seem to contradict him. If Indians were so poor that they could afford to spend no more than ninepence a year each on all British goods,[30] they could be wearing very little of even the cheapest Lancashire cloth. Had they then, profiting by the absence as yet of the British missionary and his wife, all taken to going naked? The 64 million yards of muslin imported into India in 1837[31] would not have given the population of British India one yard each.[32] If 150,000 people at Dacca in east Bengal were supported in 1824 by weaving,[33] their disappearance since

---

[27] E.g. *War of Independence*, p. 38.
[28] *The German Ideology*, e.g. pp. 57, 59.   [29] *Ibid.*, pp. 73–4.
[30] *War of Independence*, p. 30.   [31] *Ibid.*, p. 18.
[32] A *sari* is 5 or 6 yards long. Two Indian friends agree that a family of five today, in modest comfort, would use no less than 80 yards of cloth a year.
[33] As n. 31. V. I. Pavlov, *The Indian Capitalist Class, a historical study* (English edn., Delhi, 1964), p. 120, refers to this passage, but points out that most of Dacca's cloth had gone to the court or army, or been exported. Marx had used the Dacca weavers as an example in his lecture on Free Trade at Brussels, 9.11.1848.

then had no bearing on the fate of the village artisans with whom Marx's argument is concerned: the towns of old India he regarded—too sweepingly, it may be—as only marginal to its economy. Lancashire cloth could only have made its way in coastal areas close to the ports, or where rivers gave admission to bulk commodities. India's extreme dearth of means of transport throughout the first half of the century was itself a dyke against the inundation of manufactures that Marx imagined. In the whole of the south, there was scarcely a road worth the name, even for military purposes, and many districts found it impossible to fetch even salt from the coast.[34] In later years it was reported, very likely with truth, that numbers of weavers and other rural craftsmen—menials, not partners, of the farming fraternity—shook the village dust off their feet, not because they were forced out of work but because railway and other construction jobs offered them a better life.[35] Handicrafts rural or urban have often died out very recently, or are still struggling.[36] At this day in all kinds of places in India and Pakistan the traveller hears of artisans just being overtaken by their slow but relentless pursuer, the machine.[37]

The other force that Marx saw operating on the old village was in his view not less cruel, but less blankly negative, for it was setting up private ownership of land, and this appeared to him in 1853 'the great desideratum of Asiatic society'. It was emerging in two forms, each so far as the masses were concerned 'abominable':[38] the *zemindari* system of big landed estates, and the *ryotwari* under which land-tax was collected from cultivators each treated as individual proprietors, or at least, on the theory of the government being universal landlord, as individual tenants. On this theory the government was free to demand rent as well as tax, and shear them doubly close to the skin.

[34] *First Report . . . [on] Public Works in the Madras Presidency,* in Parliamentary Papers, 1852–53, Vol. LXXIV, p. 181; cf. pp. 7, 284.

[35] L. C. A. Knowles, *The Economic Development of the British Overseas Empire* (London, 1924), p. 289. Cf. pp. 309, 318, on the weavers' resistance to imported cloth.

[36] Statistics have been very imperfect. See S. Kuznets, etc., ed., *Economic Growth: Brazil, India, Japan* (Durham, N.C., 1955), chap. 4: 'Long-Term Trends in Output in India', by D. Thorner.

[37] A friend recalls that a generation ago in his village in Bihar there were a dozen weavers; now there are none.

[38] *War of Independence,* p. 20.

When the issue came up again for debate as a result of the Mutiny, Marx (reluctantly agreeing for once with Bright, though finding fault with his reasoning) wrote of the ryots as suffering from grinding over-taxation.[39] On the big estates, especially in Bengal, the peasantry suffered from rack-renting and sheer robbery.[40] Marx could fittingly describe the zemindar as a caricature of an English landlord, the ryot as a caricature of a French peasant.[41]

What sort of private landowning he thought desirable and feasible is never made clear; presumably, capitalist farming. And if the only way forward for India was indeed, as he assumed, through capitalism, countryside as well as town would have to come under its control; and all the exploitation that was going on under British auspices could be reckoned another part of the necessary price of progress, since it would accumulate capital and drive the peasantry into wage-labour on the land or in industry. The Marx of the 1850s judged any price worth paying to get rid of Asia's senseless torpor, even the brutal surgery of imperialism. In later, less sanguine years, he showed signs of drawing back from this ruthless logic. When he returned to general history after the years of struggle with *Capital*, the great work he lacked energy or confidence in the end to complete,[42] primitive communism engaged his thoughts a good deal. He may have experienced a need of reassurance that man really was socialist by nature, by heredity. His sympathy with the Narodnik dream of a direct transition from *mir* or village community in Russia to socialism can be interpreted, as Hobsbawm suggests, as a shrinking from the price in human suffering implied in any overwhelming of an old rural society by capitalism.[43] The spectacle of India, as well as of Russia, may have influenced him.

From another and less clouded point of view, the constructive mission ascribed to British power by Marx began with the country's political unification. That the old India was incapable of uniting and defending itself was to him self-evident. Its

[39] *Ibid.*, pp. 169–74.
[40] See, e.g. Anon., *The Zemindary Settlement of Bengal* (Calcutta, 1879).
[41] *On Colonialism*, pp. 73–4.
[42] As H. Collins and C. Abramsky observe: *Karl Marx and the British Labour Movement* (London, 1965), pp. 296–8.
[43] Hobsbawm, p. 50.

equilibrium had rested on mutual repulsion of all its parts (one may fancy the Holy Roman Empire floating in his mind), so that it became 'the predestined prey of conquest', and its history if it had any was a history of being overrun. Some foreign rule being at present inescapable, British was better than Persian or Russian, for it rested on a higher level of material achievement than India's, and hence could not be simply engulfed.[44] At the same time Marx equally took it for granted that India was a single country, and potentially a single nation; the more readily—or even uncritically—because for him nations and nationalism were merely parts of history's scaffolding, used and then dismantled. His own native land was awaiting unification; so was Italy, with which he once compared India.[45] Britain was transforming India from a geographical expression into a reality, capable in 1857 of waging its first national struggle.

Thus Marx was prepared to welcome the annexation of Sinde (1843) and conquest of the Punjab (1849),[46] as completing the expansion of British power in India and closing the old gateway of invasion, the north-west frontier. This time it was being bolted and barred against Russia, and even though Marx sometimes derided the Russian menace to India as a bogy,[47] it is hard to believe that his hatred of tsarism did nothing to reconcile him to the presence in India of Russia's grand enemy. The Afghan war of 1841–42 on the contrary he considered 'infamous',[48] the Burmese war of 1852 'senseless'.[49] Burma (but not Afghanistan) lay outside the ancient limits of India, and there was no Russian threat on that side. Nor was there in Oudh, annexed in 1856; and Marx, who ought logically to have welcomed annexation of all surviving principalities inside India, and usually did so, was at some not very useful pains to prove that its seizure was *illegal*.[50] He blamed it and the Afghan affair on the machinations of his *bête noire* Lord Palmerston, whom he persisted in viewing as a Muscovite secret agent and author of practically all evil. Oudh apart,

---

[44] *War of Independence*, pp. 32–3.   [45] *Ibid.*, p. 14.   [46] *Ibid.*, pp. 26–7.
[47] *The Eastern Question*, p. 533.   [48] *Ibid.*, p. 573.
[49] *War of Independence*, p. 31; cf. *On Colonialism*, pp. 70–71.
[50] *War of Independence*, pp. 150–56. Cf. *On Colonialism*, pp. 65, 67, where he reproaches English liberals for regretting the elimination of Indian princes.

Marx found another reason for welcoming the completion of conquest: hitherto the British had been able to divide and rule, to play off one Indian state against another, but now that game had come to an end. He often underestimated the tenacity of religion—one of the great powers of history, its Hapsburg empire so to speak; he did not foresee that the old form of divide and rule would be replaced by a more insidious one, the playing off of Hindu against Muslim.

Having arrived at this point, the constructive mission was about to unfold its next chapter, the economic and social regeneration of India. This would be set in motion by John Bull's own requirements. India had become indispensable as a market, notably for the cotton industry. But a colony ruined by plundering and neglect made a poor customer. Its nine-pence a head spent on British goods was a sorry figure compared with the fourteen shillings a head of the West Indies. Hence the 'industrial interest' in England felt 'the necessity of creating fresh productive powers' in India; of making canals to facilitate the growing of cotton and other commercial crops, and railways to lower the cost of transporting them. In short, the time had come to commence 'the transformation of India into a repro-ductive country'.[51]

Far from looking upon capitalism as beneficial at first, baneful later, Marx thought of it as doing nothing but harm in the first place, at home and abroad, and now at a later stage as preparing to do some good at least abroad. Be that as it may, he certainly explained the whole wrangle over renewal of the East India Company charter in 1853 as a tug-of-war between the 'millocracy' or industrial bourgeoisie and the obstructive 'moneyocracy and oligarchy', or the City and landed gentry.[52] There was doubtless a great deal in this view. It may have left out some factors of a less immediately economic sort. Marx thought of all Britons in the East as so many Clives or free-booters, still greedily cramming their swag into capacious knapsacks. But a gradual change had been stealing over the Company's servants, moulded for a generation now by Evangel-icalism and Utilitarianism and the rest of the ideology that capitalism had acquired since its caveman days, and some of

[51] *War of Independence*, pp. 34–6.
[52] *Ibid.*, pp. 30–31; cf. *On Colonialism*, pp. 24–5.

them were carrying out intentionally, not as mere tools of history, a sort of bourgeois-revolutionary, anti-feudal policy. Like any such large establishment, the administrative corps could not but develop a certain momentum of its own.[53] While there were provinces still to be snapped up, the old predatory habit of advancing the frontier in a vain effort to get rid of financial deficits kept the ascendant; now, newer ideas and men could begin coming to the front. They had on their side the growing interest in technology, stimulated by the advent of the railway age which opened horizons as fascinating as the atomic age a century later. A separate Public Works Department was being organized, to take development out of the palsied hands of the Military Board which had hitherto made nonsense of it. Work started on the Ganges Canal, of which the Roorkee engineering college in 1847 was an outgrowth. Lord Dufferin as governor-general wrote rhapsodically of what railways could mean for India. Here, as much as in the narrow minds and counting-houses of Lancashire, may be recognized the springs of a new programme.

Part of what aroused Marx's interest in India was the outburst of discussion, about the mid-century, on economic development there. Change was very much in the air. Nearly a century after Plassey, the country depicted in the reports and plans of the reformers was amazingly undeveloped; now, ironically just before its past sins of omission and commission were overtaken by the retribution of 1857, British rule was turning over a new leaf. What Marx seems to have been expecting was methodical development of a plantation-economy of the kind the Dutch were to create in Java (though Holland was of course not like Britain an industrial country), supplying cotton and other raw materials, with coal-mines, to fuel locomotives, thrown in. About the coming railways he was as enthusiastic as Dufferin. They would enable food to be moved from surplus to needy provinces, they would make the army more mobile and enable it to be reduced (this has an odd sound, just before the Mutiny). Marx did not count on all this leading to industrialization of India by the British; but he was hopeful of something even better, industrialization by

[53] Marx did stress the power, but only of inertia, of the large India House bureaucracy in London: *On Colonialism*, pp. 62–63.

Indian enterprise. Once railways started, and railway work-shops were set up, in a country endowed with coal and iron, it would be impossible to prevent technology from sprouting further, and industry making its appearance. Indians would be perfectly equal to the technical requirements; they had revealed 'particular aptitude', for example as engineers at the Calcutta mint.[54] And in the long run this, he clearly thought, was what would get India moving once more, and would pave a highway towards both economic and political independence.

Marx's vision, then, was not of an effete Asiatic society changing, adapting itself, evolving into a modern one—as Japan was about to do. He was thinking in catastrophic terms, of a new Deluge followed by the building of a new world. He had full confidence in the ability of Indians to learn, but to learn Western science; he complained of their being supplied with education by the British 'reluctantly and sparingly'.[55] Macaulay's dismissal of Hindu learning, of geography made up of 'seas of treacle and seas of butter',[56] was not much more peremptory. For several decades now Ram Mohun Roy and his followers had been endeavouring to put India's intellectual house in order, while making room in it for Western knowledge. But of this aspect of the 'Bengal renaissance' Marx seems to have had no inkling.

His notion of the Indian slate being wiped clean and promptly covered with fresh writing—

> as if the world were now but to begin,
> Antiquity not known, custom forgot

had too close an affinity with the *tabula rasa* thinking of 1789. Burke had seen one half of the truth when he argued against the National Assembly that men and nations cannot, for good or evil, be so transmogrified. An exile from an abandoned religion and a country not yet united, brooding between the British Museum and Hampstead Heath with only family, Engels, Shakespeare, Cervantes, for constant companions, Marx contemplated his world from above oftener than from within. Bigotries of cult or nationality belonged for him, like dynasties or Horse Guards, to the realm of Maya. In some ways it came more naturally

[54] As n. 51.   [55] *War of Independence*, p. 33.
[56] Minute on Indian Education (1835).

to him to think of society as a machine, in a universe governed by Newton, than as, in Burke's sense, an organism. Bourgeois rule in the West he believed had 'destroyed as far as possible ideology, religion, morality, etc.', or reduced them to 'a palpable lie'.[57] But the past is never mere dead rubble to be carted away; it has living and multiplying cells, among which any potent new contact stimulates reactions. Romanticism, Evangelicalism, were two of the antibodies generated by capitalist industry.

In the *Communist Manifesto* its authors light-heartedly laughed religion out of court, as no longer capable of throwing dust in the workers' eyes. All such abstract, unreal teachings, Marx had written still earlier, had been thrown off, or never seriously embraced by 'the mass of men', and for the proletariat 'nationality is already dead'.[58] In fact, the workers everywhere carried over with them from their past many shreds or habits of feeling, nationalistic in particular, that would gradually enable their rulers to integrate them into a new bourgeois order. There is a close parallel between the way Marx had been thinking of the proletariat in the West and the way he was now thinking of the colonial masses in the East. The Juggernaut of industrial capitalism had rolled over them both. Antiquated habits and the outlook on life that went with them might still linger, but only by inertia, and would vanish with little further delay. Here too Marx was travelling too fast. On the one hand, he was overestimating Britannia's efficacy as a new Kali or goddess of destruction. Grinding taxation was in a measure balanced by cessation of internal strife; the hum of machinery was still faint. On the other hand the subtler influences by which the West today corrodes the mental furnishings of an old society—cinema, radio, gadgetry—were missing. Marx counted on railways and factories to dissolve caste prejudices, 'those decisive impediments to Indian progress',[59] and railways were indeed to be lauded in days to come as bringing an 'electric shock' to India.[60] Even this was a comparatively mild shock; trains could not reach into the recesses of the countryside as the

[57] *The German Ideology*, p. 57.
[58] *Ibid.*, pp. 32, 57; cf. p. 67.
[59] *War of Independence*, p. 36. In 1881 we find him complaining of the railways being 'useless to the Hindus' (*On Colonialism*, p. 304).
[60] Knowles, p. 322.

bus does nowadays. Caste was to wane very slowly, even
sometimes to grow afresh, not only because technology came
slowly but also because in the social dislocations accompanying
it men would cling to whatever forms of mutual aid and comfort they could find shelter in.

Marx was not aware that one effect of the British presence
had been to invigorate a Muslim religious revival which was
one of the powder-trains leading towards the Mutiny. In his
gloomiest mood he would not have guessed that India's march
towards independence would take the form very largely of rival
Hindu and Muslim communal excitement. In his own familiar
Europe, he was painfully conscious at times of the persistence
of archaic ideas. 'The tradition of all the dead generations
weighs like a nightmare on the brain of the living,' he wrote
bitterly in 1852 of the rise to power of Napoleon III.[61] Far away
in Asia things of this type did not force themselves on his
attention in the same way. As a result, in his impatience for the
new broom and the fresh start, he did not see how important it
was that the better, healthier ideas of an old society should be
preserved as binding links between one epoch and another.
Remarkably enough he could find it in his heart to declare that
it would be less damaging to India's self-respect for a worthless
feudal aristocracy to survive than for there to be no class of
eminent Indians at all.[62] But it might even more humiliate and
demoralize India if no Indian ideas were to survive, and all
wisdom to be a foreign gift. When the better side of the past is
written off, the worse is promoted. English rule and English
education meant for India a break, an interruption, that China
and Japan did not undergo; past and present were never
dovetailed as men like Ram Mohun Roy hoped, but lie side by
side today, amid a chaos of castes and railway-carriages, sacred
cows and chemical works, nonsense and sense, more separate
and incongruous than anywhere else in the world.

The proletariat, and now in another sense the colonial
peoples, were the new forces that would liberate mankind
from the series of class societies that had enslaved it, like
Buddha bringing emancipation from the cycle of birth and
death and rebirth. Each seems at times in Marx's conception

[61] *The Eighteenth Brumaire of Louis Bonaparte*, p. 1.
[62] *On Colonialism*, p. 68.

G

to lack inner strength or volition, to be an inert battering-ram for History to knock down the walls of the capitalist Bastille with. Because Marx was in such haste to turn his back on the past he saw his progressive forces, sometimes at any rate, too mechanistically; because of this, in turn, he had to deny his own finer intuitions, to copy Bentham's clockwork psychology and 'springs of action', and to think of working-class and Asia as kept in motion only by the crude pressure of increasing misery.

In 1853 Marx had drawn up an orderly chart of British India, and was looking forward to its regeneration 'at a more or less remote period'.[63] In 1857, the Mutiny broke out. He could be excused for not foreseeing this, because hardly any of those who knew India foresaw it, though there had been many uneasy premonitions. All the same, in some ways the outbreak went against the grain of his preconceived notion of a society paralysed, if not actually pulverized, by the British steamroller. In the political sphere he had written of a 'levelling of all that was great and elevated in the native society',[64] yet the leadership, such as it was, in 1857 was that of princes and aristocrats new or old, under the banner of the descendant of Akbar and Tamberlane—that 'little shrivelled yellow old man' on whom Marx had poured scorn as symbol of the dead past.[65]

Under the surface agitation over things like greased cartridges, Marx discerned significant currents; and it is a notable fact that he viewed the Mutiny as in some sense a 'national' rising. He thus anticipated the present-day Indian view of it as the starting-point of the independence movement. But he laid less stress on this aspect of it than Indian Marxists have sometimes done,[66] and his caution was reasonable; 1857 may be said to have been nationalistic in the same rudimentary way that the Taiping rebellion was socialistic, and the starting-point of the modern Chinese revolution. It was the army alone that Marx recognized as a new, coherent force, 'the first general centre of resistance' of modern India;[67] and this mercenary army was to be quickly reconstructed afterwards,

[63] *War of Independence*, p. 37.   [64] *Ibid.*, p. 33.
[65] *On Colonialism*, pp. 68–9.
[66] See the centenary volume of studies, *Rebellion 1857*, ed. P. C. Joshi (Delhi, 1957).
[67] *War of Independence*, p. 40.

and to serve the British Raj faithfully down to almost the very end. Even at the time, he was struck by the sepoys' lack of solidarity, and ascribed their defeat at Delhi to dissensions between regiments, and between Hindu and Muslim, as well as between the soldiery and the traders whom they looted.[68]

Marx was aware of an agrarian as well as national flavour in the Mutiny, but, again realistically, he did not credit the peasantry with a line of action of its own. In spite of the huge Taiping revolt, it was not to peasant movements that he was looking for progress in Asia, and he did not guess their coming importance. It should be recalled that in western Europe the most active peasant movements of recent times had been of a reactionary clerical-feudal or monarchist complexion, as in the Vendée, Calabria, and Carlist Spain; while in central Europe in 1848–49, though peasants had sometimes risen against feudal burdens, some had been mobilized in the service of Hapsburg reaction. This record must have helped to concentrate Marx's hopes on the new class, the proletariat.

Marx found no time during the rush of events to ponder the fact that the scene of most widespread resistance to the British was the province of Oudh, round Lucknow, which they had only just taken over, and where, under a feeble local monarchy, the *taluqdars* or revenue-collectors had been lately turning themselves into big landlords. These men had no place in Marx's earlier scheme of things, in which all the soil belonged to State or rural commune. Before the end of the conflict he was recognizing them as mushroom feudalists who had risen by encroaching on both the peasantry and the King of Oudh, and who had joined the sepoys out of fear of the British trespassing on their 'rights'. There had been talk of sweeping these usurpers away altogether: it was encouraged by the new reforming mood at Calcutta as well as by desire for more revenue, and Marx felt constrained to admit that the arguments in favour of it were 'very plausible'.[69] He would have been entitled to conclude that Oudh in 1857 bore some resemblance to the Vendée. As to Engels, he was always

[68] *Ibid.*, p. 112.
[69] *Ibid.*, p. 160. See Jagdish Raj, 'Introduction of the Taluqdari System in Oudh', in *Contributions to Indian Economic History*, 1, ed. T. Raychaudhuri (Calcutta, 1960), pp. 46 ff.

inclined to button himself up in his Prussian uniform when he wrote on military matters, but he may only have been saying bluntly what his friend was surmising when he dismissed the resistance in Oudh as 'a miscellaneous rabble, collected by insurgent zemindars'.[70]

Their attention was monopolized by the fighting areas, most of them little touched by modernity, along the Gangetic valley from Delhi to Bihar. About Bengal Marx was curiously silent. Engels remarked disparagingly that 'Bengal proper is easily held, because its people have fallen terribly'.[71] Militarily they had, long before Plassey, and they had been a long time under British rule. But this meant too that there had been time for closer ties to form between some Bengalis and the ruling power, and to enlist their sympathy in 1857 (no doubt with many misgivings) on the British side.[72] Landowners were content, and relied on British protection. Of more moment for the future, here alone was there a numerous intelligentsia—partly of the same social stratum as the landowners—permeated by Western education. It believed far more deeply in Britain's civilizing mission than Marx himself, or most Englishmen, and it was the only class capable of leading India into the modern age as he desired.

In the excitement of the contest an instinctive fellow-feeling with the rebels checked for the time being any sober estimate of what India stood to gain or lose. After it was over, unluckily, he was not at leisure to draw lessons from the Mutiny or decide how it fitted into his previous picture of India. He had an occasion to begin a reconsideration when writing his final Indian article in 1858, about the debate on the India Bill transferring authority from the Company to the Crown. But the dust had not yet settled, and as often he was unable to banish his King Charles's head; he gave too much of his energy to detecting in the Bill another sinister design on the part of that fiend in human shape and mutton-chop whiskers, Lord Palmerston.

It may seem however to follow from the logic of Marx's

[70] *War of Independence*, p. 130. This estimate is in line with that of Jagdish Raj, *op. cit.*, pp. 55–6.

[71] *War of Independence*, p. 203.

[72] See Benoy Ghose, 'The Bengali Intelligentsia and the Revolt', in *Rebellion 1857*, pp. 103 ff.

thinking about India that the Mutiny was a premature explosion of feeling, provoked so far as the masses were concerned by the harshness of British rule, colliding with and frustrating its more beneficial tendencies. If a mode of production and its ruling class cannot be dislodged before they have exhausted whatever development they are capable of,[73] the same may be true of a colonial régime like the British in India. On Marx's analysis its potential development, so far from being exhausted, was only just starting. He was, it may be added, prepared to acknowledge in war, as its 'redeeming feature', the ultimate test of peoples and societies.[74] The Mutiny failed; but it brought about a new alignment in India, not in all ways favourable to progress. After 1848 in Europe, autocracy was obliged to take into partnership the defeated bourgeoisie: conversely after 1857 viceregal autocracy had to take into partnership, as less dangerous than the masses, the defeated feudal interests. The Oudh *taluqdars* in particular were to remain a cancer of India down to the close of the British epoch.

Misgivings about the future he had lately been so hopeful of must have cast shadows across Marx's mind while the news came in during 1857. Quite early in the struggle he saw with foreboding the approach of 'a most terrible tragedy';[75] meaning thereby, perhaps, a contest that, whatever the fortunes of war, India could not win.

Marx's prediction of an industrialized India, and its very lagging fulfilment, has a bearing both on his understanding of India and on his doctrine of how industrial capitalism came into being in its original habitat, England. These themes were in his mind in the same years, and here as in other ways his thoughts about East and West intertwined. He did not enquire why industrial capital had not developed in India spontaneously, and to Asian society as he saw it the question could have little relevance. Yet of the three necessary conditions that he listed in 1857-58—labour made available by detachment of peasants from the soil; specialized craft skills; accumulation of money from trade and usury[76]—the second and third were undeniably present in old India, while as to labour there were

[73] As n. 2.   [74] *The Eastern Question*, p. 576.
[75] *War of Independence*, p. 43.   [76] Hobsbawm, p. 46.

at any rate numerous urban craftsmen, village artisans, and a large vagrant population. Clearly also there was a connexion, of the 'putting-out' type, between merchant capital and handicraft production.[77] We talk of the world market that made Britain's industrial revolution possible, but Indian cloth had something like a world market long before: it sold in Persia, in east Africa, in Indonesia.[78]

Eight or nine years later, when he finished the first volume of *Capital*, Marx had worked out a fuller account of the genesis of capitalism.[79] To have labour available is not the same thing as to know what to do with it. All sixteenth-century Europe teemed with vagabonds—disbanded retainers or dispossessed peasants—, but only Tudor England, with its flogging-and-branding magistrates and its Puritan discipline, kneaded the loose mass into a useful labour force. Marx sometimes seems to run the two stages together causally, as if Ancient Pistol was dismissed and Hodge evicted in order that capitalism might not lack hands. It would be more accurate to say that capitalism was starting in order to cope with a social problem that had arisen independently of it: it was the reaction of a whole society, in other words, rather than the initiative of a single class. Marx never did quite say this, and may have come closer to saying it in his early sketches than in his mature statement.[80] State power continued to be a crucial factor through the Mercantilist period, in France and, more bureaucratically, further east, and again later by fresh methods in Japan and tsarist Russia. Capitalism did not grow, it was made. Only a modern mixture of deception and self-deception allows it to fancy its ancestors a line of sturdy free enterprisers harassed by official meddling like Hitler's generals by their commander-in-chief.

In old India the military-bureaucratic State, alien by origin and always least Indian when most powerful, had no tendency of this kind. It had no interest in the sea, or in naval power to protect and enlarge India's foreign markets. It guaranteed the subsistence of the towns by squeezing food out of the countryside by means of its land-tax, but kept them parasitic on itself:

[77] See e.g. Pavlov, *op. cit.*, chap. 1.
[78] See Bal Krishna, *Commercial Relations between India and England, 1601 to 1757* (London, 1924), chap. 1.
[79] *Capital*, Vol. 1, Part viii.
[80] *The German Ideology*, pp. 50 ff.; *Formations*, pp. 111 ff.

the town was under no compulsion to sell to the village, while
the village, drained by taxation, could not afford to buy from
urban craft industry more than a trickle of things, chiefly silver
ornaments for hoarding. In this situation the business community remained separate from the rest of society; the same
phenomenon that Marx observed in old Europe, where pursuit
of wealth was left to 'a few trading peoples . . . in the pores of
the ancient world like the Jews in medieval society'.[81] Specialized groups—Jain, Marwari, Chetty—were the moneyed men,
or Armenians and other foreigners.[82] It was the same in the
Ottoman empire, and even in China a prevalence of leading
merchants from one or two provinces can be observed.[83]

If Marx tacitly assumed that British enterprise would not
industrialize India, he was to prove quite right, in the face of
what might at the time have seemed reasonable anticipation.
Mills in India would have some patent advantages, and the
country's strangeness and remoteness were not likely to daunt
British businessmen or engineers, who were hurrying on the
industrial revolution all over Europe, and running cotton-mills
from Malaga to St. Petersburg. Dispersal of energy and skilled
man-power over Europe, and then North America, may have
helped to divert attention from India. Pioneering difficulties
might be more daunting to new-fledged Indian businessmen,
and fear after 1857 of another upheaval would discourage
investment by them at least as much as by British capitalists.

Politicians at Westminster, still mostly drawn from the landed
class with its paternalistic attitudes, might be reluctant to see
unemployment increased in Bolton by increased employment
in Bombay. To have this brought about by an opening of
Indian mills, instead of British, would be still more objectionable. Cotton textiles were the obvious thing for India to begin
industrialization with, as Britain had done; Lancashire's
reluctance to be supplanted in the Indian market was the most
tangible obstacle in the way.

[81] *Formations*, p. 84; there is a similar phrase in *Capital*, Vol. 1, p. 91, and
again in Vol. III, p. 388.
[82] See the early chapters of L. C. Jain, *Indigenous Banking in India* (London,
1926).
[83] See a valuable discussion of the failure of true capitalism to emerge in
old China, in L. Dermigny, *La Chine et l'Occident. Le commerce à Canton au
xviii*e *siècle, 1719-1833* (Paris, 1964), pp. 58 ff., 321 ff., 817 ff., 1,434 ff.

Marx could argue that India would be starting from the level of the locomotive instead of the spinning-jenny; industrial technology once in being, new countries could adopt it ready-made. He was studying Spain, where liberals after the revolution of 1854 were hopefully expecting their country to be hauled non-stop into the future by steam traction;[84] and he may have transferred some of this hopefulness to India. Both he and the Spaniards were crediting railways with a bigger horse-power than they really possessed. In 1857 Engels wrote an article on the theme of how a genuine modern army must be a slow growth in any Asiatic country, demanding moral equipment as well as uniforms and rifles.[85] Marx might have been expected to reckon similarly with the manifold social, cultural, psychological adjustments necessary for a real transition to industrial society.

The prime requisite for industrialism was a corps of industrialists. Marx seemed to take it for granted. By defeating the military powers of India—Muslim, Maratha, Sikh—Britain had, it is true, cleared the way for commercial elements to come to the front. But for the traditional money-spinning groups, Jain and Marwari and so on, this only meant a return, after an interval of disorder, to business as usual, the old grooves of speculation. They had been used ever since the Muslim conquest of India, or from earlier still, to living as camp-followers of an alien government, keeping in the background, practising esoteric arts by which they could become opulent, though never secure. Banking in their hands continued in British times to be not much more than money-lending.[86] The Parsees who flocked into Bombay were exceptional. Still only half-Indian after a thousand years in India, these descendants of refugees from Persia had not previously been a specialized business group, and now, as if wakened by the British touch from a refreshing slumber of centuries, they showed extraordinary readiness for experiment. They followed the British into the opium trade with China as adventurously as Bengalis followed them into English literature and political theory, and

[84] V. G. Kiernan, *The Revolution of 1854 in Spanish History* (London, 1966), pp. 154, 195.

[85] In *Marx on China*, pp. 45 ff. As with India, some other articles and letters on China are to be found in *On Colonialism*.

[86] Jain, *op. cit.*, p. 185.

eventually it was a Parsee firm that founded Indian steel. But the more westernized they grew, the less Indian they were.

The more truly Indian and hidebound had as a rule mediocre success when they ventured out of old lanes, starting tea-plantations or coal-mines for instance in the wake of the British. Emancipation from the past proceeded much more slowly than Marx expected. Religion of a specific minority type had been one ingredient in the crucible where Western capitalism was first formed; in India religion and the social habits that went with it were, as Catholicism had been in Europe, a dead weight on change, an incubus from which China and Japan were comparatively free. An analogous question arises in the same epoch in Ireland, where the Protestant trader often seemed able to thrive under the same conditions as the Catholic who could only sigh and blame the government.

Meanwhile, industrialization in Japan and Germany (as in socialist Russia and China in later years) was being accelerated by a strong national afflatus, an impulse to make up for lost time, to cast off the reproach of barbarous backwardness—of being 'a dark people', as Russians used to call themselves. A genuine entrepreneur cannot, any more than a statesman, be reared on narrow self-regarding calculations alone. He too is a social animal; he needs a fostering climate, the oxygen of public approval; he must have his admiring audience, like an actor or artist. Absurd as the modern company-director's cant of 'service' often sounds, a historical reality underlies it. Urges and incitements from his environment are as much required to make a man toil at building a factory as at building a pyramid, a party, or a Grand Army.

Since there was no Indian State, there was no tariff policy to protect Indian industry.[87] Several independent countries shared the same disability. Turkey was shackled by the Capitulations, and Japan had a long struggle to throw off the 'Unequal Treaties' imposed on it in its days of weakness. Japan made headway in spite of the handicap. For one thing, it could indulge in imperialistic forays abroad which, profitable or not, helped to draw the jarring classes together. Indian soldiers fought abroad far oftener, up and down Asia and Africa, but

[87] See R. Dutt, *The Economic History of India in the Victorian Age* (7th edn., London, 1950), chap. xii, 'History of Tariffs'.

the glow and glory were Britain's, India only paid the bill. Unlike India, Japan enjoyed political autonomy: unlike Turkey it had a ruling class bent on industrialization, both for public and for private advantage, and an active merchantry, with a long and close connexion with the ruling class, and Japanese in a sense in which no comparable group was either Turkish or Indian. And far more than either of the others, Japan was already a nation. Here again the national State appears as the parent or guardian of capitalism, its creator much more than its creation.

One other area where these factors counted was that of labour recruitment and discipline. Marx leaves it to be supposed that he thought the disintegration of the village commune would release the necessary labour. But surplus labour-power might easily form a stagnant pool in the countryside instead of flowing to distant mills. For construction work on roads and railways, local resources usually sufficed; for one purpose vital to British investment, manning the Assam tea-plantations, a new labour force had to be got together by hook or by crook. Here the State power was fully exercised, and helped the planters to construct an elaborate recruiting organization with agencies all over India, drawing to a considerable extent on the aboriginal tribal reservoir; it also enabled them, especially in the earlier decades, to treat their coolies virtually as serfs.[88] Mining was unimportant from the British point of view, so no such effort was applied to recruiting miners,[89] or would have been made in favour of any primarily Indian industry. In Japan regimentation of labour was comprehensive; employers backed by law and police could shut up workers from the villages, many of them women, in company barracks, and at the same time indoctrinate them with willingness to work for company and fatherland.

Bengal, whose first generation of technicians had caught Marx's eye, kept the lead intellectually, but showed small taste for industry. It might have been different if British capital had been setting a more spirited pace, or even if British capitalism had been more dynamic at home, and Oxford and

[88] On the early stages see W. N. Lees, *Tea Cultivation . . . in India* (London, 1863).
[89] See e.g. G. M. Broughton, *Labour in Indian Industries* (London, 1924), p. 75.

Cambridge had fed Indian students on applied science instead of Cicero. It would be interesting to know how an India run by Germans or Yankees would have turned out, and some computer may one day tell us. As things were, other openings had superior attractions for educated Bengalis. Their province, which had been racked to pay for Britain's conquest of the rest of India, was now getting something in return, in the form of a junior partnership; whatever government posts were not monopolized by Britons were likely to go to them. Britain, like the Bourbon monarchy, allowed the middle-class man to buy his way into its service, or if not his own way, then his son's, by investing his savings in the young man's education. Other savings must have gone on being drawn into government loans, as those of the old French rentier were.

Worst of all, a vast deal of money that might have fermented into industrial capital was sucked into the land, like a river of central Asia seeping away among desert sands. The estates erected by the British in Bengal were being let and sub-let and sub-let again by their owners; the failure of British-sponsored landlordism to evolve into rational agrarian capitalism, as expected by the makers of the Permanent Settlement, fore-shadowed the failure of industrial capitalism to spring up, as expected by Marx. Not only the right kind of landlord, but the right kind of man to serve as wage-paying farmer, was missing in the countryside, as the entrepreneur was missing in the towns. There was the same story, the same clinging to habits of usury and extortion and absenteeism, in the Spanish countryside, where the selling off (to itself) by the Liberal bourgeoisie of Church estates and village commons had results parallel with those of the *zemindari* system in Bengal. Marx might have been forewarned by Spanish experience ever since 1833 that a half-baked middle class in a backward country will not put its money into industry so long as it remains free to buy land and rack-rent tenants.

The longer industry hung fire, the more problematical it became, because technology was growing more complex and costly. Japan had started just in time. By 1914 India was the world's fourth biggest manufacturer of cotton textiles, and mining and heavy industry had made a start, but this meant little when set beside the huge and increasing population. In

1928 the Comintern in its colonial thesis was proposing to miss out the stage of capitalism in such lagging areas, by dint of an alliance of progressive forces there and socialist parties in the metropolitan countries. Independence when it came at last in 1947 brought to power in India a bourgeoisie still, like that of Spain, bearing strong marks of its past.[90] The pace of industrialization became more brisk, but only as a trot is brisker than a walk; the 'private sector' of industry was to devote less energy to expansion than to preventing the 'public sector' from expanding.

Marx had no time to speculate about how Indian capitalism would behave, or how it would benefit the Indian masses; possibly also no inclination, from an unconscious desire to get technology in India without paying the price in capitalist misery. The nobility or gentleness he found in the Indian character had no place among the satanic virtues he held to be the stamp of a successful bourgeoisie. In one enigmatic allusion, he wrote that the new technology would do the Indian people no good until India became independent, or Britain socialist.[91] What a socialist Britain should do with India, he did not specify; why capitalism should be any less villainous in an independent India than in independent Britain or France, he did not explain. If he really expected it to be less villainous, he was sadly astray.

It would not be easy to extract from Marx's comments on India a socialist doctrine on imperialism. Clearly they do not point towards Hobson's idea of Britain evolving into a 'rentier-State', living off the profits of colonial factories and workers;[92] nor towards the theory of 'decolonization' discussed among Marxists in the 1920's, although they might be said to look forward to the same result by a different route. Marx's silences are at times as striking as his utterances. There is copious detail on New Zealand, nothing on India, in the final section of Volume 1 of *Capital*, 'The Modern Theory of Colonization'. It was the nature of the capitalist relationship that he was concerned to elucidate here. But his analysis of capitalism in

[90] See e.g. V. Anstey, *The Economic Development of India* (4th edn., London, 1952), Introd., and pp. 272 ff.
[91] *War of Independence*, p. 37.
[92] J. A. Hobson, *Imperialism* (London, 1902), part II, chap. V, section IV.

Britain might seem to stand in need of further consideration of the colonial empire and its contribution, clearer light on his epigram that 'to be free at home, John Bull must enslave abroad'.[93]

In a less explicit yet deeper fashion, India's fate may have helped to mould Marx's philosophy of capitalism. A ruling class often recapitulates in its colonies the more lurid episodes of its early career. The suppression of peasant or tribal revolts in Bengal had something in common with the suppression of peasant revolts in Tudor England, likewise with the aid of foreign mercenary troops; the mass executions after the Mutiny were akin to the Cromwellian reprisals after the Irish Rebellion. The spectacle of Western capitalism in Asia, red in tooth and claw, must have helped to inspire in Marx a conviction of the absolute, incorrigible badness of capitalism altogether. One of his articles has a peroration on 'The profound hypocrisy and inherent barbarism of bourgeois civilization', displayed more nakedly in colonies than at home. Imperial exploitation writes large, he declared, 'the inherent organic laws of political economy now at work'.[94] His mind may have been working from imperialism to these laws, as well as outwards from economics to empire. Emotionally at any rate, British India supplied him with a magnified illustration of man's inhumanity to man in class society. Increasing misery there may have helped to convince him that the masses at home too were doomed irrevocably under capitalism to grow poorer. To suggest this is to attribute to Marx some thinking of a not exclusively logical character; but this great thinker did not always, as Nietzsche advises philosophers to do, keep his thoughts on ice.

How much of a motive Lancashire's voracious need of markets supplied for the continuing subjugation of India in the first half of the nineteenth century, is a question Marx does not clearly pose. It would be about as easy or as hard to prove that Napoleon conquered Europe to oblige the French manufacturers (a proposition Marx would certainly not always have endorsed[95]). The disorder prevailing before the arrival of

93 *On Colonialism*, p. 202.
94 *War of Independence*, pp. 37–8.
95 See Marx and Engels, *The Holy Family* (1844; English edn., Moscow, 1956), pp. 166–7.

the Union Jack can scarcely, it might be thought, have hindered reception of British goods more than the absence of roads which the EIC did so little to remedy. John Bull looked on at the process of conquest complacently. From time to time he was called on to pay some expenses, but that could be treated as part of the national pastime of beating the French, or the Russians, and patriotic pride was already to him what family pride was to Pooh-Bah. As a rule the campaigns were self-sustaining; they were paid for by Indian peasants, or loans from Indian financiers, and most of the casualties were borne by sepoys, who could well be spared, or by Irishmen, Highlanders, and younger sons, who would never be missed.

Of more practical significance for the time when Marx was writing is the question whether India, if it had ever been necessary to Britain economically, was still a necessity, or only a luxury. Marx gives no categoric answer, such as Adam Smith had given to the same kind of question, but Smith's conclusions were of a piece with his more tentative ones; there is often a straight line between Marxism and the early, ingenuous phase of bourgeois economics. 'Dreadful misfortunes' were what Smith, as much as Marx, saw as the result of contact with Europe for the native peoples of Asia and the Americas.[96] He was arguing chiefly from the case of the North American colonies then just breaking into revolt, as Marx was concerned chiefly with the Indian Mutiny. Smith argued that Britain's foreign trade pattern had been distorted by the selfish interests of groups of traders, to whom the wider interests of Britain as well as of the colonies were sacrificed.[97] Several scattered observations by Marx are in the same vein, and suggest that he was willing to think of imperialism as a morbid excrescence on capitalism rather than (as Lenin—of course at a later stage—considered it) an integral, inescapable part of capitalism.

Marx was impressed from the first by India's precarious finances, its deficits only bridged by the opium profits from China. When the Mutiny came he was convinced, a trifle hastily it may be, that all the immense cost of its suppression would have to be met by the British taxpayer.[98] He noted with

[96] *The Wealth of Nations* (1776; World's Classic edn., 1904), Vol. 2, p. 236.
[97] *Ibid.*, pp. 184–5, 202–5.
[98] *War of Independence*, pp. 31, 47.

gloomy relish that Indian bankers would lend no more to the Company (they were also extremely reluctant to lend to the rebels[99]), and that loans were having to be floated in London, which would be the starting-point of a heavy 'Anglo-Indian Home Debt'.[100] It might have struck him that this would create a fresh vested interest in favour of India being held on to. For the British public, however, it seemed quite clear to him now that India was a dead loss. Moreover it was dragging Britain into expensive quarrels with neighbouring countries. Who then gained? Marx reckoned some 10,000 officials or officers—about 6,000 planters or men of affairs in India—pensioners—and EIC stockholders drawing a guaranteed $10\frac{1}{2}$ per cent profit.[101] He found room too for the English aristocracy, who kept British India involved in wars 'in order to find employment for their younger sons'.[102] As to Lancashire, its Indian market was costing John Bull 'a damned high price'.[103] 'India is now our best ally', he could even write to Engels—not thinking of the Indian masses as an ally of the working-class at home, but of the Indian empire as a millstone round the neck of the bourgeoisie.[104]

Vested interests, Adam Smith complained, conjured up a myth of America's indispensability to England.[105] The fiction that loss of control of America must mean irretrievable ruin for the British people had quickly turned out, in the light of experience, to be the merest moonshine; but the habit of living on a myth is not easily shaken off, and the blank space left in popular emotion was soon filled by India. In point of fact, the U.S. Civil War was to reveal that the cotton industry had made Britain perilously dependent, not on India, but on America. Many countries offered markets, one country alone an adequate supply of raw cotton. But the lesson was a few years too late. The Mutiny had come to the help of the vested interests, by plunging the whole question in hysteria. If taxpayers had begun to ask themselves, like Marx, what they were getting out of

[99] N. K. Nigam, *Delhi in 1857* (Delhi, 1957), pp. 82, 95.
[100] *War of Independence*, pp. 124 ff.; *On Colonialism*, pp. 145–8.
[101] *War of Independence*, pp. 86–90.
[102] *On Colonialism*, pp. 63, 70.
[103] *War of Independence*, p. 209 (9.4.1859).
[104] *Ibid.*, p. 208 (14.1.1858).
[105] Vol. 2, pp. 210–11.

India, the passions now let loose, the tales of sepoy atrocities, the murders of English women, the frenzied howls for revenge, put an abrupt end to any cool discussion for many decades to come. From now on, holding India at all costs was a national dogma, subject to as little rational scrutiny as the annual liquefaction of St Januarius's blood at Naples. Unluckily, the Mutiny came just after the Crimean War had whipped up jingo excitement, and it coincided with wars with Persia and China; these made India necessary at least as Britain's base of operations in Asia, and as the bulwark of British prestige without which John Bull's customers everywhere would no doubt throw his piece-goods back in his face.

Carrying Marx's train of thought a step further, one might conjecture that possession of India and similar captive markets was for Lancashire more and more a superfluity, a feather-bedding; and that this retarded the flow of capital and invention into newer, more advanced industries, such as Germany was soon developing, and thus held Britain back at a less advanced technological stage. Venturing one step further still, one might conjecture that all the later stampede of colony-grabbing up to 1914, for which the Indian empire supplied the malign model to Britain and its rivals alike, was a fit of atavism rather than a logical dictate of the pure thing-in-itself of capitalism.

What might prove less difficult to demonstrate is that some sparks from the explosion of 1857 fell into a magazine of patriotic powder in Britain, whose existence in the working-class as well as middle-class consciousness Marx had not suspected; and that the lingering spirit of Chartism, if it had not been put to flight by the charge of the Light Brigade, was finally routed now. In that case, instead of the bourgeoisie being weakened by any drain of Indian costs, it was being greatly strengthened, and the way prepared for class collabor-ation all round. The half-truth, or quarter-truth, that the Lancashire mill-hand had the same interest as the master in upholding Britain's civilizing mission in India, may have done as much as anything else to make revolutionary socialism in this country impossible.

From these points of view the storm and sack of Delhi by the British army on 18 September, 1858, which may have been a painful blessing for India, was a disastrous triumph for England.

Marx's jottings on China offer some sidelights on what he was thinking about India. Here too his interest first displayed itself in 1853, in a long article followed a few years later by a running commentary on the second Opium War where some of his views emerge more maturely.

In China he observed, and found detestable, the same stagnation, immobility, as in pre-British India, made ridiculous by Chinese self-satisfaction, 'delusions of Celestial perfection'.[106] Here if not in India, he noted from the first the factor of over-population. This he thought must have been the prime cause of the unrest flaring up in the Taiping rebellion, but he assumed at the same time that foreign imports must have worsened the situation by crippling hand-spinning and weaving as in India and western Asia.[107] By 1859 he had revised this judgment, and was impressed by China's imperviousness to Western competition: it made its own rough cloth cheaper than Lancashire could under-sell it, because each household produced its own supply in its spare time, at no labour cost at all.[108] This concept of 'Asiatic society' in China 'depending upon the combination of minute agriculture with domestic industry'[109] invites comparison with Marx's picture of India. He equated the two economies when he spoke of China having the 'same combination of husbandry with manufacturing industry' as India. He spoke of this also as an impediment to imports of foreign cloth in both countries, and gave a new turn to his theory of the disruption of rural India by adding that there the British, having seized political power, were able to undermine a 'peculiar constitution' of landed property, and to turn part of the soil into plantations growing opium, indigo, and so on.[110]

In 1853 Marx was indulging both the hasty optimism he sometimes gave way to, and his taste for epigram, when he declared that Chinese events would do more than any nearer home to quicken revolution in Europe.[111] He was expecting not

[106] *Marx on China*, p. 55.
[107] *On Colonialism*, p. 13.
[108] *Marx on China*, pp. 90–91.
[109] *Ibid.*, p. 87.
[110] *Ibid.*, pp. 91–2. This anticipates a passage in *Capital*, Vol. III, pp. 391–3.
[111] *Ibid.*, pp. 1 ff.

socialist revolution but fresh democratic risings of the 1848
pattern, provoked by economic hardship: turmoil in China
meant loss of customers for Western industry, already suffering
as it was from over-production. This was giving far too much
importance to the China market, whose capacity he soon, and
rightly, came to think overrated.[112] He was pointing to a more
serious danger for Britain when he said China was likely to
grow its own opium, to avoid silver payments to India, and
this would put a further strain on Indian finance.[113]

On a larger view, Marx was very conscious during these
years that his world was expanding, acquiring new dimen-
sions—California, Australia, the Far East—, as if, he remarked,
the sixteenth-century age of exploration and discovery were
happening over again.[114] The old China was collapsing, he
wrote in 1857, under Anglo-French pressure and internal
revolt, and this meant 'the opening day of a new era for all
Asia';[115] but by next year he was afraid that 'bourgeois
society' was going to strengthen and consolidate itself by
extension into new regions of the earth, leaving socialism
suffocated in its narrow Western cradle.[116] So far as can be
seen, what he had in mind was not a further spread of Western
imperialism but a proliferation of autonomous capitalism, such
as he expected in India and did witness in north America.
This would mark a new enough era for Asia, if not a socialist
one. In 1894 Engels was to rejoice in the thought that defeat
in the war with Japan must finally shake to pieces the old
China and 'the old economic system of small peasant agriculture, where the family also made its industrial products itself',—
and that industrialization must follow. With unquenchable
optimism, forty years after he and Marx had first thought of it,
he prophesied once more the ruin of Western capitalism, but
now in a new way: Chinese industrial competition would be so
overwhelming that Europe would be submerged by the deluge
of Chinese goods.[117] It was a bugbear of many Westerners by
then, a new spectre haunting Europe. Like Marx earlier with
India, Engels took for granted that China once forcibly prised

---

[112] *Marx on China*, p. 87.   [113] *Ibid.*, pp. 9, 66.
[114] *On Colonialism*, p. 286 (to Engels, 8.10.1858).
[115] *Marx on China*, p. 51.   [116] As n. 114.
[117] *On Colonialism*, p. 313; cf. p. 311.

loose from its past could perfectly well industrialize itself. But capitalism was to prove even more stunted there than in India.

Like Marx's doctrine of imperialism, his conception of historical change, in the glimpses we have of it in these writings, has some ambiguous features. These are not cleared up by the *Pre-Capitalist Economic Formations* written at the same period. In this rough scheme of universal history, Marx was working, as Hobsbawm says, 'in highly abstract terms', and was more concerned with 'long-term transformation' than with minutiae of transition from one stage to another,[118] such as India was undergoing. To relate his general hypotheses to the concrete detail of the articles on India, or of Indian history as we know it, is far from easy.

Marxists are accustomed to look on every system as containing inner contradictions, and as changing primarily in response to these tensions. Marx's writings on Asia reveal that he conceived of much, or most, of human history as escaping from any iron law of change, into a timeless vegetative condition. It was the discontinuity, the jerkiness, of social evolution that impressed him, its lack of momentum, its habit of running down. Mankind was advancing only in sporadic rushes here or there, and Marx, who called on philosophy to change the world, gave his interest to these active sectors, or to the reasons that kept the others immobile.

A philosopher of a different order, writing on southern Africa, is likewise struck by finding history not in steady motion but 'subject to only partially explicable and almost invariably violent mutations'. He thinks of societies like the Bantu accumulating over long ages, like clouds, 'great invisible charges' of electricity, suddenly discharged.[119] Marx might have accepted this as a picturesque summary of a French or an Industrial Revolution. But he recognized no similar accumulation of energy in societies, like those of Asia, apparently quiescent.

About one of these at least, Japan, it may be a permissible speculation that the country was on the brink of some radical

[118] Hobsbawm, pp. 11, 13.
[119] L. van der Post, *The Lost World of the Kalahari* (Penguin edn., 1962), p. 69.

transformation when foreign guns, by toppling the old régime, allowed a new order to take shape more rapidly. External force might then be said to have played the part of 'midwife of history' that Marx assigned to revolutions like 1789. In India there had been at any rate sufficient ferment to call forth talents that the old society had no tasks for, aptitudes that would qualify Indians when the time came to assimilate modern modes in law, philosophy, administration, if not in industry. Every society, and the oldest the most, heaps up a surplus of moral and mental endowments beyond what its practical functioning requires. Marx might be said to have implied something of the sort when he praised Bengalis for their facility at engineering. Yet no such thought seems to be in his mind; he thinks, as Hobsbawm says, of Asiatic society resisting change 'until wrecked by the external force of capitalism'.[120] Certainly, he was not impressed by the claim the British had been fond of making, that they liberated the Hindu majority, among whom modern aptitudes were most evident, from the dead hand of Muslim rule. India had to be conquered by Britain—Russia needed to be defeated by western Europe—in order to be dragged out of the quagmire on to the highroad of history, not in order that pent-up energies within them might be set at large.

At times Marx's eagerness for a clean sweep is strikingly close to Maoism in its latest (autumn 1966) phase, its indiscriminate denunciation of everything traditional in Chinese life. Anyone turning his eyes today from China to India might well conclude that it would have been better for India to have all its memories blotted out. 'Every imprint of the past find and annihilate!' the great Indian poet of this century made God say to His angels.[121] But no-one has discovered how such blotting out can be done. The Africans dragged across the Atlantic in chains—the most drastic experiment in collective amnesia ever tried—carried Africa with them; nothing could be more Chinese than Maoism.

The Christian cannot be awakened from sin by any effort of his own, but only by Grace; Marx's Asia could only be roused from stupor by the intervention of Europe. What then

---

[120] Hobsbawm, p. 38.
[121] *Poems from Iqbal*, trans. V. G. Kiernan (London, 1955), p. 43.

is to be said of former, unavailing revolts there? In medieval Europe, Marx had written earlier, risings against oppression were peasant risings, and 'totally ineffective because of the isolation and consequent crudity of the peasants'.[122] If so, this must have been still more true in Asia. Marx might then have concluded that the Chinese or Japanese peasant, who rebelled often, was less sensible than the Indian who more often took refuge in religion. But a remote consequence is perhaps seen in our day in the slow, hesitant adoption of progress by India, compared with the Far East. Risings like those of medieval Europe may not have been barren; they shook the fabric of government, forced rulers to seek new methods, kept history moving. Cumulatively they altered social psychology and prepared for a new society at some time in the future. In Marx, and often in Marxist historians after him, there can be felt an unreconciled dualism between a historical scheme which made nearly all revolts useless or (as impeding the advent of new, more advanced régimes) worse than useless, and an impulse to applaud every struggle against oppression, as Marx did in 1857.

The Mutiny itself was something round which patriotic feeling could grow in years to come, and its memory helped India to gain independence in 1947. But at the time and for long afterwards its failure, and the extreme British reprisals, pushed many Indians back into their past, as the beaten sepoys drew off sullenly into their jungles. Westernizers and Western ideas were compromised by their association with the foreign despotism. The *afrancesados* of a generation or two earlier, Spaniards in love with French enlightenment, had been discredited in the same way by the brutal Napoleonic occupation of Spain. This ominous precedent might have led Marx to wonder whether one country really can be kicked or dragged forward by another. In Asia, the two countries that have progressed most, on divergent lines, are two that managed to preserve their independence. But China and Japan, like Spain, were nations already; India, to its misfortune, was not.

Marx's writings on Asia may often seem to throw more light on him than on it. But he was, after all, a pioneer in trying to look at Indian history scientifically; almost the first man to foretell an independent India, the first to see that its real

[122] *The German Ideology*, p. 46.

emancipation must come from industry. Indian socialists in our day have been inspired by the recollection that Marx tried so earnestly to understand their country. They have still far to go in developing or correcting his rough ideas, and the divisions and crises that have been overtaking them are not unconnected with a failure to strengthen their armoury sufficiently in this way. Some of them, fortunately, have been growing aware of the need for a fresh and more thorough exploration.

6
Marx, Engels, and the Indian Mutiny

Englishmen of the Mutiny years came to very diverse conclusions about what had caused the sudden eruption, and Indian historians differ as widely among themselves now. In the period of the national movement stories of the Mutiny helped to rouse patriotic emotion, and for this purpose it was all the better for being a mysterious event into which anyone was free to read whatever he wanted. Patriotism, itself in many ways an illusion, has often fed on myths. Socialism, having more ambitious aims for the future, requires a more exact understanding of the past; in modern Asia where it interacts with the naive nationalism that peasants easily come to feel, though not to originate, it has to make a special effort to achieve this.

Briefly the choice among presentday views of the Mutiny lies between seeing it as on the whole feudalistic and retrogressive, or popular and forward-looking. Of the first R. C. Majumdar may be taken as an accredited exponent, of the second S. B. Chaudhuri.[1] Marx and Engels arrived at no clear-cut diagnosis. They saw of course, as everyone saw, that the rebellion revealed very strong anti-British feelings, not confined to the sepoy army, though also far from universal; but on balance their opinions or conjectures fit more readily into the first of the two hypotheses.

Clearly the annexation of Oudh in early February 1856, in Lord Dalhousie's eyes his crowning service to India one month before he laid down office as governor-general, had a crucial

---

[1] R. C. Majumdar, *The Sepoy Mutiny and the Revolt of 1857* (Calcutta, 1957); S. B. Chaudhuri, *Theories of the Indian Mutiny 1857–59* (Calcutta, 1965).

importance. From this old British protectorate or vassal kingdom a great number of sepoys had always been recruited, and it was to be the biggest storm-centre of the rebellion. Marx found reasons of his own for disapproving of the annexation,[2] but of local conditions and of how the people would be affected he could form only a rough idea. Rumours of the coming event had been causing excitement in Oudh for months beforehand. Dalhousie was convinced that the ordinary people were bound to welcome it. Empire-builders have always been able to convince themselves that the people they meant to annex were thirsting to come under their enlightened rule; and Dalhousie was a religious man with a great deal of Curzon's self-righteousness and autocratic temper, as well as his energy and sense of duty.

He had not been to see Oudh himself, but he came from a Scotland still crammed with the mouldering castles where men like his own ancestors lived with their bands of retainers and kept the country in turmoil. That was precisely the condition of Oudh now, full of strongholds occupied by feudal magnates each with his miniature court and army, a small replica of the parasitic court at Lucknow. The ramshackle monarchy kept a disorderly army of 60,000 men, an enormous burden for so limited a territory, whose sole function was the collection by force of arms of revenue to be spent on pomp and luxury at the capital. All this double load fell, Dalhousie correctly saw, on the peasantry, whom he sincerely pitied.[3] What he did not see was that, since the Company was always hard up and its land-taxes consequently were far too high, its rule might be only an exchange of evils.

The preliminary revenue settlement made in Oudh in 1856 was less sweepingly anti-feudal than the progressive party among the British would have liked, and left a good half of the province still under the taluqdars, or feudal lords.[4] But it

[2] 'The Annexation of Oudh' (May 1858), in Marx and Engels, *The First Indian War of Independence 1857–1859* (Moscow, 1959).

[3] See his letter of 5 February 1859, in *Private Letters of the Marquess of Dalhousie*, ed. J. G. A. Baird (Edinburgh, 1910), p. 399.

[4] For a detailed account of how the annexation affected the taluqdars and peasants, see Jagdish Raj, 'The Introduction of the Taluqdari System in Oudh', in *Contributions to Indian Economic History*, ed. T. Raychaudhuri (Calcutta, 1960), pp. 46 ff.

was enough to alarm them, especially as revenue due from them would now have to be paid in full instead of being dodged as it had been before. Anything that could upset or dislocate the new government would be welcome to them; it would give them a breathing-space if no more, and a hope of being able to get better terms. Nothing could be more convenient to them than trouble in the sepoy army. There had often been mutinies before; the difference in 1857 was that the trouble was far bigger and was not due to the usual matter-of-fact grievances, but was instigated by whatever agency set afloat the rumour that the British meant to deprive the soldiers of their religion.

They were in a generally restless mood, ready to believe any ill of their foreign masters, even a story as absurd as this. No one was in a better position to set the story afloat than the taluqdars, on whose estates a great many of the sepoys' families lived. Other feudal interests, lords and princes outside Oudh, and jehadists of Muslim revivalism, joined in, either by previous arrangement or to profit by a situation they saw developing. Many of the big landowners may have been astonished and frightened by the violence of the army's explosion, and the possibility of its getting ideas into its head that would be bad for them as well as for the British. As a class their tactics were to make themselves as powerful as they could during the breakdown of order, until the British in their death-struggle with the army were compelled to think of buying them off, and then make haste to change sides. In the end they emerged with nearly all Oudh more firmly in their clutches than before. Of all concerned in the conflict, they alone, the most selfish and reactionary, did well out of it.

The villagers they preyed on were then left with no better protection than a few pious phrases from ministers far away in London. What their feelings were during 1857–8 is less easy to make out. They had long been engaged in a running struggle to defend themselves against the encroachments of the taluqdars; but the British in 1856, while doing enough to antagonize the lords, did too little to win the confidence of the peasants. Ignorance and conservatism, if nothing more rational, might make them prefer the evil they knew to the one they did not. And the sepoys were their relatives or neighbours. But situated as they were, they really had little choice; the taluqdars held the whip hand.[5]

In all that we see of martial preparations in Oudh during the struggle, it is the taluqdars and rajas collecting forces and guns and strengthening their forts. Similarly in numerous cases we see dispossessed landowners recovering their estates from new men, but scarcely ever lands being taken over by their actual cultivators. India compared with China had a less mature tradition of peasant revolt, though peasants had often in old days too been drawn into risings started by their superiors —particularly in this same Gangetic region in the time of the Sultans of Delhi, when the villager must have felt anti-Muslim, or anti-Turk, much as in 1857 he felt anti-Christian, or anti-British. The contrast between India and China is heightened by the fact that the Mutiny came towards the end of the Taiping Rebellion, an upheaval on a vaster scale and one definitely of peasants and artisans with a crude social programme. It is open to speculation that if the British army (one of whose officers eventually helped to suppress the Taipings) had been as feeble as the Chinese army, the Mutiny likewise might have spread wider and deeper and developed a more distinct social and agrarian character.

In the Communist Party of India's important commemoration volume of 1957, its editor seems closer to the mark when he rejects any conception that 'the Indian peasantry during this struggle decisively burst through the feudal bonds', than when he speaks of class strife being 'subordinated to the broad need of national unity against the foreign usurper'.[6] A reader familiar with the party's history may detect some traces or echoes of its own past in its interpretation of the national past; and in its language of 1942–7 the word 'patriotic' and the watchword of 'national unity' were very much to the fore. At odd moments in 1857 the thought of an Indian nation can be glimpsed, but only as socialism can be glimpsed in the class struggles of the fifteenth and sixteenth centuries in central Europe.

What stands out is that those provinces which had a strongly marked local nationality of their own, and had been free to

[5] Raychaudhuri, *op. cit.*, pp. 56–7.
[6] *Rebellion 1857*, ed. P. C. Joshi (Delhi, 1957), pp. 200–201.

assert it since the breakup of the Mogul empire—Bengal, the Punjab, Rajputana, Maharashtra, the South—were from the point of view of a united India non-national, or even anti-national, because 'India' had always meant an empire imposed on them by force. During the rebellion they were all either neutral or even pro-British. Only 'Hindostan', the Hindi-speaking region or Gangetic valley that had been the platform of the old empires, wanted an 'India', but could visualize it in no other form than as the resurrection of a buried past whose fitting symbol was the decrepit Bahadur Shah, descend-ant of the Moguls. Hindostan was populous, and held the strategic central position; but almost alone of the main regions of the subcontinent it had no sense or tradition of unity of its own, because it was too big and sprawling, and too mixed in religion and culture, with cities partly Muslim in a mostly Hindu countryside, and because its memories were of empire more than of national revolt against empire.

Martial spirit and absence of national cohesion made Hindostan a prime recruiting-ground for mercenary soldiers, somewhat as Germany had been for early modern Europe when the sole German 'national' framework was that vaguely splendid relic, the Holy Roman Empire. By supplying troops to the Company, as it had formerly done to the Moguls, Hindostan was in a certain sense rebuilding its empire; and the Sikh attitude in 1857-8, far more anti-sepoy than anti-British, showed how violently one of the other provinces might react to this kind of sub-imperialism. Judging by the much better showing of the sepoys at Delhi than at Lucknow, they found more inspiration in the capital of the old empire than in the capital of the kingdom to which many of them belonged by birth. Oudh as a state was a meaningless abortion, an accidental fragment of Hindostan to which no loyalty could be felt.

All India's growing-points now were on the coasts, in contact with the outer world that all its emperors had neglected: Hindostan lay inland, land-locked, deaf to the stirrings of the age. Not until the days of Nehru and the Congress would it find its historic role again, as the hub of an Indian wheel, and then in a new style. In 1857 Bengalis reading their Shakespeare and thinking of their investments in Company loans must have contemplated the Mutineers much as Englishmen in 1745, with no great love for George II, contemplated the wild Highlanders pouring down from their northern fastnesses to dethrone him and bring back a banished dynasty. A good many affinities might be discovered between the last outburst of the old feudal Scotland in 1745 and that of the old feudal India in 1857; and the brutalities of the repression in 1857–8 can be better comprehended when the atrocious treatment of the Highland wounded, prisoners, non-combatants by the English army after the battle of Culloden in 1746 is remembered.[7]

'Nowhere', Marx wrote to Engels during 1857, 'is the relationship between factors of production and the structure of society more clearly illustrated than in the history of the army.'[8] It is remarkable that although old India was perpetually at war, in the end its level of military proficiency was scarcely higher than that of pacific China. This went with a stagnant society neither truly feudal, in the European sense, nor modern; its soldiers were a floating mass of professionals, without even the loyalty of the employee to his paymaster, since they were paid so irregularly. Company wages were very low, but they were regular, and there were pensions; they gave India its first taste of an impersonal, methodical relationship of capital and labour. It was the bourgeois and unwarlike British who organized the first effective army in modern Asia. Their own army designed for service in Europe provided a model; it too was one of mercenaries, recruited largely from the conquered Highlands and Ireland. Recruitment from foreign sources had always been commonplace in Asian armies. Equipment in the sepoy army was poor enough, and the men were badly fed, housed in unsanitary quarters, dressed up under the tropical sun in preposterous uniforms, heavily overloaded on the march; they had low-grade, often absentee British officers.[9] Yet they, along with British troops in no better condition, conquered India. In military history there are only shades and degrees of stupidity and inefficiency.

Marx and Engels were aware that the 'Bengal Army' was

[7] See J. Prebble, *Culloden* (London, 1961).

[8] W. H. Chaloner and W. O. Henderson, *Engels as Military Critic* (collected articles; Manchester, 1959), Introd.

[9] See Amiya Barat, *The Bengal Native Infantry* (Calcutta, 1962), pp. 72 ff., 166–7, 171.

composed mainly of high-caste Hindus from outside Bengal.[10] These were peasants, serving as infantry, like the rank and file in all European armies of the eighteenth and nineteenth centuries; this made them amenable to a grind of drill and discipline unknown to India's old-style armies, mostly made up of horsemen who liked to think of themselves as gentlemen of fortune, a mob of individuals instead of an integrated mass. This class shift gave the sepoy army a more 'popular' character; it may in a dim fashion have felt a kind of anti-feudal class-consciousness as it helped a Company of merchants to trample on rajas and overturn thrones, as if taking an oblique revenge for the way its fellow-peasants in Oudh were trampled on by the taluqdars. On the other hand, as Brahmins and Rajputs who took service partly because they thought it derogatory to their caste dignity to handle the plough and till the field themselves,[11] these men were tiny landowners rather than actual cultivators. This fostered their martial spirit and self-esteem, but it must also have rendered their attitude towards feudal rulers and landlords an ambivalent one: they had something in common with the aristocracy, and might the more easily be got to follow its lead in a crisis like 1857.

There was the same ambivalence in the army's attitude towards its British employers, who paid it faithfully and led it to victory, but treated it with contempt and often injustice. It was true, as Marx wrote, that in this army the British created India's 'first general centre of resistance' to them,[12] but only in a certain sense. Like the western-educated élite in Bengal, then and much later, it was ready and eager to help the British to run India, if they would only behave reasonably and give it the status of a junior partner. It had no experience like the War of Independence of 1808–14 which Marx spoke of as having 'transformed and revolutionised' the Spanish army.[13] On the contrary its latest exploits had been attacks on the independence of three peoples each with a strong identity, the Sikhs and Afghans and Burmese. It may have learned some-

[10] War of Independence, p. 45.
[11] M. R. Gubbins, An Account of the Mutinies in Oudh (London, 1858), p. 432.
[12] War of Independence, p. 40.
[13] Marx and Engels, Revolution in Spain (collected articles; New York, 1939), p. 81 (1854).

thing from contact with them; but what it learned may have been not so much 'patriotism' as an aspiration towards something like the privileges of a military aristocracy, or praetorian force, that the Khalsa army had won for itself in the Punjab. It may have had some knowledge of the similar privileges enjoyed by the janissaries in Turkey, until their destruction by the Sultan in 1826.

All the limited mutinies before 1857 had been over professional grievances, though misconduct by British officers might give resentments a racial (rather than 'national') colour. These officers had at times set the example by going on strike for better pay and conditions, and there was a moment in 1767 when European privates in Bengal sharing their officers' discontent had to be held in check by loyal sepoy units.[14] Here was another variant of the politics of divide-and-rule. European privates were paid scarcely better by the Company than the sepoys,[15] and must have suffered still more from the climate and hardships of this alien land from which few returned home. A united front between Indian and European rank-and-file would have been a portent indeed, though probably not a happy one for the rest of the country. In early days they were closer together, and in 1764 did show symptoms of combining; at any rate they were both grumbling together. But as soon as the white soldiers were bribed with a bigger share of a donation, they were glad to display loyalty by turning against their Indian fellow-sufferers.[16]

Many later struggles gave the sepoy army a strong trade-union spirit, and an experience of secret combination, which might turn into patriotism, but only in an altering national environment. It had also the esprit de corps of the camp and the battlefield, and a professional pride in its victories—nearly all of them over fellow-Indians. All this helped to make the army an entity with a consciousness of its own, strengthened by the fact that men joined it, in order to gain the modest rank open to them, and the pension, for very long terms of years. It was the family in which a sepoy's whole active life was passed. Its hold on him was the firmer because all India's own insti-

[14] A. Barat, *op. cit.*, p. 33.
[15] A. Barat, *op. cit.*, p. 138.
[16] A. Barat, *op. cit.*, pp. 16, 18.

tutions above the level of caste or village had crumbled away, leaving a vacuum.

When 1857 came an Englishman in Oudh heard of sepoys saying that they must do what the army did. 'The feeling of the authority of the "Fouj ki Bheera", or "general will of the army", was to individual men, or regiments, almost irresistible.'[17] Its unity and cohesion in the hour of trial were impressive; and it was a democracy, for there were no longer, as there had been in early British days, any Indian officers above the lowest grade. But in Hindostan, unlike the Presidency towns, there was no background of public controversy, debate on 'national' issues, to give it the kind of political consciousness that inspired Cromwell's army in the English civil war. Hence it could hardly do otherwise than trail behind the feudal interests, the only powerful voice to be heard. Princes and taluqdars stepped into the position that the Company was losing. Hence also the loudest slogan was that of 'Religion in danger', an unreal one because in fact religion was the one thing in India *not* in danger from the British, who were there to pick their subjects' pockets, not their souls.

Some ideas of a more rational sort were canvassed among the rebels, and some of their proclamations included public grievances against the government, but even these set religion in the forefront.[18] The feudalists could make no more valid appeal to the soldiers, and the soldiers no more valid appeal to the masses. After all, if British taxation was too heavy, a large part of the proceeds went to paying sepoy wages and pensions: the army had no wish to lose these, and must have been fearing that with the completion of the conquest of India there would be reductions in its strength for the sake of economy, as had happened before in intervals of peace. Even the Cromwellian army with its high political consciousness fell foul of the public over the question of taxation for army pay. Defence of Indian religion might be said to represent a defence of India, though against an imaginary danger, but only in an atavistic form; and it was a poor guarantee even of unity of action, since there were two religions, and any excitement might set them

[17] M. R. Gubbins, *op. cit.*, p. 111.
[18] See texts in N. K. Nigam, *Delhi in 1857* (Delhi, 1957), pp. 83-4, 86-7.

against each other. There had been serious communal clashes in Oudh itself as lately as 1855.

As a fighting force the sepoy army had been criticized not long since by an unconventional English officer as too slavishly an imitation of European armies.[19] This made for weaknesses which in 1857 turned to Britain's advantage. It was too much in the habit of fighting in large masses, too little accustomed to flexible tactics and initiative. Asia, especially India, had always been accustomed to vast cumbrous armies, and there was something like herd instinct in the flocking together of the rebel regiments at Delhi. Discipline and combination had enabled the sepoys to defeat other Indian armies, but against a European opponent made them rigid and immobile. Such regular officers as they had were oldish men promoted by seniority, the least fit of all to work out new tactics for a novel war, or to take independent charge of small combat groups. A later British military commentator noted that the sepoys scarcely ever tried a night attack.[20] 'The Indian Mutiny was remarkable for the readiness displayed by the enemy in accepting battle; had it been otherwise its final suppression would have been far more arduous.'[21] The sepoys 'often fought with desperation', but it was their opponents who kept the initiative and took the offensive 'almost as a matter of course'.[22] In retreat they were relentlessly pursued, and heavy toll was taken of them by quite small numbers of assailants.[23]

If they had marched on Calcutta instead of shutting themselves up in Delhi, things might have turned out differently. As it was, the war became very much a matter of siege and defence of fortified towns. The Turkish soldier's preference for fighting in defensive positions had a similar cause, shortage of competent officers, other than foreigners. But the sepoys had not been trained for this kind of warfare: India had been conquered by long marches and pitched battles. Still less had they been trained for any kind of improvised fighting; and they were all the less able to turn to guerrilla tactics now, after their main forces were crippled, because of their caste rituals, the lumber

[19] H. T. Lambrick, *John Jacob of Jacobabad* (London, 1960), p. 358, etc.
[20] Col. C. E. Callwell, *Small Wars. Their Principles and Practice* (War Office, London, 3rd edn., 1906), p. 444.
[21] *Ibid.*, p. 104.   [22] *Ibid.*, pp. 154, 405.   [23] *Ibid.*, pp. 174, 209, 211.

of separate cooking-pots that each man had to carry, the taboos that had made them so unwilling to serve overseas. The rigid British army framework made it possible for men so handicapped to function as efficient regulars; nothing could turn them into effective guerrillas. Ironically it was the more individualistic British who were able to adapt themselves to local scattered fighting. Hodson and John Nicholson deserved Dalhousie's praise of them as splendid 'guerrilla chiefs'.[24] Another paradoxical reminder of how Europe and Asia have changed places with each other since then is that the British were able to operate a good intelligence service, the sepoys had none.[25] Altogether, considering their advantages, the sepoys made a poorer fight of it than the Sikhs had done a few years before; but all their disadvantages must be kept in view if Engels' hard verdict on them is to be understood.

Marxists in Europe are growing more aware than they used to be of their need to know something about history outside Europe; Marxists in Asia have at least an equal need to know more than they have usually done about history in Europe. It may therefore be worth while to look at Marx's comments on the Mutiny in the context of what he was saying about events elsewhere, chiefly in Europe, in that decade. For Marx himself India was not an isolated problem, but part of a complicated world-pattern. Asia and Europe he was coming to think of, it is true, as contrasted regions, the outcome of distinct lines of evolution. Still, they were two aspects of one universal problem, and human beings were members of one race with one destiny. That the 'Asiatic cholera' sweeping Europe in that epoch originated as he believed in India, and was the result of imperialist exploitation and poverty there, seemed to Marx 'a striking and severe example of the solidarity of human woes and wants'.[26]

Marx studied current events most intensively in this decade of the 1850s, the middle or pivotal one of his intellectual life. He was concerned with them partly as a journalist earning his bread, partly as a revolutionary trying to plot the tides of

---

[24] *Private Letters*, p. 414.
[25] This is emphasised by N. K. Nigam, *op. cit.*, pp. 142, 144, etc.
[26] *On Colonialism*, p. 75 (1853).

H

history. His philosophy of history, never completed or half-completed, was taking shape as he pored over his newspapers; happenings of the moment and long-term trends jostled together in his mind, and he like all lesser Marxists often found it hard to keep them apart. His topical writings, hasty articles or letters or jottings, are full of suggestive hints and speculations, but there are no worked-out doctrines in them.

In the years just before the Mutiny the European happenings that he and Engels were chiefly concerned to study were the revolutions of 1848–9, with the consequent rise to power of Napoleon III in France; the Liberal revolution of 1854 in Spain; and the Crimean War of 1854–6, an affair of Asia as well as of Europe, with Turkey as the bridge (or handcuff) between the two. India had begun to occupy Marx in 1853, when the Charter of the Company came up again for renewal and debate. China entered his vision with the second Opium War which began in 1856, and Persia to a smaller degree with the Anglo-Persian war of 1856–7. In each case he went to great pains to study the historical background, if it was not already, like that of France or Germany, fairly familiar to him. Spain in Europe and India in Asia were the two countries he delved into most thoroughly, and just about the same time.

Modern Spanish history began with the long struggle, from 1808 to 1814, against Napoleon's attempt to add Spain to his empire; and between this and the Mutiny it is not hard to find similarities. Spain unlike India was old as a united nation, but it was by west-European standards a very backward one. It led the way in the turning of the peoples of Europe against the French domination established by the armies of the Revolution, and then of its heir Napoleon, as they marched across the continent overthrowing worm-eaten monarchies and opening the way to progress, but antagonizing by brutality and arrogance the peoples they professed to be liberating. In the end these peoples rallied round their old tyrants to get rid of the new ones; rather as Hindostan turned against the British conquest in 1857. The Spanish resistance was heroic, but it was also uncompromisingly reactionary; it was royalist and clerical, fanned by benighted priests and their feudal patrons. 'Religion in danger' was its grand rallying-cry. At the end Spain was rewarded for six years of sacrifice by the restoration, to the great delight of the illiterate majority, of the Inquisition, the power of the big landowners, and the decadent monarchy which lasted until the civil war of the 1830s.

'The absolute monarchy in Spain,' Marx wrote in 1854 as he looked back over these years, 'bearing but a superficial resemblance to the absolute monarchies of Europe in general, is rather to be ranged in a class with Asiatic forms of government.'[27] Questions about how State and society in Asia and Europe differed were already much in his mind. In the anti-French ranks, he noted, peasants and priests and inhabitants of small inland towns, 'all of them deeply imbued with religious and political prejudices, formed the great majority';[28] upper-class conservatives kept the lead. Most of the fighting was done by guerrilla bands in the countryside (*guerrilla*, 'little war', and *Liberal*, were two Spanish contributions of that period to international speech). It is very noticeable that Marx's estimate of guerrillas as a political factor was by no means flattering. It seemed to him self-evident that after having for years 'freely indulged all their passions of hatred, revenge, and love of plunder, they must, in times of peace, form a most dangerous mob'.[29] The romantic aura that invests the guerrilla today did not exist for Marx. In his age politically progressive struggles were fought by organized, disciplined bands, whose exemplar was the new-model army of the French Revolution, or by urban workingmen at their barricades. Irregular armed movements were for the most part, as in Spain, popular but reactionary; movements of peasants, who in western Europe were, by and large (and in France itself once the Revolution of 1789 was over), an anti-progressive force. No guerrilla struggle can last long without a potent ideology, and the only one known to these peasants was the ultra-conservative Catholic religion.

In the War of Independence there was a small active minority of 'Liberals', middle-class urban progressives, who got another chance after 1814 because the army was drifting away from reaction. In 1854 the Liberal revolution which first set Marx studying Spain was initiated by a section of the army,

[27] *Revolution in Spain*, p. 26.
[28] *Ibid.*, p. 32.
[29] *Ibid.*, p. 55.

led by the pseudo-progressive general O'Donnell.[30] In such a retarded country soldiers might take the lead, for want of anyone better, as they do in sundry parts of the world today. If the army could give the signal to the country in Spain, why not in India? On the other side it must not be forgotten that the counter-revolution of July 1856 was also the work of the army, led by the selfsame general O'Donnell.

In 1848–9 the restless forces damped down after 1815 by the Holy Alliance exploded in a confused medley of revolutions over half Europe. Some of these cancelled each other out. In the multinational Hapsburg empire, especially, reaction was able to make use of backward Slav minorities to defeat the Austrian and Magyar progressive movements. This was something that Marx and Engels and many other Germans could not forgive the Slavs for. Whatever the rights and wrongs of this controversy, Marx obviously had no belief in a divine right of all nationalities to go their own way at all times. His instinct was to judge a national struggle, either in Europe or in Asia, on its merits as a contribution or a hindrance to general progress. (It is by this criterion that he would have judged the Kashmir dispute of today.) In Europe the 1850s and 1860s were a time of agitation and wars for national independence or union, which Marx welcomed when they seemed likely to break down obstacles to progress, but did not rhapsodize about in themselves. Would a restored Poland last long, he asked? 'One thing is certain: it would put an end to what is hollow in the enthusiasm for Poland, which for the last forty years has been affected by everybody and anybody calling himself liberal or progressive.'[31] Free Poland would be run by serf-owning noblemen.

Ram Mohun Roy had taught the new class of Indians with modern education to keep a close eye on western politics. Watching European events in 1848–9 a reader at Calcutta could not fail to be impressed by two things—the solid stability of British institutions, and the tangle of contradictory forces on the continent that ended, in the Hapsburg empire above all,

[30] I first read Marx's writings on Spain in the inspiring atmosphere of the 'commune' of the CPI at Bombay, about 1944. I have since tried to re-examine the events he was observing in my book *The Revolution of 1854 in Spanish History* (1966).

[31] Marx, *The Eastern Question* (collected articles, ed. Eleanor Marx Aveling and Edward Aveling; London, 1897), p. 505.

in the failure of them all and the triumph of the old regime. Between British India and the Hapsburg empire a number of resemblances might be pointed out; and it can be supposed that in 1857 recollections of 1848-9 helped to encourage Englishmen, and to discourage educated Indians from siding with the rebels. It was the salient difference between the two upheavals that in Austria-Hungary the most progressive elements were in the vanguard, in India they stayed at home.

Of all Marx's writings the most bewildering are the vast heap of articles written between the spring of 1853 and that of 1856 on the 'Eastern Question', the rival interests of European powers in the decaying Ottoman empire. In 1853 Turkey and Russia engaged in another of their recurrent wars, and next year Britain and France joined in to prevent a Russian victory. The Crimean War dragged on until 1856. Marx looked on tsarist Russia, which had helped to suppress the revolutions of 1848-9, as the bulwark of all European reaction, and was passionately eager to see it defeated. What he hoped for at bottom was that the war would turn into a revolutionary struggle involving the whole continent. But it was a confused, tortuous business, and even Marx could not make very much sense of it.

Part of its topsyturviness was that despotic Russia, instead of the liberal West, stood for liberation from Turkey of oppressed Balkan nationalities. Marx showed as little sentimental concern for these Balkan peoples as in 1848-9 for the Slavs; and equally little for the Armenians under Turkish rule, for he was eager to see Turkey driving the Russians back in Asia Minor too.[32] Yet Marx did not share the official Western faith that the Turkish empire was capable of being revived and modernized. At the outset in 1853, before a general war was in prospect, he gave what may be taken as his authentic opinion of Ottoman rule in Europe. He saw it then as hopelessly rotten, and any Western talk of maintaining it as absurd. This had nothing to do with the Turks being aliens, intruders in Europe. 'This splendid territory', he wrote of the Balkans, 'has the misfortune to be inhabited by a conglomerate of different races and nationalities, of which it is hard to say which is the least fit for

[32] *Ibid.*, pp. 592, 611 ff.

progress and civilization.' Hence the Turks, though a small minority, might have seemed the best able to give the peninsula the order and the unified control that Marx felt it needed. But by now they had proved themselves quite inadequate for the task, and become merely a hindrance.[33] It was from the point of view of the collective European interest, which for Marx overrode that of any local nationality, that he thought it still worse to have the Tsar at Constantinople than the Sultan.

He looked upon Ottoman administration as by origin an amalgam of 'eastern barbarism' with 'western civilization'[34]; as such it had started with certain potentialities, though these turned out to be defective. If the Balkan peninsula and its jarring peoples offered a 'mission' to some ruling power from outside to set them in order, the same might manifestly be said of India. Marx's logic would lead him to see Turks in medieval India, or Moguls in modern India, performing the same function. But if the Ottoman empire, with the benefit of close proximity to 'Western civilization', was a failure, there must be a strong presumption that any similar empire of Asian conquerors far away in India had been capable of only a still more limited and temporary success. Nor did Marx when he looked at Asiatic Turkey and saw revolt breaking out there in 1854, as well as in the Balkans, feel hopeful of its leading to anything better than anarchy. 'The rebels . . . constantly descend from the mountains, invade the villages . . . plunder the inhabitants and caravans, violate the women, and murder every one that resists.'[35] This was exactly what Englishmen always said would happen in India if they were not there to prevent it.

If Marx saw nothing objectionable in principle to law and order being imposed on a region of Europe like the Balkans by an Asiatic government, he could have no reason to object in principle to law and order being imposed on a region of Asia like India by a European government. Except in the excitement of a Crimean War, he in fact regarded even tsarist rule as a step forward for Asia, or for those parts of western and middle Asia where it was spreading in the nineteenth century.

[33] *Ibid.*, pp. 2–4.
[34] *Ibid.*, p. 81.
[35] *Ibid.*, p. 468.

It does not follow that he would have considered Russian rule in India as good as, or no worse than, British. How he viewed the chronic scare in Britain about a Russian threat to India is doubtful. Late in 1853 he like official London saw both the Persian move against Herat and the Russian move towards Khiva as endangering the Punjab.[36] In 1854 he discounted such alarmism: 'There are always some vague and alarming rumours afloat about Russian progress in Central Asia, got up by interested Indian politicians or terrified visionaries.'[37] Even if he (correctly on the whole) thought the Russian threat to British power in India a bogy, things would be different if the British were driven out by a revolt, and India then fell back into its old political condition. A Russian entry, sooner or later, would then be not at all improbable.

In 1808–14 the Spanish people fought the French with the aid of a British army, commanded by a general who had learned his trade in India. It would have been a neat retort if a French army had gone to aid the Indian rising, or had attacked England, in 1857. If Napoleon III had not so very recently been Queen Victoria's partner in the Crimea, he could scarcely have resisted the temptation to settle accounts for his uncle and for France's old friend Tipu Sahib. Barely a year after the Mutiny was over Britain was forming a Volunteer Corps to resist an expected French invasion. Had the sepoys waited until then, they would have had fewer reinforcements from Britain to cope with.[38] Or had they started their rising eighteen months earlier, while the Crimean War was still going on, Russia must have seized the chance to strike at Britain from the rear by giving them support. It was possibly the most important consequence of the Crimean War, which settled nothing in Europe, that in 1857 France was neutralized and Russia crippled, and India fought alone. Persia and China were not more then trivial embarrassments for Britain. The rebellion could scarcely have been worse timed; whoever chose the moment for it can have known little about world politics.

[36] *Ibid.*, p. 158.
[37] *Ibid.*, p. 533.
[38] As it was, in 1857 Marx noticed and shared a feeling that Britain might find itself dangerously denuded of troops, in view of the precarious European situation (*War of Independence*, pp. 69–70).

Yet in India the Crimean War aroused keen interest. Marx might have been expected to ponder this aspect of it; Dalhousie could not help doing so. He had hoped for the sake of tranquillity in India that war would be avoided,[39] and when it came he was very reluctant to let any of his European troops be removed.[40] (At the beginning of 1857 there were fewer than 30,000 in all India, an extraordinarily small total.) At first he found comfort in the thought that Indian Muslims were 'immensely pleased at our taking the part of the Sultan',[41] but this ceased to comfort him as the stalemate in the Crimea went on and British prestige dropped. There were rumours that the queen had been forced to flee from England and was hiding in India, and Dalhousie felt 'more and more the need of some great success'.[42] It came at last with the fall of Sevastopol in September 1855, and he hastened to circulate a jubilant proclamation of the news to every town and village in the country.[43] But the mischief had been done. Britain with two allies was being forced to struggle long and hard against a single opponent, and in the end for fairly small rewards; and it could not be kept a secret that the war-effort was hampered by a vast amount of bungling. No legend of invincibility could survive this.

Marx is not to be taken quite literally when he speaks of the Mutiny being 'intimately connected' with Britain's Chinese and Persian wars of 1856, as part of a 'general disaffection' of Asia.[44] His disapproval of these wars does however emphasize how little he wanted to see any further expansion of British imperialism. He had nothing good and much bad to say about the Opium Wars with China. If Britain or Europe had any Far Eastern 'mission' in his eyes, it was simply that of a gadfly, to irritate nations that had fallen asleep and sting them awake. Politically China, by contrast with India or the Balkan

---

[39] *Private Letters*, p. 304 (12 June 1854).
[40] *Ibid.*, p. 355 (23 Sep. 1855).
[41] *Ibid.*, p. 313 (12 Aug. 1854).
[42] *Ibid.*, p. 357 (6 Oct. 1855). Cf. Sir J. W. Kaye, *History of the Sepoy War in India* (London, 1865), Vol. 1, p. 342, on the current rumours of British collapse and Russian invasion.
[43] *Private Letters*, p. 362 (15 Dec. 1855).
[44] *War of Independence*, p. 40; cf. p. 153.

peninsula, stood in no need of unification. It did no doubt at present stand in need of order, being in the grip of an immense internal convulsion. Marx's curiosity was aroused by the Taiping rebellion, and at first along with many westerners he thought it held a promise of progress. Certainly he had no wish to see western conservatism intervening against it. But he could form no very clear view of it, and by this time it was past its best days.

His approval—tacit or implied—of colonial wars was restricted to those by which Britain brought India under a single control. For him as for the world, India was a unique case. There was no other big British possession as yet in Asia. By the time he came to take an interest in it the conquest was so nearly an accomplished fact that he seems to have assumed that it might as well be completed quickly. For the achievement it represented he was not without respect. He admired the eccentric genius of Sir Charles Napier, who added Sind.[45] Pining in 1854 for sterner action against Russia, and lamenting that decadent Europe had ceased to be equal to 'a decent, hearty, hard-fought war', he contrasted the deeds of Europeans in colonial campaigns with their present torpor. 'The troops that have conquered Algeria . . . one of the most difficult theatres in existence, the soldiers who fought the Sikhs on the sands of the Indus, and the Kaffirs in the thorny bush of South Africa . . . there they are, helpless and useless. . . .'[46]

Implicit in Marx's approval was the conception of 'India' as in some sense a logical unit, a nation potentially if not actually. He may have overestimated the degree of moral unity it possessed already, or the speed with which this could be engendered by political unity imposed from outside. Marx was apt to underrate the force of religious divisions, whether of Muslim against Christian in the Balkans or of Muslim against Hindu in India. He made too little allowance for the strength of local feelings and feuds within India. In 1857–8 the Niazis, a tribe of the north-west, were to aid the British, grateful to these new rulers for having 'emancipated them from the thraldom of the Sikh';[47] while the Sikhs aided them against the

[45] *The Eastern Question*, pp. 573–74.
[46] *Ibid.*, p. 452; cf. p. 506.
[47] W. P. Andrew, *Our Scientific Frontier* (London, 1880), pp. 84–6.

Hindostanis, as the Hindostanis had formerly served them against the Bengalis. For India the game of playing off one community or people against another would have far more damaging results than the older one of manipulating princes.

Marx's general feeling about India was a compound of two opposites. One was respect for Indians, as a civilized race with great accomplishments in antiquity and a capacity for new ones in the future. He had been reading about the links between Sanskrit and the European language family, and could even refer to ancient India as 'the source of our languages, our religions'.[48] He believed that modern Indians were quick to learn, and a new class could and should be given appropriate training and brought into the administration—not the futile old gentry, whose exclusion from it was deplored by British conservatives.[49] With everything Indian between antiquity and future, on the contrary, Marx felt only impatience. Growth had been paralysed by caste divisions, and also by division into a myriad villages, each a tiny self-sufficient commonwealth uniting agriculture with handicrafts, deaf and blind to all outside its own narrow limits.

There were English officials of the newer, anti-feudal school who wanted to preserve, in Oudh for instance, the joint or 'coparcenary' village holding of land, by ridding it of the encroachments of feudal landlords. This did not appeal to Marx as a way forward. He thought of the village commune in India as Engels spoke of it many years later in Java, where it was preserved by the Dutch and made the basis of their 'Culture system', or centralized extraction of wealth from the peasantry. Engels argued that 'primitive communism furnishes there as well as in India and Russia the finest and broadest basis of exploitation and despotism'.[50] India in short had got into a blind alley, from which it had no strength to extricate itself; so stupefying that it was worth while to be dragged out of it even 'through blood and dirt, through misery and degradation', by capitalism and foreign rule.[51]

[48] *War of Independence*, p. 37.
[49] *On Colonialism*, pp. 66–9 (1853).
[50] See two letters to Kautsky in 1884: *On Colonialism*, pp. 309–10. Marx had wavered for some time on this point, when studying the Russian *mir* or village commune.
[51] *War of Independence*, p. 37.

Marx could acknowledge some negative benefits of foreign rule in India of a less painful kind. 'A general war was declared against *dacoity, thuggee, infanticide, human sacrifice, suttee*, etc.', we read in his *Notes* on Indian history, for 1849–51.[52] But in 1853 India stood, he was convinced, on the threshold of a more constructive epoch, because British capitalism itself was entering a more mature phase. This was being inaugurated by Dalhousie, who worked himself nearly to death over his projects of improvement. His health never recovered, and he died in 1860; it would not be too much to say that, after his own fashion, he died for India. In his *Notes* Marx made a derisory reference to the list of achievements Dalhousie drew up as his farewell message:—'*Answer to this rodomontade, the sepoy revolution.*'[53] But in his articles of 1853 Marx took the new programme seriously, and in the next two or three years it was showing some remarkable results. In April 1854 the Ganges Canal was opened at Roorkie, and Dalhousie could boast that it was far the longest main channel in the world, both for irrigation and for navigation. In February 1855 the new telegraph lines from Calcutta to Madras, Bombay and Attock were thrown open to the public, and the first stretch of railway, 122 miles long, was inaugurated. Bengalis thronged to enjoy the thrill of a ride. In all these fields India was ahead, in irrigation far ahead, of a backward western country like Spain.

It is much to be deplored that as 1853 went on Marx's attention was jerked away from India and modern imperialism to the far less profitable conundrums of the Eastern Question, on which he wrote in the next three years nearly three times as much as he wrote altogether on India. His newspaper-readers in New York wanted news piping hot, and Marx himself was always torn between the talk of the hour and the riddle of the ages. It was the Mutiny that brought him back to India—in a particularly bad temper with Britain for fighting, as he saw it, only a phoney war against tsarist Russia in the Crimea.

He was as much taken by surprise as anyone else, and found no short cut to an explanation. The Mutiny was an event, as British India was a possession, unique in the history of im-

---

[52] *Notes on Indian History (664–1858)* (Moscow, n.d.). This is a mainly chronological outline made by Marx for his own use.
[53] *Ibid.*, pp. 176–7.

perialism. Nothing like it occurred in the long history of Dutch Indonesia, where local troops had been enlisted since very early days, though for some years after 1857 there were fears of a similar explosion in Java.[54] Clearly Marx was drawing on fresh recollections of the Crimea when he wrote now of 'the desperate obstinacy with which Mussulmans are accustomed to fight behind walls'.[55] To him as to most Europeans, Turk and Muslim meant much the same thing. He compared the British holding on to isolated points in India with the French reduced to the same straits in Spain during the Peninsular War. Having so lately been writing about a Spanish revolution, he spoke of sepoy regiments 'pronouncing',[56] i.e. making a *pronunciamiento*.

The Mutiny has often been reproached with being too much an insurrection of soldiers, too little one of a nation. But to Marx it was in a sense a reassuring feature that an army, a coherent and disciplined force, was in the vanguard. Watching Spanish events in 1854 he had welcomed symptoms of 'wholesome anarchy' in the provinces, as tending to save the revolution from being sabotaged by the politicians at Madrid.[57] But 'anarchy' in relatively orderly Spain meant peasants refusing to pay rents, not a descent into blind social chaos; whereas in Asia (as in Asiatic Turkey lately) he may have thought such chaos a likely result of any breakdown of authority. His allusion in the *Notes* to the Santhal rising of 1856-7—the precursor of the Mutiny, at least in its total unexpectedness— as an affair of 'a half-savage tribe ... put down, after *seven months' guerrilla warfare*',[58] scarcely suggests that he placed much hope in rebellion of so primitive a type.

In retrospect Marx seems to have thought of the Bengal Army primarily as a professional organization on bad terms with its employer. Relations had been bad for years, he wrote in his *Notes*: the men were 'bound together by caste and nationality; one common pulse in army ... officers powerless;

---

[54] 'Multatuli' wrote his novel *Max Havelaar* (1860; trans. W. Siebenhaar, N.Y., 1927), an exposure of Dutch exploitation of Java, with the aim of averting a conflict there like that of 1857 in India (pp. 202-4).
[55] *War of Independence*, p. 107.
[56] *Ibid.*, p. 46.
[57] *Revolution in Spain*, p. 119.
[58] *Notes*, p. 176; cf. the reference to the Santhals in *War of Independence*, p. 109.

laxity of discipline....'[59] In his first article on the Mutiny, in June 1857, he mentioned the famous greased cartridges, and sepoy fears about religion, as the reported cause of the trouble;[60] he did so without comment or query. He was soon convinced that there had been conspiracy in the army on 'an immense scale', and also that anti-British feeling was widespread among the masses. How things would now develop he did not profess to know. An Indian rebellion he remarked could not be expected to follow the same lines as one in Europe.[61]

He must have been relying on Engels, always his military guide, when he wrote in July 1857 that it would be 'preposterous' to imagine the rebels holding Delhi for long, and disparagingly called them 'a motley crew of mutineering soldiers who have murdered their own officers'.[62] By the end of that month he was writing in a different strain. It had always been said that 3,000 English troops could at any time beat 30,000 Indians, and now their failure to take Delhi was helping the rebellion to spread. It was no mere mutiny, as the British public was trying to believe, but 'a national revolt'.[63] This was much nearer to his own bent of mind than his previous words; still, the passage stands alone in his articles, and cannot safely be taken to represent his considered judgment. Allowance must be made for the fact that emotionally Marx responded to any revolt against any of the governments he detested; and also, here and throughout his many series of articles for the New York *Daily Tribune*, for the fact that he was writing for a remote American public with no responsibility for what was being done or might be done, and therefore could indulge his natural love of epigram and rhetoric more freely. He was, as it were, communing with himself, sometimes experimenting with theories, sometimes blowing off steam.

His mind came back to Spain when he met the clamour of the British press about Indian atrocities by pointing out that the British public applauded similar atrocities committed against the French by its Spanish guerrilla allies in the Peninsular War.[64] In September, two years after the fall of Sevastopol,

---

[59] *Notes*, p. 176; he adds that 'fakirs' told the men that the new cartridges were a design against their religion.

[60] *War of Independence*, pp. 40–41.   [61] *Ibid.*, p. 65.

[62] *Ibid.*, p. 44.   [63] *Ibid.*, pp. 54–57.   [64] *Ibid.*, p. 91.

Delhi was stormed by the British. Marx surmised that the rebel failure had been due to dissensions between regiments, between Hindus and Muslims, and between the sepoys and the trading class of Delhi which they were forced to lay under contribution now that they were without regular pay.[65] Here he seemed to be taking a narrower view of the rebellion, as essentially an army affair, but he was still eager to find symptoms of other regions joining in,[66] and hopeful of a better leader coming forward. For a while he had his eye on Sindhia—'young, popular, full of fire'—as the natural leader for all Marathas.[67] In other words he had more hope of leadership being provided by one of the old ruling families than emerging from the ranks of the sepoys. His *Notes* reveal his disillusionment: Sindhia figures there as an 'English dog-man', together with the maharaja of Patiala whom Marx likewise despised for standing by the British.[68] At the same time he does not appear to have formed a much higher opinion of any rulers or ex-rulers who took part in the rebellion, and in the *Notes*, where he goes into detail about the motives of Nana Sahib and the Rani of Jhansi, he treats them in both cases as merely personal and selfish.[69]

After all, the most remarkable thing about what Marx said of the Mutiny is that—although intensely absorbed in it—he said so little. It might well baffle him and throw him into a painful dilemma. He could feel enthusiasm for what was heroic in it, but to fit it into a rational historical pattern was another matter. On its constructive side the British mission that he thought so indispensable to Indian progress had only just begun. Spain won its struggle in 1814 only to sink back into the past. This was not fatal, because Spain however backward was part of western Europe, and could not be kept sealed off for long against modern ideas. It would take much longer for these ideas to find their way into a remote India free of western control.

At any rate, of Marx's thirty-three articles on India, twelve belong to 1853; four of the fifteen written in 1857, and all six

---

[65] *War of Independence*, p. 112. N. K. Nigam, *op. cit.*, pp. 66 ff., confirms the forcible raising of money from traders.

[66] *War of Independence*, p. 114.   [67] *Ibid.*, p. 71.

[68] *Notes*, pp. 180, 185.   [69] *Ibid.*, p. 176.

of those written in 1858, deal with the general background of Indian affairs; and among the remaining eleven on the Mutiny itself several are only fragmentary comments on current news. All the eight articles on the course of the Mutiny from November 1857 to September 1858 are by Engels. Marx, it would seem, was giving up the problem in despair, and leaving it to his friend to follow events on the military level. He was turning away from it as if he felt that he had lost the clue and must go back into the past to recover it. He plunged into a study of fundamentals of economic theory, far removed from the hurlyburly at Delhi or Lucknow. Of the resulting treatise, composed in 1857–8 but never published by him, one section consisted of a highly abstract analysis of world history and its socio-economic phases.[70] Here he had much to say about 'Asiatic society', on the lines of the conclusions he had already been coming to about the old Indian society and its static nature, its incapacity for further evolution.

Engels had a considerable reputation as a military critic, and among his many hobbies the study of war was perhaps the favourite. He revelled in military technicalities and terms of art like Tybalt in *Romeo and Juliet*. 'Ah, the immortal passado! the punto reverso! the hai!' In the Marx family circle he was nicknamed 'The General'. All his thinking was in terms of regular warfare practised by well-trained modern armies: the guerrilla style of our day lay beyond his horizon. In this he was a man of his time. It was the experience of nineteenth-century Europe, as it marched over Asia and Africa, that irregular opponents were seldom formidable against disciplined troops and flexible coordination of all arms by a unified command. Not only was this more efficient, but it generated more courage, or a steadier type of courage, than the most warlike of wild enemies, men like the Bedouin or the Pathan, could muster.[71] Europe's most dangerous antagonists were not guerrillas but the elaborately organized Sikhs in Asia and Zulus in Africa.

[70] First English edition: *Pre-Capitalist Economic Formations*, ed. E. J. Hobsbawm (trans. J. Cohen, London, 1964).

[71] On the erratic quality of Bedouin courage see Sir R. F. Burton, *A Pilgrimage to Al-Madinah and Meccah* (1855), Vol. 2, pp. 87–8 (Bohn Library ed.); cf. on Highland fighting Prebble, *op. cit.*, p. 110.

Engels had done a spell in the Prussian army, the best trained in Europe, though he had his baptism of fire in the insurrectionary movement of 1849 in western Germany, which the Prussian army helped to put down. He was now a mill-owner, and running a mill must remind even a socialist daily and hourly of the importance of order and method. It is a striking testimony to his orthodoxy as a military man that when serving in the Volunteer Corps, formed in Britain in 1859 during the French scare, he was entirely in favour of its being a well-drilled replica of the regular army, nothing in the least like a democratic, decentralized force of skirmishers. His call to the nation was exactly the same as Lord Tennyson, the Poet Laureate's—'Form, riflemen, form!' Yet this meant sub-ordinating the volunteers to the generalship that (besides being politically reactionary) had proved itself so ludicrously incom-petent in the Crimea, and its fossilized headquarters the Horse Guards. We in the north of England, he wrote in one of his enthusiastic articles on the movement, unlike the carping Londoners 'have always been on capital terms with our natural military superiors'.[72]

The fate of the popular militia formed in Spain in 1854 might have cautioned him. It was crushed in July 1856 in a two-day battle against the regular army in Madrid, largely because it had imitated the army too closely in organization and training. When the big socialist parties of the Second International came to be formed, the faith in disciplined mass strength, firmest of all among the Germans, was carried over from military into political thinking, and helped to make parties too heavy and rigid to retain their revolutionary fire. At the other extreme the Spanish anarchists who rejected all party organization whatever were translating into political terms the guerrilla tactics that modern Spain had found most congenial in time of war.

Turkey in the Crimean War, and then the Persian and Chinese wars of 1856, drew Engels' expert eye towards Asia. He took for granted that the way for Asia to learn to defend itself was to scrap its old-style armies and build new ones on the western model, trained to begin with by European officers; just as Marx wanted to see Asia scrapping its past and building

[72] *Engels as Military Critic,* p. 10.

a new society on western technology. He recognized that to form a reliable army was a slow, difficult task, in the swamp of corruption and obscurantism that was 'Asiatic barbarity'.[73] This struck him forcibly in the spring of 1856 when 600 Indian cavalry of the Bombay Army, whom he thought very poorly of, routed 10,000 modern-trained Persians. The spectacle neither induced him to dismiss Persians as 'a nation of cowards', nor to despair of western training in Asia. He recalled that the new Turkish army had done poorly in its earlier stages of modernization, yet had fought well against the Russians in the war just finished. In another twenty years a Persian army might be as efficient as the Turkish now was.[74] In reality the Turks, as later wars were to show, never made more than very limited progress. Engels looked on an efficient cadre of officers and NCOs as the vital factor;[75] he did not raise the more fundamental question, whether an Asiatic state could have a modern army without a political and social revolution first.

Japan was about to embark on such a revolution; no other free Asian country did, and no other made any serious military progress in the nineteenth century. Engels did make a shrewd prophecy when he recognized in the war of 1856 the quickness of ordinary Chinese to learn. Their gunnery on the Canton river was astonishingly improved since the last time the British tested it, he wrote. 'In everything practical, and war is eminently practical, the Chinese far surpass all the Orientals, and there is no doubt that in military matters the English will find them apt soldiers.'[76] His political comment on this contest could serve either as epilogue to the Spanish War of Independence or as prologue to the Indian Mutiny: these Chinese were fighting a national, popular war in defence of a traditional society steeped in 'overbearing prejudice, stupidity, learned ignorance and pedantic barbarism'.[77]

Engels was a revolutionary, but a *mutineer* went against the grain with him. Moreover the opinion he had formed of the sepoy army before the Mutiny was not flattering. Indian troops he thought—underrating a good deal the part they had played

[73] *On Colonialism*, p. 111, This article on 'Persia and China', of May 1857, is printed also in the collection of articles *Marx on China 1853–1860*, ed. Dona Torr (London, 1951), pp. 45 ff.
[74] *On Colonialism*, pp. 112–14.   [75] *Ibid.*, pp. 112–114.
[76] *Ibid.*, p. 110.   [77] *Ibid.*, p. 115.

I

in the conquest of India—were useful to the British chiefly by their ability to march faster in hot weather and on poorer food than European troops could.[78] Indian soldiers of the old un-drilled type he regarded as beneath contempt. 'An army of 5,000–7,000 Englishmen has always been thought fully sufficient to go anywhere and do anything in the open field in India. That stamps the opponents at once.'[79] It should be added that Engels thought poorly enough of the British army and most others. Englishmen and Russians were 'the worst light infantry in Europe'.[80] Presumably Frenchmen or Germans would have made even shorter work of India. As for general-ship, he admired Sir Colin Campbell and praised Sir Charles Napier very highly, but derided others like Windham, one of the Crimean blockheads.

During the Mutiny Engels must often have looked back on his own experience in the armed uprising of 1849. In his articles on that episode, written in 1851–2, he had laid it down that 'insurrection is an art quite as much as war', and that once started it must be pushed on boldly and rapidly. 'The defensive is the death of any armed rising', while aggressive action wins the support of 'those vacillating elements . . . which always look out for the safer side'.[81] When he saw the bulk of the rebel army shutting itself up in Delhi he must have felt that it was committing a cardinal error. He was convinced on the other hand that the British committed a blunder by tying up their forces round Delhi, for political reasons of prestige, while disaster threatened their rear in the Ganges valley. Delhi he considered of no strategic importance, and the attempt to take it by siege foolish.[82] It is then a trifle surprising to find him in his first article reporting its capture as quite an easy feat. He credited the sepoys with individual bravery, but held them 'utterly without leadership' above the company level, destitute

[78] War of Independence, pp. 162–63; cf. p. 178, and p. 202 where Engels tells Marx that the Madras Army was 'recruited exclusively from riffraff'. Engels laboured under the extraordinary delusion that sepoys could march 40 or even 60 miles a day. In fact 10 miles a day over a long distance might be beyond them (A. Barat, op. cit., p. 230).

[79] War of Independence, p. 207.

[80] Ibid., p. 207.

[81] Germany: Revolution and Counter-Revolution (London edn., 1933), p. 100.

[82] War of Independence, p. 101; cf. the letter of Engels, 24 Sept. 1857, which Marx was following in this article: pp. 201 ff.

of 'the scientific element without which any army is nowadays hopeless'.[83]

Scientific principles of warfare were the speciality of his native Prussia, inventor of the General Staff, and the sepoys' total lack of them made it harder for Engels to sympathize with them. Of course he had to depend on the newspaper reports slowly trickling into England, often garbled, or distorted by the anti-Indian hysteria. He was far more scathing about the fall of Lucknow to the British in March 1858 than about that of Delhi. The rebel force there had been growing demoralized, he thought, with some of the sepoys slipping away and raw recruits taking their place.[84] This combination might well accentuate the weaknesses of both elements. Engels had seen the same thing in 1849, when the army of one small German state, Baden, joined the rising. 'As in every insurrectionary war', he had written about this, 'where armies are mixed of well-drilled soldiers and raw levies, there was plenty of heroism, and plenty of unsoldierlike, often inconceivable panic.'[85]

Some of the new faces in the ranks at Lucknow must have belonged to men of the royal army of Oudh, disbanded by the British in 1856, one of the worst collections of riff-raff in Asia. Some of the others may not have been there of their own free will. 'The great Talookhdars had sent in their contingents', writes Kaye;[86] and all the village levies in the province seem to have been got together by the feudal chiefs.[87] When the feudal chiefs of the Highlands raised their clansmen for the rebellion of 1745, they made sure of every man volunteering by threatening to burn his house over his head if he did not. If a good many of the defenders of Lucknow were there under similar pressure, their disposition to run away when the crisis came is understandable.

Engels demonstrated with a wealth of the technical detail he loved that the defenders of Lucknow were utterly ignorant of

[83] *Ibid.*, pp. 117 ff.
[84] *Ibid.*, p. 139. Engels surmised that the sepoys had been given a plan of defence, which they could not properly execute, by Europeans in Delhi: *ibid.*, p. 123.
[85] *Germany: Revolution and Counter-Revolution*, p. 107.
[86] Sir J. W. Kaye, *op. cit.*, Vol. 3, p. 529.
[87] Cf. S. B. Chaudhuri, *op. cit.*, pp. 156 ff., which scarcely bears out the idea that the villagers were volunteering.

how to construct and defend fortified positions. Worst of all, he thought that unlike the sepoys at Delhi they let their courage ooze away, until in the end 'there was but one grand and unanimous act of bolting'. He went on to generalize about the triumphs of the bayonet in Asia.[88] This too belonged to accepted military doctrine. The bayonet was the weapon that required most training and steadiness; these were Europe's strongest points, and it was not by superiority in long-range weapons alone that it was winning its empires.

But Engels was also a military man of his time in cherishing an ideal of civilized, as well as scientific, warfare. He condemned the sack of Lucknow in very strong language, as 'an everlasting disgrace' to the British army, the only army he pointed out that still clung to the 'time-honoured privilege' of freedom to loot a captured city.[89] It was the only army that did most of its fighting outside Europe. About this same time he wrote an encyclopaedia article on Badajoz, the Spanish town stormed by Wellington's forces in 1811 and given up to military execution. There the victors, he said, perpetrated horrors 'which might well make the angels weep, and which obscured, if they could not efface, the glory of their wonderful achievement'.[90] Badajoz and Lucknow must have been in his mind together.

After Lucknow fell Engels predicted a long, toilsome effort by the British to wear down scattered resistance. 'The whole Kingdom of Oudh bristles with fortresses.'[91] But these were as he saw feudal strongholds, rallying-points for the zemindars and their ragtag and bob-tail.[92] He does not seem to have expected much in the way of a genuine guerrilla struggle: on the contrary he expected the beaten sepoys to degenerate into bandits, with the people against them.[93] He pictured 'Oudhians' rather vaguely as a 'warlike tribe', brave but capable only of ragged fighting 'in the normal Asiatic manner'. In his eyes even an irregular force ought to have some definite shape and leadership, and, as he had written to Marx, 'we have not heard in a single instance that any insurrectionary army in

---

[88] *War of Independence*, pp. 143 ff.   [89] *Ibid.*, pp. 146–7.
[90] Published in 1858; text in *Revolution in Spain*, pp. 161 ff.
[91] *War of Independence*, pp. 149, 161.   [92] *Ibid.*, p. 130.
[93] *Ibid.*, p. 136.

India had been properly instituted under a recognized chief'.[94]

Engels still thought the end far off until he heard of places like Bareilly being surrendered without a fight, but by September 1858 he felt that the heart had gone out of the resistance. He saw three factors at work to weaken it. Too many sepoys were content to levy contributions from the areas they controlled, instead of harassing the British and cutting off food supplies from their urban bases. Secondly the 'chiefs' or 'landholders' were going over to the government, which was now ready to compromise with them. Thirdly he believed that the British reign of terror was intimidating, though further embittering, the country.[95] Altogether, Engels seems to have concluded by this stage that the sooner things were brought to an end, the better.

The next colonial campaign he had occasion to study was the fumbling Spanish invasion of Morocco in 1859–60. In his essays on it, while not referring to the Mutiny specifically, he compared the mobility and energy displayed by the British in India and the French in Algeria with Spanish sluggishness. But he found fresh evidence to prove that a disciplined modern army with its screen of skirmishers was more than a match for any number of irregular attackers on any ground.[96] Two years later he and Marx were watching the Civil War in America, where two improvised regular armies were in conflict. In one of their articles they wrote that if the South resorted to 'guerrilla warfare and brigandage' (two things always associated in their minds) it would be the doing of the poor whites, and would only alarm their superiors, the rich southern planters, who would then be glad to see them suppressed by the North.[97] In the same way they may have supposed, and with good reason, that real peasant militancy in Oudh would have frightened (or did help to frighten) the taluqdars into the arms of the British.

On the U.S. war the opinions of the two friends soon diverged. Engels never failed to be impressed by good soldiering, whatever politics it went with, and he felt sure that the half-hearted North must be defeated by the southerners. These

[94] *Ibid.*, p. 207.
[95] *Ibid.*, pp. 186–90.
[96] *Revolution in Spain*, pp. 193–4.
[97] Article of 30 May 1862, in the collection *The Civil War in the United States* (N.Y., 1940).

men might be slave-owners, but they were in 'bloody earnest. . . . Besides, they fight quite famously.'[98] Marx demurred. 'It seems to me that you let yourself be swayed a little too much by the military aspect of things.'[99] He might have said the same in 1857, but he did not. In America he wanted the North to win, and believed it would. In India he might want to see the British beaten, but he could not expect, and perhaps could not hope, that the rebels would win.

Nearly all the thinking of Marx and Engels, as they groped their way through the press of nineteenth-century events, explorers making their own maps as they went along, was provisional and speculative. Sometimes ambiguities in it stand out more noticeably when we see them theorizing about the new political arena of Asia. There was an unresolved discord in Marx's thinking about empire, between the idea of a western 'mission', and hatred of conquest as a reinforcement of class power abroad and at home. At times, particularly about 1853, and particularly in India, he was prepared to think of a 'civilizing mission' not much different from the one that Winwood Reade had in mind when he declared: 'Asia is possessed by a few kings and by their soldiers . . . the masses of the people are invariably slaves.'[100] Even if Marx found it harder later on to believe that Asia would be any better off under western rule, western interference might be better for it than to be left in the coma it had been sunk in for ages. Engels lived to welcome the effect, as he forecast it, of Japan's attack on China in 1894, the final disintegration of the old immobile Chinese society.[101]

Marx did not overcome the contradiction in his thinking (or between his thinking and his feeling, as in 1857) on imperialism, and turned away from the problem of its consequences both for Asia and for Europe, the effect of India on Britain as well as of Britain on India. He went on reading about India at intervals, and may have intended to write about it

[98] Letter of 30 July 1862, *ibid.*, pp. 1,123–4.
[99] Letter of 10 Sept. 1862, *ibid.*, p. 1,127.
[100] W. Reade, *The Martyrdom of Man* (1872), p. 415 (Thinker's Library edn.). He censures 'the sickly school of politicians' who say that every country ought to be left to itself; for Asia conquest means emancipation.
[101] Letter to Sorge, 10 November 1894: *On Colonialism*, p. 313.

again some time or other.[102] But in the end he and Engels bequeathed to the socialist parties only a puzzlingly uncertain guidance here—especially when we recall that their writings on Asia were fugitive pieces which have only in recent years been salvaged from oblivion, and which they themselves did not think mature enough to be worth collecting. It is possible that they thought of imperialism after 1857 as a process that had more or less reached its limits, as something rooted in an earlier phase of history, and of less significance for the future. If so, they were to be contradicted by the lessons of the decades before 1914 when imperialism became the burning issue, and the worst impediment to the international socialist movement.

Before this happened, there was a lull of a quarter-century in imperial expansion. It can be explained (as by Lenin) in terms of the inner laws of capitalist evolution, or (more simply) in terms of political and 'accidental' factors. One of these was the Mutiny itself. Had it succeeded, whatever the result might have been for India the effect on the world would have been great. Europe might have lost its taste—shared so far by only a few nations—for empire-building; all the more if the spirit of revolt had spread, as it might, from India to the next most profitable colony in Asia, Indonesia. Even as a failure the Mutiny must rank as an event of world history, for it must have had some damping influence on all expansionists in the West, including the U.S. Engels wound up his commentary on it by predicting a general clash of British and Russian interests across Asia, with battles in Central Asia in which Britain would be hamstrung by India's hatred.[103] The clash of interests did develop, but less immediately than he expected; and the battles were never fought, partly because the British in India were very conscious of the danger of a rebellion in their rear.

They were occupied for a good many years after 1857 with rebuilding their political position in India, and with forging a new northern army. India was to Britain what the Illyrian provinces of the Balkans were to Rome, and without this reservoir of cheap soldiery, added to that of Ireland, its huge

[102] The *Notes* are stated by their editor (pp. 9–11) to belong to 'the last years of his life'. They include minutiae of names, titles, etc., which could scarcely have been of value to Marx unless he had in mind some plan of publication.

[103] *War of Independence*, p. 190.

empire would have been an impossibility. In the first Opium War nearly the whole of the Madras Army had been employed. Indian troops were again indispensable when expansion was resumed in Malaya in the late 1870s and then Egypt in 1882 and Upper Burma in 1885. By that time a political movement of modern type was under way in India: the new sepoys had nothing to do with it—and were only occasionally required to take action against it.

Other western countries too were inactive in Asia during the post-Mutiny years, partly because Britain was inactive: governments always watched and imitated each other, and when one moved the rest flocked after it like fierce sheep. In addition they each had preoccupations of their own. There was a series of wars inside Europe until 1878. The France of the Second Empire sought to regain hegemony over its own continent. Russia was temporarily knocked out by the Crimean War and then absorbed in internal problems of reconstruction. Britain itself was for several years in fear of French invasion. In the 1860s the U.S. was busy with its civil war, and its first intervention in Asia, the forcible opening of Japan to trade in 1853–4, was not followed up until the end of the century with the seizure of the Philippines.

All this gave Asia a breathing-space after 1857, which it ought to have profited by. Its failure to do so lends weight to Marx's hypothesis that the old order in Asia had reached a dead end. Only Japan seized the opportunity, after change was forced on it by first American and then British and French warships in the 1850s—that decade so rich both in great events in the East and in studies of world affairs by Marx and Engels. Between then and the start of a new phase of imperialism about 1880, Japan got through the critical stages of modernization. In a very roundabout way the Indian Mutiny may be said to have helped to make Japan's survival possible. It is a great pity that Marx's full attention was never drawn to the rise of this new power, far more meaningful in the long run than the decline of the Ottoman empire, at the other end of Asia, on which he lavished so much thought and ink.

If there was a discord or doubt in Marx's mind about empire in India, it was an extension into Asia of one that beset him at home in Europe. Mankind, the family of human beings, was like Asiatic society too inert to move forward spontaneously. It could only be dragged forward, by the dominion of a capitalist class; and capital could only be accumulated, as empires could only be nourished, by the exploitation and misery of the masses. The panorama of history unrolling itself before him was a harsh one, something like the Calvinist theologian's grim scheme of eternity. Even then there still remained the problem of how capitalism, having done its work, was to be got rid of. Considering the high respect Engels always showed for the power of modern standing armies, one is compelled to wonder how he and Marx ever expected them to be overcome by revolutions, unless first disrupted (as the tsarist army was in 1917) by foreign war. The relatively easy suppression of the Mutiny, in spite of the rebels having superiority of numbers, and fighting on their own ground, and being so far away from Britain, might well discourage them about the prospects of any future revolts in Europe, whether national or proletarian.

Later generations of Europeans hankered for an easier, smoother road than the one charted by Marx. He himself, as youthful excitement and hopefulness wore off (when the Mutiny ended he was a man of 40), must have had moods of dejection. If he felt a growing doubt about human beings, their readiness to revolt against tyranny, their ability to revolt successfully—and about whether revolts might be premature and self-defeating—it is less strange that in his later years he turned from scrutiny of actual history to analysis of capital as a thing in itself. Capitalism was a complex machinery made by men but independent of men's wills; its internal contradictions would, like a lurking death-wish, ensure its destruction, or compel its makers to destroy it, at the hour when humanity was ready to dispense with it.

7
India and the Labour Party

Many questions suggest themselves about the influence that India may have had on the Labour Party, a good deal stronger in all probability than the party's influence on India; about India as one of the taproots of the peculiar British social-democratic mentality. It could be argued that the Labour Party talked nonsense from the cradle, but there is a sense in which it can be said to have fuddled its wits by thinking about India, and then to have become unable to think realistically about anything. There was genuine anti-imperialism in the early movement, just as there was anti-war feeling, and both helped to get it going. But just as men like Ramsay MacDonald hated the thought of war but were little concerned to explore the causes of it, so they were sorry to see anyone in the empire ill-used, but had little interest in imperialism, in what made empires and kept them at work. Hence it came about that while they day-dreamed of transforming the empire into a true federation, in reality the empire was transforming them. They were soon growing content to change it by giving it a new look, contemplating it in a new light, as Hegel did with Prussian autocracy. From this point it was natural to go on to think of revolutionizing British society in the same painless way, of dealing with capitalism by altering the colour of the spotlight.

Effective contact with the Indian masses was impossible, and confronted with their vast bewildering misery Labour might well come to think of humanity at large as an amorphous, incalculable mass, at best a crowd of children, at worst a bloodthirsty mob. This was already how too many Labour men, really Liberals with an interest in social welfare, instinctively viewed the masses at home, and the Indian myriads, chronically haunting their thoughts, deepened their mistrust. In India, again, to work for progress with and through the people was impossible; they could only think of working through the existing bureaucracy, in its way a respectable and efficient one. The Labour Party had no difficulty in crediting it with other virtues—neutrality between government and people, willingness to be used as an instrument of radical change—which it did not possess. From this illusion it was a short step to endowing the civil service at home with similar virtues, and to believing that all the changes Britain required could be carried out by merely pressing the right civil service buttons. A purely bureaucratic approach to India reinforced a bureaucratic approach to Britain. Labour has always disliked any kind of mass struggle, at home as in the colonies; it thought suffragettes very undesirable people, as it did the agitators in Bengal and Maharashtra.

Meanwhile the tendency engendered by British history to think in spacious terms, of decades instead of years and centuries instead of decades, to be unwilling to recognize that history now was speeding up, was deepened by contact with India, which seemed to think in aeons, or rather to be above thinking of time at all. India's problems were extremely complex; preoccupation with them helped to make Britain's too look intricate beyond the wit of man, and to slow down still further Labour's habitual mode of progression, each foot held cautiously poised in the air for ten minutes before being brought back to the ground. If the Indian people had to be matured so very gradually for independence, the British people must be ripened slowly for socialism. Any fretful impatience was to be checked. Tories could justify their repressive policies in India by pointing to Labour's—to which Labour could only fatuously reply that though the method might be the same when it was in office, the spirit was different. Even this difference was not always claimed; Wedgwood might be heard consoling a political prisoner in India by telling him that his Tory jailers had the best of intentions at heart. More frankly Labour took refuge in the formula that a government must govern, i.e. that

Labour in office must rule India on Tory lines, and could indulge the luxury of thinking about reform only when in opposition. 'Realism' swathed in mental fuddle at the India Office easily spilled over into realism in other departments of State. Today the Labour Government's stock excuse for its Tory policies is that it has, after all, to govern.

Bureaucratism screened itself behind an exaggerated reverence for Parliament. Parliament's awe-inspiring authority over a world-wide empire helped to foster a kind of mystical respect for this inmost repository of power—not to mention that MPs touring India were always treated, though seldom regarded, with profound respect by officialdom. In their conviction that debates in the hall at Westminster represented the omnipotent tide of history, these men resembled a child holding a sea-shell to its ear and thinking that it was listening to the ocean. If this oracle could answer the riddle of India, it could surely cope with Britain's miniature puzzles, such as how socialism was to be inaugurated. But for Parliament to bring its full wisdom and benignity to bear on India, it was clearly to be desired that all parties should speak with the same voice. It would be unjust to India to treat it as a party issue. . . . This specious bi-partisanship, steadily adhered to, was bound to spread into a similar approach to home affairs. From telling Indians that Tories were not such bad fellows as they looked, Labour began telling itself or its voters the same thing. When MacDonald deserted the party and formed a 'National Government' (one of whose chief items of business would be India), he might be said to have simply carried this train of thought to its logical conclusion.

Britons took very little interest in India while it was their responsibility, and have taken still less interest since. It may be wondered how many of them will want to read a precise survey, or obituary, of Labour Party policy towards India before independence and partition came about in 1947; a study as it might be called of the dead bones of something that was never very much alive. All the same, anyone to whom socialism or the Labour movement are a concern ought to read such an account of the meanderings of Labour thinking, because the Labour Party, though not India, is still with us, and still meandering.

Labour leaders and spokesmen did little about India, but talked and wrote a great deal, and there is a ponderous literature of books, pamphlets, memoirs, by them or about them and the Indian leaders they were in contact with. All this, and a vast quantity of files and journals and conference reports, M. Georges Fischer in his *Le parti travailliste et la décolonisation de l'Inde* (Paris, 1966) has painstakingly sifted, and he has made use too of some unpublished materials from India Office records. He displays a thorough command of the British political scene and its ins and outs, never an easy thing to acquire about any foreign country. He has written a similar study of the 'decolonization' of the Philippines by the U.S., and draws our attention briefly at a good many points to developments there and elsewhere in the world that had some relevance to India. He notes for example that the anarchical condition of China in the 1920s and 1930s lent weight to gloomy predictions of what would happen if the British left India. He writes with a judicial detachment almost too complete, commenting now and again on the inconsistencies or fallacies of Labour reasoning, but on the whole perhaps appearing to take it too seriously, too much at its face value.

The work is arranged chronologically, with the First World War as the main dividing-line; the epoch before 1914, when the Labour Party was comparatively youthful and elastic, is in a way the most interesting, but the years between 1918 and 1939 are the most important and occupy the biggest share of space. An introductory survey reminds us that few Liberals wanted to give India up; and the Labour Party separating itself off from Liberalism—even then the ailing offspring of an elderly parent—started with the idea not of breaking up the empire but of transforming it, socializing it, from within. There was discussion of a federation of working-class movements in all the empire countries, to be led by the British: an attractive vision, but too much akin to Labour illusions today of a Common Market of monopoly capitalists magically transformed by the presence in it of a Britain occasionally run by a government whose members occasionally make speeches about socialism.

After the Great War, with the prevailing sensation of ship-wreck and collapse, there was a more convulsive clinging to empire. It was the time of the Waste Land, and colonies, all

Europe felt, were convenient fragments to shore against its ruins. Businessmen felt this in one way; Labour leaders, groping for something solid, and never conscious of *socialism* as a solid, in another. Spiritually the contrast between Tory greed and Labour idealism was doubtless strong; materially it was too slight for India to be much aware of. In 1925 the TUC struck a more radical note on colonialism, but the General Strike of the following year seems to have done nothing to make Labour see class conflict in Britain and India in the same perspective. Economic relations, Indian markets and Lancashire jobs are not Fischer's subject, but the consequences of the Slump starting in 1929, for any chance of concessions to Indian nationalism, deserve more prominence. Another landmark that might have been made to stand out is the Labour schism of 1931, when its leading group headed by Ramsay MacDonald went over divested of disguise to the capitalist camp. The rest of the party might have been expected to be stung into some show of fighting spirit; instead it seemed cowed by electoral defeat, bewildered by economic crisis, less able than ever to think radically about India. It had been taught, after all, to think of capitalism not as the enemy but as a sometimes annoying neighbour.

The event that does stand out in this main section of the book is the Simon Commission of 1928. One of the things that strained Indian trust in Labour's goodwill, a trust quite lively before 1914 but steadily curdling into scepticism, was Labour's willingness to join in a Commission to pronounce on India's destiny, made up of Englishmen alone and universally repudiated and boycotted by Indians. This did not prevent the seven members from being a very happy family, the two Labour men collaborating cordially with the rest, whose chief, Simon, had been one of the arch-enemies of the General Strike. One of these two worthies was Attlee. Of the few actors of that day still on the stage now he comes out of the record badly enough (one who comes out better is Fenner Brockway). Attlee found only one or two trifling points to differ from his Tory colleagues on. It was much the same when their report came before Parliament. There were shades of opinion on the Labour benches, but no more than on the Conservative side, where men like Hoare stood apart from the wild men like Salisbury (a familiar name on such occasions of imperial history) and Churchill. Even a Tory must take some twinge of comfort from being able to feel that he is not as other Tories are—not one of the worst of them, not a real malignant. Compromise as Fischer remarks is the essence of the parliamentary method; at Westminster it usually meant Labour giving up its principles and Conservatism giving up a few commas or semicolons— though Labour might have defended itself as to India by saying that it had no principles to abandon. Moderate Tories exerting themselves against Tory extremists had an excuse for not being as progressive as they might have liked to be, and sensible Labour MPs could feel that it was right to go along with them. These players in the Westminster comedy were so much accustomed to being taken seriously in Britain that they were always surprised when their performance failed to convince Indian spectators equally.

With the Second World War, Indian disillusionment with Labour became complete. Britain's governing class, Tory or Labour, was still determined to hang on to India as long as India could possibly be hung on to. As late as the election of 1945 only 8 per cent of Labour candidates thought India worth a mention. Bevin was promising no more than that India should be transferred to the Commonwealth Office—and this was the man who as Foreign Secretary was soon to show his true colours by helping to restore French imperialism in Indochina and Dutch in Indonesia, and using Indian troops for the purpose. When Labour took office in 1945 many of its leading spirits were still convinced that Dominion Status could not be conferred on India hastily. They had to change their minds before long, simply because it became obvious that the only alternative to getting out was to be thrown out.

Brailsford, recognizing the inevitable, breathed a sigh at Labour's having to renounce the hope of leading India and Burma and Ceylon to socialism—as if this had been the party's dearest, most cherished wish, when in half a century it had not 'led' India or Burma or Ceylon half an inch towards socialism, and twenty years later has scarcely begun to lead its own country there! Yet the man who heaved this flatulent sigh was one of the best men in the movement. Labour had not given India socialism; it was to take great pride, instead, in having helped to bestow—or impose—on India a parliamentary system which had nothing to do with socialism, and which as Fischer says in an alien environment was often to be a mere sham. With it went a bureaucracy carefully chosen and trained by Toryism, which has been a further obstacle to social progress. By its strategic retreat from those colonies Labour was helping to check the spread of communism there: the boast was Attlee's. In other words, since communism was in Asia the only kind of socialism, Labour's last thought was not to aid socialism, but to trip it up.

Fischer's concentration throughout is on the leaders; he is satisfied that they alone really counted, because the rank and file were indifferent. Whether he is right or not, a parallel study of the rank and file is to be desired, along with the question of how far apathy was the fault of the leadership. He reminds us that the party's working machinery, and the influences and impulses activating it, were complex, and that it is over-simple to explain everything in terms of manipulation by a group of managers. Managers do manipulate, nevertheless, in every party, and moments did occur when the membership showed signs of discontent with official policy on India, and leaders had to stand by with soft soap—very much as in later days over Vietnam.

In his ordinary mood, it may be allowed, the British workman did display a massive, good-humoured indifference to the plight of his Indian brethren. If in some ways the British ruling class can be said to have behaved towards India less badly than it might have done, the British working class behaved far worse, judged by the standard of the old ideal of international frater-nity, than it ought to have done. We are at liberty to think of the demoralization in the movement as a reciprocal effect, the stolid mass dragging down the leadership as well as the other way round. In any case this leadership was not one that would have challenged the apathy of its supporters, or blown bugle-blasts, or even penny-whistles, for the sake of India. The Liberal party in its best days did challenge imperialism over Ireland, and if it had perished finally in the crusade would have perished gloriously. Unhappily it was brought back to life by the undertakers and set marching somnambulistically towards Flanders.

It would have been useful, as a check on Labour Party attitudes, to consider the Communist Party as well. Back in 1900 the old undivided International was calling for socialist organizations to be set up in colonial regions. Little pressure was put on the Labour Party by the International to take a more strenuous line on India, but it had some healthy effect on the party to belong to a dynamic international movement. After the post-war split this stimulus was lost: the Second International was now tame and merely European, while the workers' movements growing up in the colonies were communist, and therefore anathema to the Labour Party. British Communism recognized in principle a duty to assist the workers in India, and in practice did in some measure assist them. Whether it could have done more for them, or to enlighten British workers, are points for investigation.

The ILP was distinctly better on India than the Labour Party, trying at times to act as a ginger group. As between the trade union bosses and the more literate or bourgeois spokesmen, the comparison is often in favour of the latter, who were multiplied in the 1920s by the influx of former Liberals. Lord Olivier, Secretary for India in the first Labour cabinet, had been governor of Jamaica, and looked like a Spanish grandee; he had been at least a benevolent autocrat to his subjects. There is another distinction to be drawn between those of the middle-class group who were principally intellectuals and publicists, like Cole or Laski, and the whole-time politicians like MacDonald or Attlee, and the comparison here favours the intellectuals, though not by a wide margin considering their greater freedom of speech. The men from mine or bench mostly had less knowledge of India, less interest, fewer misgivings, a more naïve egotism, all helping to draw them towards the point of view summed up in Bevin's 'jolly old empire'. The others could not be so light-hearted, even if their subtler formulae varied from Bevin's by shades often too fine for common perception.

Altogether, the broad impression left by hundreds of quotations of Labour Party utterances is a depressing one of wishful thinking, unrealism, poverty. The reader who can remember listening impatiently to some of these utterances before 1947, and now with this book in hand can look back over the full record, meticulously put together and not unsympathetically presented by Fischer, may feel some touches of regret for some sectarian intolerance of his own—but he is likely to see in the record as a whole very much what he saw at the time: a long cloud-procession of platitude and prevarication, flim-flam and flapdoodle, humbug and hot-air.

It might then be concluded that the record was not worth studying in all this detail, that the history of the Labour Party is simply irrelevant to the history of British India. Fischer makes the reasonable, though negative, claim on behalf of the party that when withdrawal was unavoidable it had the sense to withdraw more promptly than a Tory Government would have done. It might also be maintained that the party's existence put some restraint on British behaviour in India, which might otherwise have been more rough and ready. Too much shooting would have disturbed too many illusions, too many of those delicate psychological checks and balances on which depended the ability of Labour men to believe in, and therefore to keep their followers believing in, the British Raj. In fact the real subject of interest is the Labour Party much more than India, and political history much less than political psychology.

It deserves to be taken into account, of course, that Indian affairs were complicated and awkward; sheer size made them seem, more than those of any country in the world, insoluble. It is true also that Indian spokesmen advanced very slowly towards a demand for anything like complete independence, and that India was, by and large, very poorly led. Fischer is right to regard the communal issue as a real one, even if it was exploited at times by the ruling power. Yet on the one hand Labour's nervous fancy was apt to inflate difficulties and hazards, to people Indian jungles with every species of paper tiger and serpent; and on the other hand these men very seldom suffered, at any rate in public, from any sense of being unequal to their mission of showing India the way forward. Laski in a mood of exasperation might talk of India as an impossible riddle, and Cole might suggest, as ought to have been suggested

far oftener, that aid should be sought from the League of
Nations; as a rule Labour suffered rather from a too complacent estimate of its qualifications for acting as guide and
guardian, or Moral Tutor as teachers call themselves at
Oxford, or some such place, to 300,000,000 Indians. It might
not be able to convince many Englishmen that it knew what
was good for them, but it knew what was good for Hindus.
There was some profundity here of conceit, if not of thought.

In the early years quite a number of builders of the Labour
Party saw India with their own eyes. Hyndman came of a
family with Indian connections, and had himself worked in a
princely territory. He was more forward-looking than most of
the others, though erratic on this as on other topics, but he and
his Socialist Democratic Federation really belonged to an
earlier stage. Ramsay MacDonald visited India, wrote two
books on it, prided himself on his special knowledge. How much
such an inquirer really learned one is left speculating. British
India was a country where it was deceptively easy for a British
visitor to suppose that he was getting the hang of things,
because there was a small educated class everywhere which
spoke English—but extremely difficult for him really to get
the hang of anything, without the channel of communication
that Communism later on did something to provide. We have
a diverting picture of Keir Hardie (another Scot, by the way,
and the man who had staggered Westminster by turning up at
the House in a cloth cap, as if bent on immediate red revolution)
gravely conversing with a magistrate at Benares on the importance of encouraging landowners and others with a stake
in the country, as a moderating influence. Benares with its
thousand temples, swarming beggars and naked fakirs is a
place where a Briton might well forget any distinction between
cloth cap and top hat, and feel all the value of the grand
British virtue, respectability.

Moreover these Labour tourists were going out with fixed
preconceptions, with a ready-made hold-all of ideas which
they were confident would hold India too. On fundamentals
it never dawned on them that they had anything fresh to learn.
This made it easier for them to squeeze what began as genuine
sympathy for Indian toilers into a very British mould. The

conclusion they quickly arrived at was that it would never do
to give India independence prematurely, and so leave defence-
less workers at the mercy of their hard-hearted employers. As
the national movement grew, and its demands stiffened,
Labour's reaction was to shuffle backward. It became a stock
argument against the Congress that it was financed and controlled by big businessmen; an argument that Tories, from
motives of delicacy, could scarcely resort to, but were glad to
have put forward by the Labour Party in their stead. Labour
was coming down to spinning socialistic costumes as disguises
for imperialism. It felt entitled to set up as a better friend and
truer representative of the Indian masses than their own selfish
bourgeoisie. It could appeal to them therefore to be patient,
to wait until Labour should be in power at Westminster with
a sufficient majority and sufficient leisure—then something
could be done. If they must do something on their own account
in the meantime, let them stick to trade union activity, or even
start a party of their own, but not be misled into supporting
the national movement and its self-interested demagogues.

It struck Indians, however, that while Labour was so indignant about exploitation of workers by Indian capitalists, it had
much less to say about exploitation by British capitalists in India.
Another little inconsistency can be detected in the 'British
Committee on Indian Affairs' of the 1920s, made up mostly
of Labour men but relying for its expenses chiefly, as Fischer
tells us, on Indian Liberals and capitalists; to say nothing of
the remarkable meanness of taking money from India for
working or pretending to work for India. An excuse could be
found on similar lines for reluctance to grant even tariff
autonomy. The real objection to this was that by sheltering
India's young industries it would mean stronger competition
for Britain's; the alleged reason was that it would mean
stronger exploitation of workers by Indian millowners. Even
Brockway could lean to the convenient view that India would
do better to remain an agricultural country. Conservatives like
Churchill and Halifax were happy to agree that it would be
very wrong to abandon India to its capitalists, and almost at
the very end of the Raj we find Attlee quite of one mind with
Churchill that Congress was too much dominated by financial

and industrial interests. The Westminster charade could hardly become more farcical; it reminds one of Cicero's question, how any two of Rome's official soothsayers could catch each other's eye in the street without bursting out laughing.

In 1911, in the hopeful days before the first War, the Labour Party and TUC discussed a scheme for a sort of grand national consolidated trade union organization in India, to be got going by British unionists. Nothing, it scarcely needs to be said, was done. Later on as well Labour often talked of helping trade unionism in India, by sending advisers, giving money, and so on, but there always happened to be a reason why the would-be good Samaritan was obliged to pass by on the other side of the street. More urgency came into the plans when Indian unionism was seen to be coming under Communist direction, but even then it stuck at the level of urgent talk. Everything Indian was perpetually in a state of being under active consideration by the Labour Party. What the party did do was to co-operate heartily, when in office, in jailing Indian trade union organizers, who either were Communists, or—merely as energetic unionists—laid themselves open to suspicion of being such. The notorious Meerut Conspiracy trial was the grand demonstration of this. When Brockway at the Labour Party conference in 1930 hoped for a mass struggle in India against capitalists and millowners, the Labour Government spokesman was deeply shocked. It was proper that Indian workers should not be duped by the patriotic claptrap of their bosses, but highly improper that they should think of doing anything against these bosses. The Indian working class was to be encouraged to stand on its own feet, so long as it stood perfectly still.

In the same way, on the political front Brockway was prepared to welcome Gandhi's non-violent civil disobedience—a harmless safety-valve for national agitation if ever one was invented—but most of his colleagues, Ramsay MacDonald in particular, recoiled from it in horror, as something indescribably subversive and sinister. For these men Order was coming to be as sovereign a virtue as for Metternich, and statesmanship the purging of public life from any taint of the old Adam, its refining by bleedings and exorcisms to the pure innocence of a Sunday-school picnic. Meanwhile, as Nehru complained, the conduct of the British authorities in India grew considerably more brutal, a fact that Labour failed to observe, or blamed on the Congress. It is not the school-master's fault if his pupils compel him to use the birch. To this quietist philosophy, no news from India was good news.

Labour's faith was pinned, for India as for Britain, to the parliamentary method. Parliament always had the great double advantage of explaining both why peaceful socialism was bound to come in the future, and why it was out of the question just now. With the same neatness it disposed of Indian independence; and just as this could come about only by the fiat of the British parliament, so India could only be given freedom to run itself by means of a parliament of its own, the one instrument of salvation. That parliamentarianism might not necessarily be the best system for a country with totally different traditions was a thought that seldom obtruded itself. Toryism had never believed in parliamentary (or any other) self-rule for India; nor did most Liberals, John Morley for instance, before the Government of India Act of 1919, when the Liberal party was at its last gasp. Men of the older British parties, more firmly linked with the old governing classes, had less superstitious reverence for Parliament than Labour newcomers felt; for them it was a convenient method, not the Ark of a Covenant. One or two Labour men were able to grasp that for India it might be desirable to think on new lines—Lord Strabolgi, for instance, and Cole, but the thought scarcely ever entered the minds of the practising politicians.

When would India be given a real parliament of its own? When British capitalism was ready to give India up, a vulgarian might have replied. But in that political fourth dimension where so much Labour thinking was carried on, the right way to look at it—especially for Indians to look at it—was that it would happen as soon as India could prove itself fit and ready for self-government. Hence the doctrine of criteria, the tests of fitness and maturity, and the perennial Labour recipe of a fresh commission of inquiry to go out with tape-measure and stethoscope and see how much progress towards fitness had been made since last time. Tests were various, though the essential one was always respect for Order, the patient's ability to maintain a fixed immobility like that of the fakir gazing at eternity. Clearly, for one thing, India would have to be able to undertake its own defence. In 1930 only 100 out of 3,000 officers were Indian, and the Labour Government envisaged a programme of training twenty or twenty-five new ones annually (pp. 202–4). This would produce the requisite number in little more than a century. Another cardinal test was education; here such a rapid advance could not be expected, and at the actual rate of progress it would take nearer a millennium than a century to abolish illiteracy. Meanwhile the Labour Party could be trusted to keep matters, as before, under active consideration. Again this approach opened up a broad field of agreement between sensible Labour men and moderate Tories. When Edgar Snow interviewed the Viceroy at Delhi during the Second World War, while the Japanese were approaching India and the national leaders lay in jail, he found Lord Linlithgow regretfully convinced that Indians were not yet ripe for freedom—not yet ripe for this, that, and the other— not ripe yet (when the visitor as a last resort suggested this) for running co-operatives.[1]

Ripeness is all. Labour ministers could feel that they were bringing maturity nearer by keeping agitators in jail, where they could mature their opinions in peace and quiet. They themselves must have felt extraordinarily mature, too ripely developed almost to be capable of doing anything but lament the imperfections of their fellow-men. Fischer looks upon the 'doctrine of criteria' of a people's fitness for freedom as peculiarly Anglo-Saxon (pp. 199–200); but it has a close resemblance to the tests devised by De Gaulle of Britain's fitness for entry into the Common Market—'the general's technique', in the words of the *Economist*, 'of asking Britain to give constantly changing proofs of its "Europeanness"', for him as examiner to mark at his own discretion. Exactly so did the Labour party examine India for evidence of a satisfactory degree of Englishness.

On issues like extensions of the franchise Labour's view were, Fischer writes, so full of contradictions and ambiguities as to

[1] See Edgar Snow's account of his visit to war-time India in *Glory and Bondage* (London, 1946).

invite ridicule (p. 214). Labour reasoning altogether had a tendency to revolve in circles. Few of the leaders believed in universal suffrage; the poor were not ripe, of course. Surely then they ought to be left to defend themselves by other means —but that meant unconstitutional action, which was absolutely ruled out even if the heavens fell—so the poor must rely on strictly legal methods—but this meant having votes. . . .

India was being trained for nationhood, or *refined* for it like a barrel of crude spirit slowly purifying in the cellar of British administration—but to Labour's adult eye all nationalist feeling was really infantile, anachronistic, out of harmony with an age when world federation was the goal to aim at. Labour was not proposing any surrender of Britain's own sovereignty, and its habit of preaching against nicotine with a cigar in its mouth was one of the things that irritated its audience. Nationalism in India moreover, Labour could not help feeling, was unpleasantly mixed up with religion. One really could not talk to a Hindu mystic like Gandhi—any more than one could talk to an atheistical communist, or a soulless capitalist, or an ignorant coolie. Labour was always looking for someone it could talk to, someone like the Respectable Working-man it got on so well with at home. Unluckily there were no respectable working-men in India; everyone was too rich or too poor, too extremist or too apathetic, too tall or too short. In the end one could really only talk to oneself. Labour's dialogue with India did often sound like an old man's monologue, or the armchair reverie of a good man after a good dinner wishing, like the king in *The Gondoliers*, that all men could be as rich (or as ripe) as he.

One third of India was composed of Native States, ruled by princes whom the British had relied on increasingly since the Congress movement grew troublesome. It might have been expected that Labour would not take kindly to these irresponsible despots, or would wish to devise some suitability-tests for them. Its spokesmen were so scrupulous in their respect for constitutional freedom that they could never bear the thought of how it was being curtailed in the U.S.S.R. Yet it scarcely occurred to them that these Indian potentates could stand in need of any ripening or maturing. Keir Hardie had given them a good certificate, on the strength of progress-reports from two

of them, Mysore and Baroda. There were always a few reputable rulers; at the other end of the scale there were some who,
had they given a truthful account of themselves and asked
Malcolm's question—

> If such a one be fit to govern, speak,

would have invited Macduff's answer—

> Fit to govern!
> No, not to live.

In between, most of the princelings and their feudal hangers-on
were a gaudy mob of boobies or blackguards. It would have
been a miracle if they were anything else, considering their
temptations and lack of restraints. Tories have always warned
socialists against expecting too much from weak human nature.

Long after Keir Hardie, when some in the Labour movement
had misgivings, Lord Strabolgi was ready to defend the princes,
and Attlee in the Simon Commission to uphold the sanctity of
moth-eaten treaties with them. As prime minister presiding
over the Round Table Conference in 1930 Ramsay MacDonald
thanked Their Highnesses in a gush of lyrical rigmarole for
their kindness in agreeing to join a Federation with British
India, and so opening the way to progress—orderly enough
progress to satisfy the Tories.[2] One trade union boss of that
time, J. H. Thomas, flattered by being allowed to hobnob with
George V, is said to have chivalrously assured him that he was
ready to stand or fall with the monarchy. Such a man might be
dazzled even by the feeble and distant glitter of India's petty
coronets. Thomas was in any case a strong empire man; and
it would be instructive to examine how regularly the worst
elements in the Labour movement were the most imperialistic.
To the end, Fischer points out, Labour leaders failed to comprehend that the princes had become mere meaningless relics
(p. 313). He adds the illuminating remark that they thought
the British public took these absurd survivals far more seriously
than it really did; and that politicians often go on repeating a
thing even when they know it to be a myth, but mistakenly
suppose that the public cannot bear to be told it is a myth.

All in all, India fostered in the Labour party the habit of

[2] See *Proceedings of the Round Table Conference* for Nov. 1930, 'The General
Discussion'.

mistaking pious aspiration for fulfilment, promise for performance, fantasy for reality; of thinking a thing as good as
done when it has only been talked about. Communism's
besetting vice has been to keep theory and practice united by
arbitrary shackles; Labour has avoided this by leaving theory
and practice to go each its separate way, and has kept its ideals
unsullied by treating them as abstractions laid up in heaven,
too good for this world. With Bertie Wooster to think was to
act; with the Labour party very often to act was to think. I
think, therefore I am. . . . It was a philosophy India was well
qualified to teach.

Index